Professional Community S

Professional
Community Server™
Themes

Professional
Community Server™
Themes

Wyatt Preul
Ben Tiedt

BICENTENNIAL
1807
WILEY
2007
BICENTENNIAL

Wiley Publishing, Inc.

Professional Community Server™ Themes

Published by
Wiley Publishing, Inc.
10475 Crosspoint Boulevard
Indianapolis, IN 46256
www.wiley.com

Copyright © 2008 by Wiley Publishing, Inc., Indianapolis, Indiana

Published simultaneously in Canada

ISBN: 978-0-470-18208-6

Manufactured in the United States of America

10 9 8 7 6 5 4 3 2 1

Library of Congress Cataloging-in-Publication Data is available from Publisher.

For general information on our other products and services please contact our Customer Care Department within the United States at (800) 762-2974, outside the United States at (317) 572-3993 or fax (317) 572-4002.

Wiley also publishes its books in a variety of electronic formats. Some content that appears in print may not be available in electronic books.

To Rob, Scott, and Jason—your vision of a platform for online communities is enabling collaboration worldwide.

About the Authors

Wyatt Preul works as a software test engineer for Telligent Systems. Wyatt is the author of the Wrox book Professional Community Server. Wyatt has been working with and admiring Community Server shortly after version 1.1 was released. Since that time he has become a respected member of the community and active participant in the product itself. Wyatt now spends his days happily developing features for Community Server and trying to locate bugs in the product, to which he reports there aren't many. His thoughts on development, testing, and Community Server can all be found at www.wyattpreul.com. Wyatt currently lives in Philadelphia with his beautiful wife Dusti.

Ben Tiedt works as a developer lead on the Community Server Team for Telligent Systems. Ben started working with Community Server during the development of version 2.0 and recently worked on the development of the Chameleon theming engine and Dynamic Configuration feature of Community Server 2007. Ben continues to develop future versions of Community Server and also enjoys answering questions on communityserver.org and posting help and tips on his blog at getben.com. Ben is happily married to his beautiful, understanding wife Tarah and lives in Grand Rapids, Michigan.

Credits

Executive Editor
Chris Webb

Development Editor
Rosanne Koneval

Technical Editor
Dan Hounshell

Production Editor
Angela Smith

Copy Editor
Foxxe Editorial Services

Editorial Manager
Mary Beth Wakefield

Production Manager
Tim Tate

**Vice President and
Executive Group Publisher**
Richard Swadley

Vice President and Executive Publisher
Joseph B. Wikert

Project Coordinator, Cover
Lynsey Osborn

Compositor
Craig Johnson, Happenstance Type-O-Rama

Proofreader
Sossity Smith

Indexer
Johnna VanHoose Dinse

Anniversary Logo Design
Richard Pacifico

Acknowledgments

Special thanks go to Dan Hounshell who volunteered his time to assist with the editing process of this book. In addition, special thanks are due to Rosanne Koneval for her patience and support during this same editing process. Without you two this book would not be what it is today.

Contents

Contents

Contents

Contents

Contents

Contents

Introduction

Community Server provides a platform that enables communities to be easily created and continuously thrive. It achieves this task by including all of the applications that are useful for the growth of communities. In addition, Community Server is extremely flexible and is able to meet the requirements of each community. The combination of simplicity and flexibility make Community Server an ideal platform.

Who This Book Is For

This book is for web developers who are interested in customizing the presentation of a Community Server site. If you are an experienced developer, then it will be most helpful for your understanding of the materials in this book if you are experienced with ASP.NET. If you have any experience with web development in general, then you will be comfortable with the topics covered in this book.

Aims of This Book

One of the main goals of this book is to provide you with the material required to easily create a custom theme for Community Server. By reading this book you will become familiar with the various files and content that is expected to be included with these themes. Additionally, you will be equipped with the knowledge of the new controls available in the latest version of Community Server. As a result, you will be able to create custom controls for your site.

The overarching goal of this book is to provide you with enough material so that you can more easily turn a Community Server site into one that meets your requirements, particularly in the area of your site presentation.

What This Book Covers

This book covers a wide range of topics that will all assist you in modifying your Community Server site. In the first two chapters of the book you will be introduced to some of the general topics covered in later chapters. Additionally, you will be presented with steps to guide you in setting up your development environment.

In Chapters 3–4 you will learn about how URL rewriting takes place in Community Server. This content will help you learn how to add new pages to a site as well as how to modify the paths to current paths. With this understanding, you will learn how the limited number of theme files is used in Community Server.

Chapter 5 is an extremely important chapter, as it covers a large part of the new Community Server controls that are available in the 2007 release. In Chapters 6–7 you will apply your knowledge of URL rewriting and the understanding gained in Chapter 5 to creating custom themes. Each of these chapters provides you with an example of how to create either a blog or site theme for a Community Server site.

In the remainder of the chapters, Chapters 8–15, you will learn about individual topics that can help improve your theme and sites. These chapters provide you with the material necessary to create not only custom editors but also custom controls. The topics covered in these chapters are of an advanced nature and are meant to be consulted after gaining a basic understanding of the new Community Server controls and URL rewriting.

Conventions

To help you get the most from the text and keep track of what's happening, we've used a number of conventions throughout the book.

> *Tips, hints, tricks, and asides to the current discussion are offset and placed in italics like this.*

As for styles in the text:

We *highlight* important words when we introduce them.

We show keyboard strokes like this: Ctrl+A

We show file names, URLs, and code within the text like this: `persistence.properties`

We present code in two different ways:

```
In code examples we highlight new and important code with a gray background.
The gray highlighting is not used for code that's less important in the present
context, or has been shown before.
```

Source Code

As you work through the examples in this book, you may choose either to type in all the code manually or to use the source code files that accompany the book. All of the source code used in this book is available for download at `www.wrox.com`. Once at the site, simply locate the book's title (either by using the Search box or by using one of the title lists) and click the Download Code link on the book's detail page to obtain all the source code for the book.

> *Because many books have similar titles, you may find it easiest to search by ISBN; for this book the ISBN is 9780470182086.*

Once you download the code, just decompress it with your favorite compression tool. Alternately, you can go to the main Wrox code download page at `www.wrox.com/dynamic/books/download.aspx` to see the code available for this book and all other Wrox books.

Errata

We make every effort to ensure that there are no errors in the text or in the code. However, no one is perfect, and mistakes do occur. If you find an error in one of our books, such as a spelling mistake or faulty piece of code, we would be very grateful for your feedback. By sending in errata you may save another reader hours of frustration, and at the same time you will be helping us provide even higher-quality information.

To find the errata page for this book, go to www.wrox.com and locate the title using the Search box or one of the title lists. Then, on the book details page, click the Book Errata link. On this page, you can view all errata that has been submitted for this book and posted by Wrox editors. A complete book list, including links to each book's errata is also available at www.wrox.com/misc-pages/booklist.shtml.

If you don't spot "your" error on the Book Errata page, go to www.wrox.com/contact/techsupport.shtml and complete the form there to send us the error you have found. We'll check the information and, if appropriate, post a message to the book's errata page and fix the problem in subsequent editions of the book.

Key Concepts

This chapter introduces you to the key concepts covered in this book. These topics provide a general understanding of the components that constitute theme building in Community Server. The topics that are covered in this chapter include:

- ❑ Themes in Community Server 2007
- ❑ Types of themes
- ❑ Rendering diagrams
- ❑ `SiteUrls.config` and URL rewriting
- ❑ Chameleon
- ❑ Dynamic configuration
- ❑ Content scrubbing

Themes in Community Server 2007

The themes in Community Server 2007 are different from those in previous versions of Community Server. Not only has the process of creating a theme been simplified, but also the number of files that require creation have decreased. There is now a new set of controls across the site that is consistent and straightforward to use. These are significant improvements, as less is required from the theme developer.

Theme Portability

One of the major advances in Community Server 2007 over previous versions is the portability of theme settings. Not only are you able to easily install and use a theme, but you are also able to easily import specific theme settings and use them. This allows anyone with Community

Server 2007 and later to be able to alter the presentation of a theme and then to share that alteration with the world. One of the important qualities of this mechanism is that you do not have to be familiar with .NET or theme development. Instead, a novice user is able to alter their site and share this alteration.

Aside from the portability of themes in Community Server 2007, themes are now much easier to create. There is a standard set of controls that can be added to theme pages that have a consistent set of properties. Furthermore, the theme controls in Community Server 2007 support implicit binding. This means that a theme developer does not need to know how to retrieve a blog in order to display content from a blog. Instead, he or she only needs to place a blog control on a page that would normally display blog details, and the control will take care of the reset. The power of the new controls is actually quite amazing.

Standard Control Features

The theme controls in Community Server 2007 are not limiting. Instead, you are able to extend them and create custom controls that are consistent with the current controls. The new controls have many useful features, some of them include the following (please note that this is not an exhaustive list and that there are actually many more standard features for the controls):

❑   DisplayConditions — You are able to toggle the visibility of most controls using conditions, which can include custom conditions that you create.

❑   Actions — You can implement actions that take place after a form or other control type successfully or unsuccessfully does something. For example, if you want to redirect the user to a new page after he or she logs in, you can do so by placing `GoToSiteUrlAction` in the SuccessAction template on the login form.

❑   Tag — You are able to surround most controls with an html tag whenever the control is rendered. For example, if you want to surround a `ResourceControl` with a `div` tag, you can simply set the value of the `Tag` property to `div`. There is an enumerator for the tag property that provides you with intellisense whenever you are setting it.

Theme File Reduction

Less is required from users in order to change the look of their site. It is now much easier to switch themes on a live site. This enables a site to alter its presentation in order to meet the needs of the community that it is enabling. Now in Community Server 2007 there are dynamic themes. These types of themes enable an administrator to easily change how a site looks all from the Control Panel. A site can also allow blog owners to alter the presentation of their blog from the Control Panel with great ease.

Types of Themes

Community Server 2007 ships with one less type of theme than previous versions. All of the applications on a default Community Server site, except for weblogs are integrated into a site theme. Previously the Photo Gallery was able to have individual themes created just for it. Now these theme files are part of the main site theme.

Aside from the site theme there is the option to create weblog themes. This allows blog owners to select the theme that they would like to use on their blog. As a result, a site can have users that have blogs that look different from one another.

The types of themes that are available in Community Server 2007 and later include the following:

❑ Site themes
❑ Blog themes

Both sets of themes are found in the Themes folder. This is located off the root directory of a Community Server installation. Inside of the themes directory is a specific folder for containing all of the blog themes named Blogs. Also inside of the root themes directory are folders for the different site themes. In Community Server 2007 there are two site themes, default and leanandgreen.

Later in this book you will learn how to create each of these types of themes. In Chapter 6, you will learn how to create a custom Blog theme. In Chapter 7 you will learn how to create a custom Site theme. Both of these chapters will assist you in understanding what is required to create a theme in Community Server.

SiteUrls and URL Rewriting

A central component to any Community Server site is URL rewriting and the SiteUrls.config file. Both of these combine to provide very powerful features for your site.

The SiteUrls.config file contains the entries for the pages on your site. This provides a central location for controlling where URLs point to on your site. For example, if you want to change the name of a page on your site or the folder that it resides in, you can do so by changing a single URL entry in this file. This prevents a site administrator from having to touch physical page files to update the location that a link points to.

The SiteUrls.config file also provides data used in URL rewriting. URL rewriting allows for a requested page to be physically located in a different path than where it appears to be. Whenever you request http://yoursite.com/default.aspx, you are actually accessing the page at http://yoursite.com/themes/default/common/home.aspx. As you can see, URL rewriting is essential for themes to work correctly.

The URL rewriting feature allows your site to have many different themes and allows it to switch between them and yet still retain the same URL structure publicly. If you change from the default theme to the leanandgreen site theme, then your page files are going to be located at a physically different location. However, the users accessing the site do not need to type in a different path to use the different theme.

Chameleon

Chameleon is the name of the new theme engine available in Community Server 2007 and later versions. It provides many of the topics that are discussed in this book. Prior to Chameleon, there were no theme.config files to provide dynamic configuration options. Also, there were no controls that provided the same level of ease for creating powerful themes.

One of the main differences between Community Server 2007 and previous versions in regard to themes is that the previous versions contained skin files, whereas the current version does not. As a result of this change there has been a dramatic decrease in the number of files required to create a Community Server theme.

Another huge advantage to using the new Chameleon controls is that they provide inherent data binding. This means that a theme developer does not have to know how to query and get posts in order to display them. Now whenever a `WeblogData` control is added to a page, it knows to only display the data for the weblog that is on the current page.

In Chapter 5, you will learn much more about Chameleon. Chapter 5 discusses the various controls that are provided with Chameleon. This is an essential chapter that will help you learn much more about Chameleon.

Request to Rendering Diagram

In order to help you understand how URL rewriting and theming works in Community Server it is useful to look at an individual request to a site. The important thing to realize is that Community Server uses a custom HTTP module that makes URL rewriting occur. This is necessary because the module allows for custom code to execute during the processing of the ASP.NET pipeline. Figure 1-1 presents the basic steps that occur to make URL rewriting and loading of the appropriate theme page.

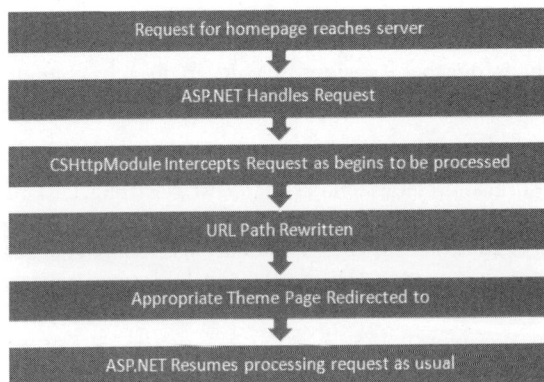

Request for homepage reaches server

↓

ASP.NET Handles Request

↓

CSHttpModule Intercepts Request as begins to be processed

↓

URL Path Rewritten

↓

Appropriate Theme Page Redirected to

↓

ASP.NET Resumes processing request as usual

Figure 1-1: Page Request Including URL Rewriting Diagram

Whenever a request comes to a Community Server site that has the `CSHttpModule` enabled, the steps in Figure 1-1 take place. Early in the pipeline Community Server rewrites the requested path to the one configured by the URL data. More information about how the appropriate path is determined can be found in Chapters 3 and 4. Basically, though, at this point you should simply realize that specific URL requests are mapped to pages on a site.

Whenever this rewriting process occurs, the selected theme is included in the rewritten path. This means that if the `home.aspx` page is rewritten on a site using the default theme, the page at `Themes/default/Common/home.aspx` will be loaded. However, if the site were running the Lean and Green theme, the `Themes/leanandgreen/Common/home.aspx` page would be processed and returned to the client.

Therefore, in Figure 1-1 there are two separate steps for rewriting a page, even though they really do occur at the same time. The first is to determine the name of the page to actually load, and the other is to determine the theme that the page is found in.

Dynamic Configuration

One of the advances that were made with Community Server 2007 is the introduction of theme configuration files. These allow a theme's developer to provide various configuration options to control the presentation of a theme. As a result, end users of a dynamic theme are able to do more than use the theme; they are able to change the various ways that the theme is presented. For example, a configuration option could be changing the background color or image on a site. This allows users to be able to select these options from the Control Panel and control the presentation of their theme without having to physically alter any files.

A theme can allow for more advanced dynamic configuration options than background color or image choices. You can use the properties that can be created in a `theme.config` file to provide a way to toggle if controls are visible or not. Furthermore, you can allow for content to be entered in the theme configuration part of the Control Panel to be rendered in a specific location in your theme. There are numerous possibilities for what you can do with a dynamic theme.

Later in the book, in both Chapter 9 and Chapter 10, you will explore how to create these `theme.config` files. Additionally, you will learn many advanced concepts that are possible inside of these configuration files, such as creating custom theme rules. After reading these chapters, you should be more than comfortable with dynamic configuration options.

Content Scrubbing

In order to keep the presentation of the user-generated content well formed and alleviate security issues, Community Server uses several different content scrubbers. This means that the markup of posts on a site can be controlled. This is useful, as it can help maintain a consistent presentation as well as prevent unnecessary and potentially harmful markup from being delivered to users.

There are several different scrubbing modules that exist to perform scrubbing. Usually, though, only one is executed whenever a post is updated or created. This means that there are scrubbing modules that are specific to types of content. For example, the `WeblogPostandArticleHtmlScrubbing` module executes before a weblog post is committed to the database. This allows different HTML tags to exist on a weblog post, while not being allowed on a forum post.

Even though you can have different types of scrubbing occurring on a per application basis, in reality the scrubbing that occurs is mostly the same for each application. One of the nice features of the common `HtmlScrubber` is that it validates the HTML tags in a post. This is important, as it helps to allow your site be validated by the World Wide Web Consortium rules.

If you are interested in learning more about the current content scrubbing that takes place in Community Server, or even how to extend this feature, you can read Chapter 11. This chapter also teaches you about well-formed markup and how to maintain this across your site.

Summary

In this chapter, you were introduced to several different concepts. These concepts included the theming changes that exist in Community Server 2007, URL rewriting, and Content Scrubbing. In later chapters you will learn much more about each of these topics, as well as many more. If you have any questions or are interested in one of these topics and want to learn more about it you can go directly to the chapter or chapters discussing the topic.

In the next chapter, you will learn about how to get started developing for Community Server. You will learn how to set up your development environment and begin using some of the development tools to assist you in creating a theme.

2

Getting Started

This chapter explains how to set up your development environment to work correctly with Community Server. This will result in your being able to eventually create controls and custom themes that can be used inside of a Community Server site. Additionally, you will be able to use this same environment to create custom modules and tasks that can also be used to customize Community Server. By the end of this chapter, you should be familiar with the following topics:

❑ Required Software

❑ Downloading Community Server

❑ Setting up a Development Environment

❑ Previewing Themes

This book assumes that you have some experience with Community Server. If you have no experience with Community Server and are interested in learning more about getting started with it, you should consult both Chapter 1 and Chapter 2 of the Wrox book *Professional Community Server*. This will provide you with basic information on what Community Server is as well as steps for troubleshooting potential installation issues.

Required Software

In order to run Community Server in a development environment, there is certain software that you should have installed. The requirements for your development version of Community Server are less than those for using it on a production server. Choosing an appropriate operating system is the first step in acquiring the software necessary for running Community Server. There are four main choices for an operating system for use for your development environment. If you are already running one of these operating systems, you can continue to the "Selecting a Database Server" section below.

❑ Windows XP Professional

❑ Windows 2000

❑ Windows Server 2003

❑ Windows Vista

If you select Windows XP, it is useful to get the professional version, as it includes some additional features that can help you with development. One important feature to make sure that you have installed with any version of Windows is Internet Information Services (IIS). IIS is the software that is used to serve and run your site; essentially it is a web server. While you can get away with running Community Server using the Visual Studio `webdev.webserver` or with the Cassini web server, it is more useful to have IIS installed. This will allow you to test your site with the application that will be running it on the production server. Windows 2000 and Windows Server 2003 both come with IIS. Therefore, you're safe choosing either of these operating systems. However, not all editions of Windows Vista come with IIS, so be sure to check first before purchasing the software. For most of my development, I use Windows Server 2003 and Windows Vista Business Edition.

Selecting a Database Server

There are three main database server options for standard Community Server development. They are listed here, and each has its advantages:

❑ SQL Server 2000

❑ SQL Server 2005 Express Edition

❑ SQL Server 2005

For most lightweight theme development, SQL Server 2005 Express Edition is a good choice. However, if you want to work in an environment that is similar to your production environment, then either SQL Server 2000 or SQL Server 2005 Development Edition is an excellent choice. One of the niceties of SQL Server 2005 Express Edition is that it is available for free.

You can optionally install all three database servers and use them for testing your site. This is not always necessary for theme development, as you are often not concerned with the backend data store. For setting up Community Server in a development environment any of these options will work well.

Aside from the database sever software itself, you should have a tool available to connect to the server and Community Server database and perform SQL commands. A free tool that is available from Microsoft is SQL Server Management Studio Express. There is also a non-Express version of this tool that has many more options that is available with different editions of Microsoft SQL Server 2005.

Selecting an Integrated Development Environment

There is really only one main choice for a development environment for developing with Community Server. You should use the edition of Visual Studio 2005 that best fits your needs. If you are going to be using Microsoft Team Foundation or developing in a team, consider using Visual Studio 2005 Team System. The remainder of this book assumes that you are using one of the Visual Studio 2005 editions.

Aside from using Visual Studio 2005 for your development, you can also use several other tools strictly for doing presentation and theme development. However, using one of these other options does not necessarily provide you with code validation and intellisense the way that Visual Studio does. Regardless, if you are tweaking the HTML or Cascading Style Sheets (CSS) code for the pages of Community Server, you can use any standard text editor such as UltraEdit, or even an HTML designer such as Microsoft Expressions Studio.

Downloading Community Server

Once you have an appropriate operating system and database server software installed, it is time to download and install Community Server. The version of Community Server that will be used throughout this book is Community Server 2007. This version introduced the new, completely reworked theming engine, which is codenamed Chameleon.

Community Server is available in different editions that are targeted to meet the requirements of many different types of sites. All of the editions that are available for Community Server 2007 have the new theming engine. You can get a copy of Community Server from the http://communityserver.org website. When you navigate to this site, you will see a link to download Community Server. If you have any questions about which edition is the best choice for your needs, you can always read through the feature matrix and licensing guide that is available on this same website. If neither of these options answers your questions feel free to make a post to the community forums on http://communityserver.org or email the sales team directly at sales@telligent.com.

Click the "All Downloads" link to be able to see the SDK, service packages, add-ons, and more.

Installing Community Server

Currently, there is a solid amount of documentation explaining how to install Community Server. You can locate many of these pages at http://docs.communityserver.org as well as http://docs.communityserver.org/kb. You can also find a good overview of Community Server, as well as helpful instructions on how to install it, in the Wrox book *Professional Community Server*. If you get stuck with any part of the installation, you should consult one of these sources.

Community Server 2007 comes in four types of packages that you can use to set up your copy. These include:

❑ **Demo** — The demo package is perhaps the easiest and fastest way to run Community Server. This package only requires that you have a SQL Express server setup and are running a version of Windows that is listed above in "Required Software."

❑ **MSI** — The MSI package is a windows installer executable package. This provides a Windows Installation Wizard to set up Community Server. This package does not require that you create a database manually, change any configuration files, or set up a website for Community Server. This is primarily used for local testing or installation onto a server that you have remote desktop access to.

❑ **Web** — The web installer package allows you to set up Community Server in an environment that you only have FTP access to. This is often used for installing Community Server into a shared hosting environment. It is the recommended installation method for most production situations.

❑ **SDK** — This is the software development kit for Community Server and is used for helping developers to both understand and develop new or improved features. You will be using this package in the next section on setting up your development environment. Most of the source code that is used to run Community Server is available in this package. Therefore, if you are interested to learn how something works in the code, you can install this package and investigate the source code. In addition, this package can be used to set up Community Server, as it provides the required SQL scripts as well as the web installer files.

Since this is an advanced book, and documentation on installing Community Server exists elsewhere, the step-by-step process will not be covered here. Again, for that information, please consult either the documentation online at http://docs.communityserver.org, the *Professional Community Server* book, or both.

Once you have downloaded your copy of Community Server, you should install it locally and use it for a while before beginning to do any development on it. You should make sure that you have acquainted yourself with the basic features and organization of the control panel before making any customizations. This will not only make you more familiar with how Community Server is structured but also give you a good idea of some of the many features that are included with this amazing platform.

Once you have installed one of these packages and are familiar with Community Server, you can begin setting up a development environment to expand and change Community Server. If you would like to understand the basics of the file structure, you can read through the following section. Before you proceed, make sure that you have all of the required software that was outlined in the previous section.

Understanding the Installation File Structure

In order to give you a basic overview of how the files in Community Server are structured you should take a look at the installation folder for one of these packages. They are all very similar and provide you with the basic structure shown in Figure 2-1. The majority of the theme development will take place with the files located in the Themes folder. In fact, this is where the code for the majority of the pages on a site is now located. If you look in any of the other application-specific folders, such as blogs, you will find files that are used for URL rewriting and that do not contain actual page content.

Figure 2-1: Installation Folder Structure

When you open a page that is not in the `ControlPanel` or `Themes` folder, you will find that they simply provide you with a link to the page that they represent. For example, if you open `blogs/about.aspx`, you will find the following contents in this file commented out:

```
The content of this page is defined by the theme associated to this
blog and is located at web/themes/blogs/[THEME NAME]/about.aspx
```

The `about.aspx` page points you to a page that can be found in any of the blog themes that ships with Community Server. Whenever you open the `about.aspx` page in one of these themes, you will find the actual code that represents this page and controls its layout.

The `ControlPanel` is another folder that contains page content. This is where all of the administration pages are located and where you can go to change the presentation of your Control Panel. Inside the `ControlPanel` folder, there is a `UI` folder that contains master pages and CSS files.

Setting Up a Development Environment

In order to setcup your development environment, you need a copy of the software development kit (SDK) that is available for Community Server. Additionally, you need Visual Studio 2005 installed as well as an appropriate database server. Once you have this software installed and the SDK package available, you can begin by extracting the SDK to an appropriate location for development. This can be anyplace on your machine, but it can be useful to have this location in an organized structure such as `C:\Development\CommunityServer 2007`.

Before doing any development, you should consider using a source control repository for your development work. It is useful for backup purposes as well as general peace of mind to have this repository located on a different machine than where your main development work is taking place. The core development of Community Server at Telligent is done using Subversion. This source control solution is open source and freely available. If you already have a source control in use, then you can continue to use it with Community Server. It is generally helpful, though, to make sure that your initial check-in is a fresh unpackage of the SDK so that you are always able to rollback to a stable point in development.

Before you open the solution file for the SDK, you should make sure that you have either SP1 for Visual Studio 2005 or the Visual Studio 2005 Web Application Project upgrade installed. This is required because the Community Server "Web" project is a web application project.

Inside of the SDK package folder, you will find a source subfolder that contains all of the source code that is available. Under the source folder you will find a solution file that you can open with Visual Studio 2005. This will open all of the available projects that ship with the Community Server 2007 SDK, which are shown below in Figure 2-2. If you are familiar with the 2.1 SDK, you will notice a couple of differences in which projects source code is available.

A couple of the differences between the 2.1 SDK and the 2007 SDK is that the `MailRoom` project has been updated and the `Reader` project has been removed. Another big update can be found in the `Controls` project, which now contains new Chameleon controls. You should become familiar with this project, as it contains many of the controls that you will use when changing the presentation of your Community Server site.

Figure 2-2: SDK Solution View

Once you have the solution open you should try compiling it to make sure that there are no errors in the package. Whenever you want to do any debugging, you should make sure that your solution is being built using the Debug solution configuration. There are a couple of ways that you can debug a Community Server site. One of the easiest is to set the Web project as a startup project, then push the F5 button to start the project.

If you are using IIS 7, you may need to change the project settings so that you are using the ASP.NET web server to run your site and debug it. Otherwise, you may need to manually attach the debugger to the w3wp.exe process. If you are running Vista, you may need to click the "Show process in all sessions" checkbox to locate the w3wp.exe process, which is shown in Figure 2-3. Remember, that this worker process is started whenever you first visit your site. Therefore, make sure that you first have a site created that points to your source\web folder as the home directory. Next, you will want to build your solution and then try browsing to your site, which will start a worker process that you can attach to.

Figure 2-3: Attach to Process Window

For the majority of your theme development, you will not need to use the debugger. However, it is an invaluable asset to have in situations where something unexpected occurs or where you simply would like to understand the steps that make an action work successfully.

Previewing Themes

Another aspect of development that is important to know is how to switch to the theme that you are developing and preview it. This will assist you in viewing your new theme from the perspective of the end user. Additionally, knowing how to not only change to your theme but also configure it through the Control Panel will give you a good summary of the options that you can provide to administrators for controlling how your theme is presented.

There are a couple of sitewide themes that ship with Community Server 2007 that you will switch between and then preview in the following steps. Before you complete the following steps, you should first log in as a system administrator.

1. Click on the Control Panel navigation menu link.

2. Click on the Administration menu link.

3. Expand the Settings menu, and click the Theme Options link.

4. Select a different theme from the Default Theme dropdown list.

5. You can optionally disable user theme selection, which means that everyone is forced to use the theme you select.

6. Click the Save button to save your changes.

Before you exit the Control Panel to preview how the different theme looks, you can use the dropdown list preview to get an idea of what it will look like. If you navigate to the Theme Configuration page, which is located below the Theme Options page, you can observe the various presentation changes that you can make from the Control Panel. Many of these configuration options allow you to change the colors and fonts that are used throughout the site. However, there are more advanced options that are available and allow you to change what images or layout your site has.

Once you have saved your settings, you can exit the Control Panel and preview your site. You can observe any configuration changes you made to the theme whenever you exit the Control Panel and browse through your site. You should also note that whenever you make these theme changes and click the Save button, the changes take effect immediately, regardless of any message displayed.

If you are interested in making configuration changes and previewing them before they are saved to the live site, you can use the Preview tab on the Theme Configuration page, which is displayed in Figure 2-4. This allows you to make configuration changes and click the Update Live Preview button to update your view of these changes. It is helpful to open a preview of the site in a different window so that when you make a presentation change you can simply click the Update Live Preview button, then refresh the window to see your changes. It is important to remember that these changes are not seen by other users until you click the Save button.

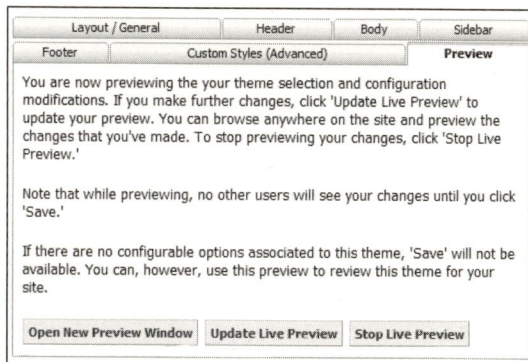

Figure 2-4: Theme Configuration Page

Summary

In this chapter, you learned about the software that you should have installed in order to begin your development with Community Server. You also learned how to download and set up your development environment for Community Server. With your development environment setup, you are able to open the Community Server SDK and begin developing not only themes but also new features. Finally, you learned about some of the files that you are able to theme, as well as about the ability to preview new themes in the Control Panel. In the next chapter, you will learn about URL rewriting and how it works in Community Server.

3

URL Rewriting

In this chapter, you will learn how Community Server uses URL rewriting to manage its handling of web pages. This chapter shows that there are numerous advantages to using URL rewriting in a platform like Community Server. By the end of this chapter you should feel comfortable with the following areas:

- ❑   SiteUrls.config File
- ❑   Location Element of the SiteUrls.config
- ❑   URLs and Transformers
- ❑   Navigation and Links

URL Rewriting

URL rewriting means that when you request a specific URL, the page that you are actually requesting on the web server is not necessarily the one that is referenced by your original request. In the previous chapter the example of the message pages was provided as a way to describe this process. In that situation when a user navigates to the page at /msgs/default.aspx, you are actually accessing the page located at /themes/default/msgs/message.aspx.

The URL rewriting in Community Server uses the System.Web.HttpContext classes RewritePath method to do a lot of the rewriting work. The RewritePath takes a request to a given page and basically rewrites it along with any additional query string information that is desired. This call to the RewritePath method is contained in the UrlReWriteProvider class that is located in the CommunityServer.Urls project and namespace. The nice thing about the fact that this is contained in a provider is that you can change how rewriting works on your site by using your own custom provider.

In order for the rewriting to work correctly, the call to the `RewritePath` needs to take place in the ASP.NET HTTP Pipeline. To accomplish this task Community Server uses an HTTP module called `CSHttpModule`. Inside the begin request event handler, the `CSHttpModule` calls the `ReWriteUrl` method, which in turn makes a call down the stack to the `HttpContext RewritePath` method. Figure 3-1 illustrates this entire process.

In Figure 3-1, a request to the `/msgs/default.aspx` page is made, and as a result `/themes/default/msgs/message.aspx` is loaded. The process that is involved to make this all possible is fairly straightforward, especially when you look at and understand the code. An important thing to take note of is that the `CSHttpModule` is required in order for any of the rewriting to take place in Community Server. This module is enabled inside of the `Web.config` file, and should not be removed or commented out.

The data that is used to convert a path to a new path is created from the `SiteUrls.config` file. The various entries in this file along with their respective attributes are useful in controlling what each requested path is rewritten to. As a result of this, Community Server can appear to contain more pages than it actually does. For example, the request to `/forums/t/3.aspx` and `/forums/t/5.aspx` will both return the same physical page on the server. However, to an end user it appears that he or she is requesting two different pages.

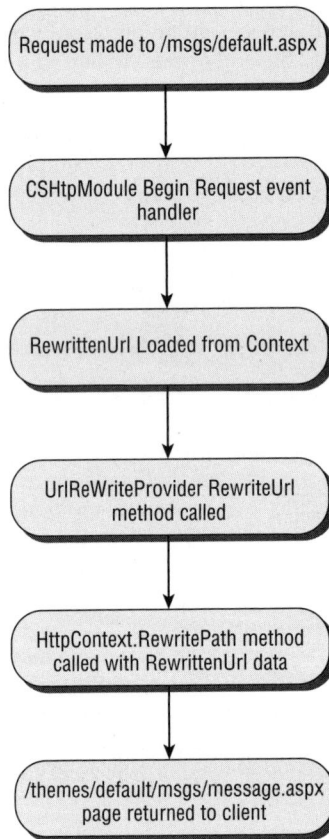

```
┌─────────────────────────────────────┐
│   Request made to /msgs/default.aspx │
└─────────────────────────────────────┘
                  │
                  ▼
┌─────────────────────────────────────┐
│  CSHtpModule Begin Request event     │
│             handler                  │
└─────────────────────────────────────┘
                  │
                  ▼
┌─────────────────────────────────────┐
│   RewrittenUrl Loaded from Context   │
└─────────────────────────────────────┘
                  │
                  ▼
┌─────────────────────────────────────┐
│   UrlReWriteProvider RewriteUrl      │
│          method called               │
└─────────────────────────────────────┘
                  │
                  ▼
┌─────────────────────────────────────┐
│  HttpContext.RewritePath method      │
│  called with RewrittenUrl data       │
└─────────────────────────────────────┘
                  │
                  ▼
┌─────────────────────────────────────┐
│ /themes/default/msgs/message.aspx    │
│    page returned to client           │
└─────────────────────────────────────┘
```

Figure 3-1: Rewrite URL Flow

SiteUrls.config File

The `SiteUrls.config` file is extremely important to Community Server, as it defines the mapping for how a page request relates to the physical pages of a site. That is to say that whenever you make a request to a given path, the `SiteUrls.config` file handles what page you will actually end up accessing. As a result of this mapping, when you go to the homepage of your site at `/default.aspx`, you are actually visiting `/themes/default/common/home.aspx`.

One of the advantages of this behavior is that it allows you to configure the location of your pages. As a result, you can actually have several different paths that are rewritten to a single page. Thus, you can have a single page that appears to be many pages by allowing it to handle multiple paths. It also allows for theme pages to be located in different directories and yet appear as though they are in the main directory paths, as in the example above of the `default.aspx` page.

This rewriting data is made available to Community Server by a provider that uses the provider pattern. The provider that is in charge of loading `SiteUrls.config` file is specified in the `CommunityServer.config` file. In addition to the `SiteUrls.config` file there is also an optional `SiteUrls_override.config` file that is merged with the `SiteUrls.config` to form a single `SiteURLs` configuration. More information about how this merging works and how you can create your own `SiteUrls_override.config` file is available in Chapter 4. These options are controlled by the following entry in the `CommunityServer.config` file:

```
<add
    name = "SiteUrlsDataProvider"
    type = "CommunityServer.Urls.UrlsData, CommunityServer.Urls"
    path = "SiteUrls.config"
    overridePath ="SiteUrls_override.config"
/>
```

If you are interested in changing the location of the override file or the original path to the `SiteUrls.config` file, you can do so by changing this entry. For example, if you want to have the configuration file simply called `Urls.config` and the override path named `Urls_override.config`, you simply need to change the `path` and `overridePath` entries. These files are, by default, located in the root folder of your site where your `Global.asax` file is also located. One more important thing to note is that these files will not be served to a web user because they have a `.config` extension. This helps prevent malicious users from finding out any important configuration settings on your site.

The code for the `SiteUrlsDataProvider` is located in the `CommunityServer.Urls` project. This project is available with the Community Server 2007 SDK. If you are interested in viewing the code that loads the `SiteUrls.config` file, you should open this project in the SDK solution. Furthermore, if you plan to create your own `UrlsProvider`, you can also get some good ideas on how to do so by looking at this same project.

Now that you have a basic understanding of what the `SiteUrls.config` does and where it is located, you should open it up with a text editor and take a look at the various sections that make up this powerful file. When you look through the file, you should notice the following core XML nodes:

- ❑ locations
- ❑ transformers
- ❑ navigation

Each of these nodes will be explained in detail in the following sections. It is important at this point to realize that there are really just three main areas that make up the `SiteUrls.config` file. However, each of these sections provides some fairly complex rewriting behavior.

Locations

The `locations` node is the first part of the `SiteUrls.config` file that you should become familiar with. It contains the bulk listing of how each path maps to its respective theme path. Inside the `locations` node you will find individual `location` child nodes. The `location` entry specifies a folder on your site and if any of that folder's child pages should be rewritten to a different path. The main `location` node can contain the following attributes:

❑ **type** — If no type is specified the `Location` object will be used by default. The `Location` object can be found in the `CommunityServer.Components` project and namespace. In Community Server 2007, the `CSLocation` is specified as the type to use.

❑ **name** — The unique name that describes the location entry. You should make sure that all of your location elements have a name attribute; otherwise, they will not be loaded correctly.

❑ **path** — The path to the folder where the pages to be controlled are located. This path should begin and end with a forward slash. The path element is required just like the name element; therefore, you should make sure to include this.

❑ **physicalPath** — This is similar to `path`; you should surround it with a forward slash. This is not a required element, and if you do not include it then the `path` will be stored as `physicalPath` in the `Location` object.

❑ **exclude** — A Boolean value indicating whether a path should be included in URL rewriting. When this is set to true, the requests to this path will not be rewritten.

❑ **themeDir** — The theme directory where the pages for the location will be rewritten to. This value will be transformed to `/themes/default/themeDir/`. In this example, `default` is the name of your theme, and `themeDir` is the value you put into the `themeDir` attribute of the `location` node.

Here are a couple of examples to help explain how the location entries should be formed. When you open the `SiteUrls.config` file, you will see an entry for the theme folder that looks like this:

```
<location name="themes" path="/themes/" exclude = "true" />
```

Once the above entry is translated into the `Location` object, it will have the following properties. These properties are for a default installation of Community Server that is located in a virtual directory named "cs" off the default website.

❑ Name = "themes"

❑ Path = "/cs/themes/"

❑ PhysicalPath = "/cs/themes/"

❑ Exclude = true

With the above properties, the pages that are located in the themes folder will be excluded from URL rewriting. If you want to exclude a page from being rewritten, you can add it to the themes folder in any subfolder. You can also exclude other paths on your site by simply adding the exclude attribute to the location node that you want to exclude from being rewritten to a new location.

url Element

An example of a location element in the `SiteUrls.config` file that does more than exclude a path from URL rewriting is presented below. This element is for the messages folder and contains specific URLs that will be rewritten to the appropriate theme page. In the example, when a user browses to either of these URLs in the `msgs` folder, it will actually load a page located in the theme folder. This is what the entire messages location looks like in the `SiteUrls.config` file:

```
<location name="message" path="/msgs/" themeDir="msgs">
    <url name="message" path="default.aspx?MessageID={0}"
        pattern="default.aspx" physicalPath="##themeDir##" vanity="{2}"
        page="message.aspx" />
    <url name="message_modal" path="modalmessage.aspx?MessageID={0}"
        pattern="modalmessage.aspx" physicalPath="##themeDir##"
        vanity="{2}" page="modalmessage.aspx" />
</location>
```

The above entry indicates that the pages located in the root `msgs` folder will be rewritten to a page that is located in the theme directory also called `msgs`. For example, if you request a page with a default installation of Community Server that is at `/msgs/default.aspx`, you will actually be loading the page at `/themes/default/msgs/message.aspx`.

The fact that a request to `msgs/default.aspx` will rewrite to `/themes/default/msgs/message.aspx` is indicated in the combination of the `location` node and the `url` element. The `location` entry indicates that the `url` entries will be found inside of the `/msgs/` folder and will have their physical path located in the `msgs` theme directory. The `url` entry for message indicates that a request that matches the regular expression pattern of `default.aspx` should be rewritten to the page `message.aspx` found in the location entries theme directory. To better explain how these attributes relate, refer to the following list of attributes that are valid inside of a `url` entry:

❑   **name** — Unique name to identify the `url` entry.

❑   **path** — The path to the original page that the request comes in on. This can be used to indicate any special query string values that are used with the incoming request.

❑   **pattern** — The pattern to match to identify that the requested URL maps to the `url` entry. If the pattern does not begin with a forward slash then the path will be prepended to the pattern to get the full path. The pattern can be a regular expression as the eventual pattern will be matched using a regular expression to indicate that the page begins with the provided pattern.

❑   **physicalPath** — The path where the page that will be rewritten to is located. In most situations, this is going to be found in the theme directory; therefore, the transformer `##themeDir##` is used.

❑   **vanity** — specifies any extra query string or page changes that you want to include when the `url` is rewritten. The vanity can include `string.Format` placeholders, since this is applied to it. The value for `{0}` will be the Theme page name, `{1}` is the theme directory, and `{2}` is the page name specified in the page attribute.

❑   **page** — The page that should be rewritten to. For example, if you specify `Test.aspx`, this will be the page that will be loaded when a request is made for a page with the related `url` pattern.

❑   **redirect** — A Boolean value indicating if the request should be redirected to the new page. If this is true, then a 301 status code will be sent to the client.

❑   **navigateUrl** — Used in conjunction with only a name attribute to specify a direct URL. This is intended to be the full URL that is associated with the `url` name. If you supply this attribute, all other attributes will be ignored, and the `url` name will be mapped to this specific URL.

There are several different options for the `url` entry, but once you break things down and see a couple of examples, it will all become clearer how each can be used. Consider the post `url` entry that is in found the forums location inside of the `SiteUrls.config`, which is shown here:

```
<url name="post"  path = "thread/{0}.aspx" pattern = "thread/(\d+).aspx"
     vanity="{2}?PostID=$1^UrlName=post" page="ForumUrlHandler.ashx" />
```

When processing the above entry, the `UrlsData` class in the `CommunityServer.Urls` project will try to replace any transforms in the path with their corresponding values. However, this `url` entry does not contain any transforms, so none are substituted (transforms will be explained in greater detail in the following section).

Whenever the pattern attribute is processed, it is prepended with the location's full path. Therefore, the pattern becomes `/cs/forums/thread/(\d+).aspx` in this scenario, where Community Server is installed into the `cs` virtual directory. This is true because the location is represented as `/cs/forums/`, and the pattern is `thread/(\d+).aspx`. The pattern is a regular expression that is used to identify if a given request matches a `url` entry. Therefore, if a request is made to a Community Server site that looks like `/cs/forums/thread/3.aspx`, it will be matched to the post `url` entry. The `(\d+)` is another way of saying any numeric value, so any digit that is used here will be matched. However, if you had a request to `/cs/forums/thread/three.aspx`, it would not be matched.

If you are not familiar with regular expressions you will be fine when you create custom `url` entries. However, it wouldn't hurt to become familiar with regular expressions (regex), as they are extremely powerful in many different situations. The digit-matching expression, `(\d+)`, and the word-matching one, `([\w\.-]+)`, are the most likely regular expressions you will need to know about when creating custom `url` entries for most situations. One tool that you can use to help test your regular expressions to make sure that they are matching the correct strings is the Regulator. This, along with Regulazy, are tools that Roy Osherove created to help make creating and testing regular expressions very easy for the .NET platform.

Similarly to how the pattern is processed, the vanity value also is prepended with the `locations` path whenever a `fullPath` is not supplied. In this scenario, vanity becomes `/cs/forums/{2}?PostID=$1^UrlName=post`. After this occurs, both the updated vanity and pattern values are searched for any transformer values that need to be replaced. In this situation, there is none, so the `url` rewrite process continues. The resulting values are all stored as a `ReWrittenUrl` object in a collection that will be used for processing requests and creating links from the values.

Whenever a link is to be created from the above post `url` entry, a call to the `UrlsData FormatUrl` method is made. When this happens, parameters are usually passed to a `string.Format()` method and are substituted in the `{0}` part of the `path` string. For example, if you are navigating to a post with an ID of 3, your resulting forum's post URL becomes `/cs/forums/thread/3.aspx`. This happens because the path entry is `thread/{0}.aspx`, and this is used in a statement that looks similar to the code below when the ID is 3 to create part of the resulting path URL:

```
String.Format("thread/{0}.aspx", "3");
```

As a post page is requested that matches the regex pattern of ^/cs/forums/thread/(\d+).aspx, and the GetReWrittenUrl method for the matched `ReWrittenUrl` object is called. In this situation, the `ReWrittenUrl` object represents the post `url` entry. As a result, the `GetReWrittenUrl` method will process the post `url` entry values and create a `ReWrittenUrl` object. The value for the post entry that will have a `string.Format` applied to it in this example is stored as /cs/forums/{2}?PostID= $1&UrlName=post. The fields that are passed to the `string.Format` method as parameters are theme name, the theme page folder, and the page name. In the example, the page was set as `ForumUrlHandler` .ashx, the theme name is default, and the theme folder is forums. Therefore, because only the third parameter, {2}, will be substituted into the post `url`, it becomes: /cs/forums/ForumUrlHandler.ashx?PostID= $1&UrlName=post. Next, the pattern regular expression is used to replace the required URL with the post URL that was created in the previous step. As a result, the URL becomes: /cs/forums/ForumUrlHandler. ashx?PostID=3&UrlName=post. After this, any additional query string parameters are appended to the URL, but because none is supplied in the example, the above URL is the URL that the user will actually be accessing when he or she makes a request to /cs/forums/thread/3.aspx.

One important consideration is that the name of the matched pattern `url` entry is added as a query string parameter called `UrlName`. This can be useful when creating new `url` entries and checking to make sure that the appropriate pattern was matched. You can check from a page that was rewritten to the `UrlName` that was used to transfer the request, to verify that the appropriate entry was used. This information is especially useful when trying to debug a situation where multiple `url` entries are rewriting to the same path, but where you expect them to go to different paths. This can also be useful to help identify what `url` entries are used and which are not on your site. You could optionally create a report that shows you the `url` entries used and those that are not used.

Transformers

In the previous section, you learned about the `url` entry and saw some of the steps that show how transformers can be used in the rewriting process. At a couple of points during the rewriting process, the transformers are utilized to replace specific keywords with their related values. These keywords exist in the transformers section of the `SiteUrls.config`. In Community Server 2007, this section is located between the `locations` and `navigation` sections and should look like this:

```
<transformers>
  <add key = "^" value = "&amp;" />
  <add key = "##themeDir##" value = "/themes/{0}/{1}/" />
  <add key = "##blogthemeDir##" value = "/themes/blogs/{0}/" />
  <add key = "##blogdirectory##" value = "{0}/" />
  <add key = "##photogallerydirectory##" value = "{0}/" />
  <add key = "##filegallerydirectory##" value = "{0}/" />
  <add key = "##blogName##" value = "(?&lt;app&gt;[\w\.-]+)" />
  <add key = "##photoGalleryName##" value = "([\w\.-]+)" />
  <add key = "##contentName##" value = "([\w\.-]+)" />
  <add key = "##fileGalleryName" value = "([\w\.-]+)" />
  <add key = "##userName##" value = "(.+)" />
  <add key = "//" value = "/" />
</transformers>
```

Often when you want to have a portion of the path value in a `url` entry replaced with the physical path of the page that will be rewritten to you should use a transformer. Usually the transformer will be used in the `physicalPath` attribute so that the resulting page path contains the complete location of the page that the user will be redirected to. Consider the `thread` `url` in the forums location that looks like this:

```
<url name="thread" path="t/{0}.aspx" pattern ="t/(\d+).aspx"
    physicalPath="##themeDir##" vanity="{2}?ThreadID=$1"
    page="thread.aspx" />
```

The `##themeDir##` is a transformer and is replaced with `/themes/{0}/{1}/` and is then prepended to the vanity value. Thus, the resulting vanity becomes `/themes/{0}/{1}/{2}?ThreadID=$1`. A string `.Format` is applied to the vanity value to get the resulting rewritten URL. If the theme was called default, then the URL for thread becomes `/themes/default/forums/thread.aspx?ThreadID=$1`. The value of the `ThreadID` query string becomes the digit that was matched using the `pattern` attribute when looking at the original URL.

In addition to the `physicalPath` attribute, the `pattern` attribute also uses transformers to perform its duties. The transformers with the regular expressions as their values are used in `pattern` attributes for various `url` entries.

You can also add your own custom transformers if you like. These can be any common string that you use throughout your `SiteUrls.config` file that you want to be consistent. For example, if you want, you can create a transformer for the digit regex and replace its usage with the transformer. Below is what the new transformer key value entry would look like:

```
<add key = "##digit##" value = "(\d+)" />
```

This would then allow you to replace a `url` entry's usage of the `(\d+)` regex with the transformer `##digit##`. As a result, you could change the forum `url` entry for thread from the entry shown first to the one following it:

```
<url name="thread" path="t/{0}.aspx" pattern ="t/(\d+).aspx"
    physicalPath="##themeDir##" vanity="{2}?ThreadID=$1"
    page="thread.aspx" />
```

```
<url name="thread" path="t/{0}.aspx" pattern ="t/##digit##.aspx"
    physicalPath="##themeDir##" vanity="{2}?ThreadID=$1"
    page="thread.aspx" />
```

As a result of this change, your thread entry will be handled the same as it is currently. The main advantage of this change is that if you want to change how your digit-matching regex looks, you do not need to change it in every place that it is used; instead, you can simply change it in the transformer section, and all the places where the `##digit##` transformer is used would be updated.

Navigation and Links

The navigation section of the `SiteUrls.config` serves as a central place to control the navigation links that are used in the sitewide navigation links. This is the navigation bar that is on pages in a Community Server site. These links consist of Blogs, Forums, Home, Photos, Downloads, and Control Panel. The navigation entries contain the URL to link to, the text to display for the link, and even what roles to show the link to. Here is what the default navigation section looks like in the `SiteUrls.config` file:

```
<navigation>
  <link name="home" resourceUrl="home" resourceName="home"
    roles="Everyone" />
  <link name="blog" resourceUrl="webloghome" resourceName="weblogs"
    roles="Everyone" applicationType = "Weblog" />
  <link name="forums" resourceUrl="forumshome" resourceName="forums"
    roles="Everyone" applicationType = "Forum" />
  <link name="gallery" resourceUrl="galleryhome" resourceName="photos"
    roles="Everyone" applicationType = "Gallery" />
  <link name="files" resourceUrl="fileshome" resourceName="files"
    roles="Everyone" applicationType = "FileGallery" />
  <link name="controlpanel" resourceUrl="controlpanel"
    resourceName="controlpanel"
    roles="SystemAdministrator,BlogAdministrator,ForumsAdministrator,
    Moderator,GalleryAdministrator,FileAdministrator,
    ReaderAdministrator,MembershipAdministrator" />
</navigation>
```

You can use several attributes for each link entry in the navigation section. Here is a list of these valid attributes as well as a description of each:

❑   **name** — A descriptive name or key for a given link entry.

❑   **resourceUrl** — The name of a `url` entry in the `SiteUrls.config` that should be used to create the URL to link to.

❑   **resourceName** — The name of a `resources.xml` entry to use for the text that will be displayed in for the link. This is useful for international sites where you have a different language and local than the default en-US local.

❑   **navigateUrl** — If you want to supply a full URL that is not provided in your `SiteUrls.config`, then you can do so with this attribute.

❑   **text** — The text to display for the link when you choose not to use a resource entry.

❑   **roles** — A comma-delimited list of roles to display the link to. If none are supplied then the default role becomes Everyone.

❑   **target** — Used like a standard target in an anchor tag. This can be used to open a link in a new window or in a specific window.

❑   **type** — If you would like to use a custom link type other than the `CSLink` object, you can do so with this attribute.

❑   **applicationType** — The application that your link belongs to so that when the application is currently being accessed the navigation link for that application can show that the application link is selected.

The Navigation section allows you to define custom links that will be added to the navigation menu on your site. For example, if for some reason you want to provide a link that appears on all of your site's main pages, outside of the Control Panel and custom blog themes, then you can define one in this section.

Below is a navigation entry that would create a new link to Google and would open this link in a new window:

```
<link name="google" text="Google" navigateUrl="http://google.com"
    target="_blank" />
```

As a result of adding the above entry, you will get a new link on your site that appears after the Control Panel (if it is visible) or the Downloads link. This link is shown below in Figure 3-2 as it appears in the default theme. If you want the link to appear at a different place in the link order, then you can move it so that it appears between the link entries you want it to. The links will be displayed in the order that they appear in your navigation section from left to right. This is why the Home link appears before the Blogs link.

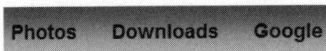

Figure 3-2 Modified Navigation Menu

Summary

In this chapter, you learned about many of the basic principles that help make URL rewriting possible in Community Server. You learned how different page requests are mapped and rewritten to their respective theme pages. Furthermore, you learned about what attributes are available in the SiteUrls.config file and how these allow you to completely control how your site paths are presented to the user.

In the next chapter, you will use this knowledge of the SiteUrls.config file and URL rewriting process to add additional pages and url entries. You will also learn how to modify the SiteUrls.config file without physically altering the file through the SiteUrls_override.config file. The information gained in both chapters is fundamental to understanding how your theme pages relate to requested pages on your site.

4

Adding New Pages to SiteUrls.config

In the previous chapter, you learned about some of the basics of URL rewriting, including how all of the various rewriting pieces come together to accomplish the process of rewriting. In this chapter, you will take this knowledge of rewriting and learn how to apply it in situations where you need to add new pages to your site that must be located in the `SiteUrls.config` file. By the end of this chapter, you should be knowledgeable in the following areas:

- ❑ Modifying `SiteUrls.config` through overrides
- ❑ Adding a Simple URL
- ❑ Adding a URL with query strings

Modifying SiteUrls.config through Overrides

Both the `SiteUrls.config` and the `CommunityServer.config` files are able to be modified without physically touching them. This is possible by a new feature in Community Server 2007 called *override files*. These files are optional and need to be created if they are to be used on your site. When an override file exists its contents are merged with the configuration file that it is intended to modify. As a result, your site configuration file will be updated with the override's contents. After the `SiteUrls.config` file is loaded, the `SiteUrls_override.config` file is loaded and then merged to create the resulting URLs data that is used to control the location of pages on a site and dictate how URLs should be rewritten.

The overrides file uses the xpath notation to identify where a configuration file needs to be changed. This notation allows for specific attributes to be updated as well as individual nodes to be added to or removed from the configuration file. As a result, the overrides file is able to customize the existing configuration file in just about everyway imaginable without physically altering the file.

One of the advantages of using the overrides approach instead of physically altering a configuration file is that it allows a site to be upgraded much more easily. Now that Community Server offers the overrides file option whenever a site is upgraded to a newer version the `SiteUrls.config` and `CommunityServer.config` files do not have to be updated manually. Before, whenever you upgraded a site, and if you made any changes to either of these files, you had to manually go through each file and make sure that your changes were added back to the upgraded copies. Now you don't have to perform this step; instead, you can let the override files update the configuration settings.

In the previous chapter, you learned about how you can actually change the names of the `SiteUrls` override file. Remember that this file is controlled through the `SiteUrls` provider that is located in the `CommunityServer.config` file. By default, the `SiteUrls.config` override file should be named `SiteUrls_override.config`. However, if you would like to change this name to simply `Urls_override.config`, you can update the `SiteUrlsDataProvider` entry to the following:

```
<add name = "SiteUrlsDataProvider"
    type = "CommunityServer.Urls.UrlsData, CommunityServer.Urls"
    path = "SiteUrls.config"
    overridePath ="Urls_override.config"
/>
```

The override file is an XML file, so it should look very similar to the actual `SiteUrls.config` file. You should begin your override file with the XML encoding and version declaration that looks like this example:

```
<?xml version="1.0" encoding="utf-8" ?>
```

The override file also uses custom attributes to describe what action to take on the node that is selected by the xpath. Here is a list of the available key attributes that you can use and a short description of what each of them do.

- ❑ **remove** — Used to delete a node or to delete an `xml` attribute

- ❑ **update** — Used to change the entry of an entire `xml` node

- ❑ **add** — Used to add a node as a child at the beginning or end of a parent node

- ❑ **change** — Used to change the value of an `xml` attribute

- ❑ **new** — Used to create a new attribute with a specified value

Because each of the above options is extremely useful in its own way, they are explained in more detail in the following subsections. The above list is a good overview of what each option can do, and the options will be made clearer whenever you see an example of one of them. Another thing to realize is that each `xpath` override node can only make use of one of the override options. This means that you cannot combine options on a single line, such as adding multiple attributes.

It is important to understand the structure of an override file. At the top level is the document node called `Overrides`. Inside of this node, you can have multiple `Override` entries. Inside of each `Override` entry is the action that you would like to take along with the `xpath` to identify the location to perform this action. To demonstrate the structure, consider the following override file as a simple template:

```
<?xml version="1.0" encoding="utf-8" ?>
<Overrides>
```

```
        <Override xpath="/SiteUrls/transformers/add[@key='##blogdirectory##']"
            mode = "change" name = "value" value = "" />
        <Override xpath = "/SiteUrls/locations/location[@name='weblogs']" mode =
            "new" name = "physicalPath" value = "/blogs/" />
        <Override xpath = "/SiteUrls/navigation/link[@name='home']" mode = "add"
            where="start">
            <link name="shop" navigateUrl="http://" text="wiki" />
        </Override >
    </Overrides>
```

Remove Override Example

The remove option is useful for deleting either a single node or a single attribute that exists on a node. For example, if you would like to delete the home navigation link that exists in the navigation section you could use the following override entry to accomplish this:

```
<Override xpath = "/SiteUrls/navigation/link[@name='home']" mode = "remove" />
```

As you can see in this example the xpath locates the entry for the home link. When using xpath, you can use forward slashes to show the parent and nodes of the node you are trying to find. In this situation, the SiteUrls.config file had the following structure, which results in the xpath value of /SiteUrls/ navigation/link[@name='home'].

```
<SiteUrls>
    <navigation>
        <link name="home" />
    </navigation>
</SiteUrls>
```

Aside from removing an actual node, you can also remove individual attributes that exist on a particular node. If you want to remove the roles attribute on the Control Panel link, so that the Control Panel link is displayed for all users, regardless of their role, you can use the following override entry:

```
<Override xpath = "/SiteUrls/navigation/link[@name='controlpanel']"
    mode="remove" name="roles" />
```

Update Override Example

Quite often you will need to change the value of an xml node. To do this you can set the override mode attribute to update. Keep in mind that the update mode cannot be used for changing the value of an xml attribute. In order to do that you should use the change mode.

Assume that you would like to update the home link so that it uses the same URL that the blog link uses. You could use the following override entry to accomplish this task, which uses the update mode:

```
<Override xpath = "/SiteUrls/navigation/link[@name='home']" mode="update">
    <link name="home" resourceUrl="webloghome" resourceName="home"
        roles="Everyone" />
</Override>
```

As you can see, the node that you want to replace the selected `xpath` node with is inserted into the `Override` node. This allows you to do some very useful things, such as insert multiple nodes where one node existed previously. If you would like to insert a new link that goes to Google after the home link on your navigation bar, you could use the following override. Notice that this override entry simply has multiple link nodes inside of it, as the override will replace the existing `xpath`-selected node with whatever is in override:

```
<Override xpath = "/SiteUrls/navigation/link[@name='home']" mode="update">
    <link name="home" resourceUrl="webloghome" resourceName="home"
        roles="Everyone" />
    <link name="google" navigateUrl="http://google.com" text="Google" />
</Override>
```

Add Override Example

The add mode allows you to insert a new node or nodes at the beginning or end of a parent node. This is useful if you would like to add a new link or `url` entry. This mode also takes an optional "where" attribute that when omitted will add the node to the beginning of the parent node. However, if you would like to add the entry to the end of the parent node, then you can supply the attribute "where" with a value of anything other than "start."

Suppose that you need to add a couple of new links on your site and you would like these links to appear before the home link; you can use the following override:

```
<Override xpath = "/SiteUrls/navigation" mode="add" where="start">
    <link name="google" navigateUrl="http://google.com" text="Google" />
    <link name="yahoo" navigateUrl="http://yahoo.com" text="Yahoo" />
</Override>
```

Again, you should use the add mode for creating new node entries as a child in a parent node. If you would like to create new attributes on a node, you should use the new mode option.

Change Override Example

The change mode is used to update the value of an existing attribute that is on a node. It requires that both a `name` and `value` attribute are supplied. The `name` should be the name of the attribute that you would like to change. The `value` attribute should be the value of that you would like to use with the specified attribute. For example, if you would like to change the roles for the forums link so that you must be a moderator to see it, you can use the following override:

```
<Override xpath = "/SiteUrls/navigation/link[@name='forums']"
    mode="change" name="roles" value="Moderator" />
```

As you can see, the change mode is straightforward, as it only allows you to change the value of a specific attribute on a selected node. It is important that both the `name` and `value` attributes be provided; otherwise, you will encounter an error.

New Override Example

The new mode is used to create a new attribute on a selected node. This is especially useful when combined with all of the other modes that exist. For example, if you want to change the text that is used for the home link, you could combine the remove and new modes into two override entries. This allows you to remove the existing `resourceName` attribute and then create a new text attribute with what you want displayed for the home link. The example below shows what these override entries would look like:

```
<Override xpath = "/SiteUrls/navigation/link[@name='home']" mode="remove"
    name="resourceName" />
<Override xpath = "/SiteUrls/navigation/link[@name='home']" mode="new"
    name="text" value="Homepage" />
```

Overrides File Review

One thing that you should realize is that while the above examples were used to change the `SiteUrls.config` file, you can create a `communityserver_override.config` file to change the `CommunityServer .config` file. Another thing to remember is that you can only use a single override file for each type of config file. This means that you cannot have more than one override file that merges with a single `SiteUrls.config`. That is to say that if you have `siteurls_override.config` and `siteurls1_ override.config` file that only the `siteurls_override.config` file will be used in the merging process.

In order to accurately locate the node that you would like to modify, you should become familiar with `xpath` notation. There are online resources to help you learn about this notation that will locate an item in an `xml` file. The above examples should have provided you with a good starting point for understanding how to locate a node.

Adding a Simple URL

Now that you have a good understanding of override files and how you can use them to alter the `SiteUrls .config` file, you can apply this knowledge to add new URL entries. The new URL entries are useful because it is essentially how you add new pages to a theme. Whenever you add a new page to a theme, you can use rewriting to have multiple URLs use your new single page. This, in turn, allows you to have URL A and URL B actually loading a single page.

To begin this process of adding a new URL entry to the `SiteUrls.config`, you should first add a new page to rewrite the URL to. For the purposes of this example, you will create a static content page that contains "About Us" information. This is a page that simply contains contact information and statements about the site owners. This page will be accessible from almost every page and will, therefore, be placed in the themes `common` folder. If you look in the `Themes\ThemeName\Common` folder, you will find pages that are used throughout the site that include but are not limited to `home.aspx`, `UserWelcome.aspx`, `error-notfound.aspx`, `login.aspx`, and `logout.aspx`. You should create `about.aspx` and place it in this folder in your theme, since this is an example you can use the default theme folder. Therefore, create a new blank page at `Themes\default\Common\About.aspx`.

Next, you should create the `SiteUrls` entry that will rewrite to this page. For this example, assume that the requested URL will be located at `http://yoursite.com/AboutUs.aspx`. This means that you should place your `url` entry inside of the common location in the `SiteUrls.config` file. Also, because this is not using any query string parameters, you will not need to make the entry itself use all of the available `url` node attributes. Instead, your new `url` entry can look like the following:

```
<url name="about" path="" vanity="{2}" pattern="aboutus.aspx"
    physicalPath="##themeDir##" page="about.aspx" />
```

Now if you make a request to `http://yoursite.com/aboutus.aspx`, you will actually be loading the page at `Themes/Common/about.aspx` that you created. You will also notice that the path value is empty, this is to prevent an exception from occurring, if you omit path you will get an error about the `url` entry not being formed correctly. With this particular combination of `physicalPath`, `page`, and the `location` value you are indicating that the page to rewrite to is at `/themes/default/common/about.aspx`.

If you would like to avoid changing the `SiteUrls.config` directly, you add this same `url` entry using the following `Override` inside of a `SiteUrls_override.config` file:

```
<Override xpath = "/SiteUrls/locations/location[@name='common']" mode="add"
        where="end">
    <url name="about" path="" vanity="{2}" pattern="aboutus.aspx"
            physicalPath="##themeDir##" page="about.aspx" />
</Override>
```

You can use this same pattern to add pages to other parts of your site. Remember that you can always change the pattern and location to point to a different place or to have multiple request locations rewrite to the same page. For example, if you would like to have all requests to `http://yoursite.com/forums/aboutForums.aspx` rewrite to the same `about` page that you have created, then you can use the following `url` override to use the forums location in the `SiteUrls.config` file:

```
<Override xpath = "/SiteUrls/locations/location[@name='forums']" mode="add"
        where="end">
    <url name="aboutforums" path="" vanity="{2}" pattern="aboutforums.aspx"
            physicalPath="/themes/{0}/common/" page="about.aspx" />
</Override>
```

You should notice that the transformer `##themeDir##` is omitted in this example. The reason for this is because if it was included the location of forums would override the theme folder so that the rewritten page would be at `/themes/default/forums/about.aspx`. However, since this is not the case, you should use the `physicalPath` provided to rewrite to the same page as in the previous example.

Now to complete this example you can add a new link to the navigation menu that uses the new `url` entry. The new link will say `About` and uses the `url` override for the about us page. Here is what this override entry could look like:

```
<Override xpath = "/SiteUrls/navigation" mode="add" where="end">
    <link name="about" resourceUrl="about" text="About" />
</Override>
```

Adding a URL with Query Strings

There are often situations where you need to pass additional query string values to the page that is being rewritten to. In addition, you may want to format these query string parameters in a way that can be beneficial to SEO. With the URL rewriting that exists in Community Server, you can easily accomplish this task.

For example, if you would like to change the profile view URL so that that username of the profile owner appears to be a folder on the server, you can use rewriting to do this. Assume that the URL you want to achieve is in the form `http://yoursite.com/members/admin/profile.aspx`, where `admin` is the username of the profile you are viewing at this address. You can use the following override to accomplish this task and use the existing profile page to pass the username to on the query string:

```
<Override xpath = "/SiteUrls/locations/location[@name='members']" mode="add"
        where="end">
    <url name="user_profile" path="{0}/profile.aspx"
            pattern="##userName##/profile.aspx" vanity="{2}?UserName=$1"
            physicalPath="##themeDir##" page="userprofile.aspx" />
</Override>
```

As you can see, the override is using the `userprofile.aspx` page that already exists. This page accepts a query string value for the `UserName` of the user you want to view the profile page for. In this situation, the path takes the value at `{0}` and uses it as the `UserName` query string to `userprofile.aspx`. The `$1` sign in the vanity is used to map to the value at `{0}` in the query string. If you have multiple values that you want to pass then each of these would increment. Therefore, `{1}` maps to `$2` and `{2}` maps to `$3` in the vanity. In this example, if you make a request to `http://yoursite.com/members/admin/profile.aspx`, the URL that is rewritten to is actually `http://yoursite.com/themes/default/user/userprofile.aspx?UserName=admin`. As you can see, the first request is much friendlier for SEO purposes, as well as for human readability.

Adding a URL for a page that accepts certain query string values is not much different from adding a simple URL that was examined in the previous section. The main difference is that the vanity and path need to be used appropriately. You can look through some of the other `url` entries in your `SiteUrls.config` file to see more examples of pages that use rewriting and custom patterns with a query string value. Again, this is not much different than the simple `url` entries above, but it is still equally as important.

Summary

In this chapter, you learned about the merging process that takes place whenever you use a custom overrides file. Furthermore, you learned about the various modes and saw examples of each that are possible inside of an override file. Aside from the exploration of how an override file works, you learned about how to add pages to your site and how to link to these pages, using custom override `url` entries.

In the next chapter, you will begin learning about many of the different controls that are possible with Chameleon. With the combined knowledge of the basics of Chameleon and adding pages to the `SiteUrls.config` file, you will begin to feel comfortable adding custom theme pages that support URL rewriting.

5

Basics of Chameleon

Chameleon is the declarative theme definition language used by Community Server. It consists of a set of standard ASP.NET server controls that can be used together to fully define the content and markup of pages rendered by Community Server.

This chapter introduces the basic types of Chameleon controls and explains how they can be used, both individually and in concert, to implement custom themes. This chapter introduces and explains:

- ❑   Implicit data binding
- ❑   Chameleon control types
- ❑   Common properties and behaviors of each control type

Implicit Data Binding

One of the basic features of Chameleon is contextual, implicit data binding. When using standard ASP.NET controls, developers are required to load data, define control data sources, and call `DataBind()` methods. Chameleon controls, in contrast, support the definition of their own data sources and automatic data binding.

Chameleon controls are mapped directly to the Community Server API so that, in general, there is one control for rendering data for each object type in the Community Server API and one control for retrieving lists of each object type in the Community Server API. These controls analyze the context in which they are placed to determine the object for which data should be rendered or the object (or objects) from which to load related information.

The context begins at the page level, using the URL of the current page. Community Server recognizes query string properties such as `GroupID`, `SectionID`, `App`, `PostID`, `PostName`, `UserID`, and others that identify objects in the Community Server API. These URL-defined objects identify the context of the page. Chameleon controls can then use this context to load related data from the Community Server API, in the process extending the context for their child controls.

Contextual Data Binding in Action

Figure 5-1 shows a context map for a page rendering a Community Server blog.

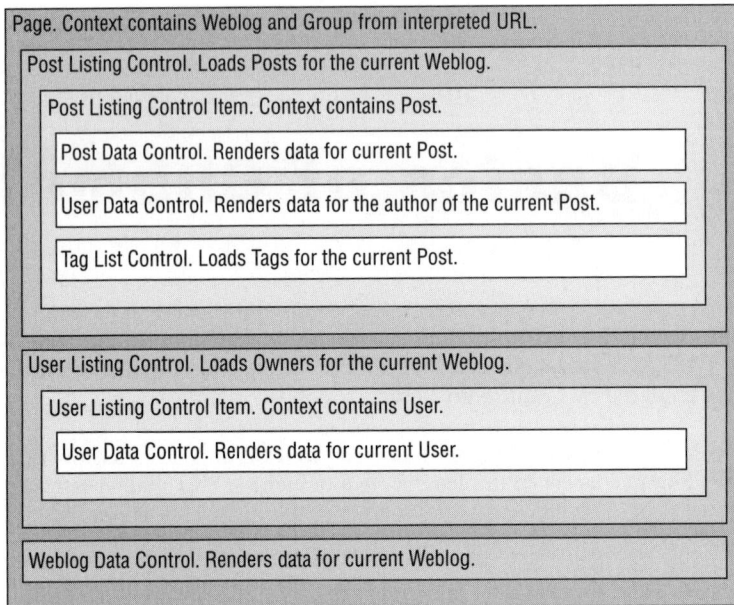

```
Page. Context contains Weblog and Group from interpreted URL.
  Post Listing Control. Loads Posts for the current Weblog.
    Post Listing Control Item. Context contains Post.
      Post Data Control. Renders data for current Post.
      User Data Control. Renders data for the author of the current Post.
      Tag List Control. Loads Tags for the current Post.

  User Listing Control. Loads Owners for the current Weblog.
    User Listing Control Item. Context contains User.
      User Data Control. Renders data for current User.

  Weblog Data Control. Renders data for current Weblog.
```

Figure 5-1: Implicit Data Binding Map

The URL contains the application key related to the blog. The page interprets the URL and includes the Community Server `Weblog` object in the current context. From the blog, the related group can be interpreted, since a blog belongs to only one group.

If, within the page, you place a control that lists posts, the post listing control will identify that the current context includes a group and a blog. Because a blog is more specific than a group, the post listing control will load posts for the current blog.

Within each template rendering each item of the post listing control, the current context then includes the current post loaded by the post listing control. From the post, the user's (the author) tags and post categories can be retrieved. Placing a control that displays user data within this context would render data related to the author of the post in the current context.

Similarly, a user listing control placed within the context of the page would identify that a blog exists in the current context and would load the users who are owners of the blog.

The relationships between objects in the Community Server API are leveraged to automatically determine the data to display using Chameleon controls.

Base Control Types

Chameleon is a set of general-purpose ASP.NET controls. This chapter will describe, in detail, the basic types of Chameleon controls and their purpose and use. Chameleon controls fall into just a few categories:

- ❑ **Single-value controls** — Single-value controls render a single user interface widget or data from a single object from the Community Server API. For example, the UserData control could be used to display the current user's name.

- ❑ **List controls** — List controls provide access to lists of data from the Community Server API and support theme-defined queries. For example, the WeblogPostList control lists posts in a blog.

- ❑ **Pager controls** — Pager controls provide support for viewing data retrieved using Chameleon list controls a page at a time instead of viewing the entire list at once.

- ❑ **Form controls** — Form controls implement behaviors that initiate a process or modify data. For example, the SearchForm is used to initiate a search and the CreateEditForumPostForm is used to create or edit a forum post.

- ❑ **Subform controls** — Subform controls interact with form controls to add new features and behaviors to existing forms. For example, the PostPollSubForm extends form controls that create or edit posts to add support for creating or editing polls in posts.

- ❑ **Condition controls** — Condition controls are the building blocks for defining custom conditional behavior, such as whether to display a specific control.

- ❑ **Action controls** — Action controls are used to define custom actions related to events initiated by other Chameleon controls, such as the successful creation of a forum post.

- ❑ **Utility controls** — Chameleon also provides a set of utility controls that make common theming tasks easier for theme developers.

- ❑ **Page controls** — Chameleon page controls provide the per-page context definition required by other Chameleon controls and expose properties for page-level data access and utility methods for page-level functionality.

A full listing of Chameleon controls and their base types is included in Appendices B through F of this book.

Single-Value Controls

Single-value controls render a single user interface widget or data from a single object from the Community Server API. For example,

```
<CSControl:UserData runat="server" Property="DisplayName" />
```

would simply render the current user's display name, such as:

```
My Name
```

All single-value controls provide support for wrapping the control in custom HTML markup and defining conditions under which the control will be rendered.

Defining Wrapping Markup

By default, single-value controls render only the content of the control with no additional wrapping markup. To define wrapping markup, each single-value control provides a flexible set of properties to control the HTML markup that surrounds the content of the control: Tag, ContainerId, CssClass, LeaderTemplate, and TrailerTemplate.

Tag

For simple content wrapping, the Tag property can be set to the name of the tag in which to wrap the content. For example,

```
<CSControl:UserData Property="DisplayName" Tag="B" runat="server" />
```

would render the current user's display name wrapped in <b></b>, such as:

```
<b>My Name</b>
```

ContainerId

The ContainerId property identifies the ID of the wrapping tag identified by the Tag property. This ID is not processed by ASP.NET and is rendered exactly as specified. Therefore, it is not guaranteed to be unique. For example,

```
<CSControl:UserData Property="DisplayName" Tag="B" ContainerId="username"
runat="server" />
```

would render the current user's display name wrapped in <b id="username"></b>, such as:

```
<b id="username">My Name</b>
```

If the ContainerId property is defined but the Tag property is not defined, the Tag will assume the value of "div" and the ContainerId will be rendered on the <div></div> wrapping tag.

CssClass

The CssClass property identifies the CSS class name to apply to the wrapping tag identified by the Tag property. For example,

```
<CSControl:UserData Property="DisplayName" Tag="B" CssClass="username" runat="server" />
```

would render the current user's display name wrapped in <b class="username"></b>, such as:

```
<b class="username">My Name</b>
```

If the CssClass property is defined but the Tag property is not defined, the Tag will assume the value of "div" and the CssClass will be rendered on the <div></div> wrapping tag.

Attributes

Any properties that do not match properties defined by the control are collected and rendered as attributes of the wrapping tag identified by the Tag property. For example,

```
<CSControl:UserData Property="DisplayName" runat="server" doesnotexist="true"
Tag="div" />
```

would render the current user's display name wrapped in `<div doesnotexist="true"></div>`, such as:

```
<div doesnotexist="true">My Name</div>
```

The support for unrecognized properties is useful when attributes must be rendered that are not explicitly supported by a Chameleon control.

If any unrecognized properties are defined but the Tag property is not defined, the Tag property will assume the value of "div" and unrecognized properties will be rendered on the `<div></div>` wrapping tag.

LeaderTemplate and TrailerTemplate

The LeaderTemplate property defines markup and controls to render before the content of the control. Similarly, the TrailerTemplate defines markup and controls to render after the content of the control. For example,

```
<CSControl:UserData Property="DisplayName" runat="server">
<LeaderTemplate>
    <div style="padding: 8px; background-color: #ccc; color: #000;">
</LeaderTemplate>
<TrailerTemplate>
    </div>
</TrailerTemplate>
</CSControl:UserData>
```

would render the current user's display name wrapped in the defined leading and trailing markup, such as:

```
<div style="padding: 8px; background-color: #ccc; color: #000;">
My Name
</div>
```

If the LeaderTemplate or TrailerTemplate property is defined along with a wrapping tag (defined using the Tag, ContainerId, or CssClass properties), the wrapping Tag wraps the contents of the LeaderTemplate and TrailerTemplate properties. For example,

```
<CSControl:UserData Property="DisplayName" runat="server" Tag="div"
ContainerId="wrapper">
<LeaderTemplate>
    <span style="color: #f00;">
</LeaderTemplate>
<TrailerTemplate>
    </span>
</TrailerTemplate>
</CSControl:UserData>
```

would be rendered as:

```
<div id="wrapper">
   <span style="color: #f00;">
   My Name
   </span>
</div>
```

The `LeaderTemplate` and `TrailerTemplate` properties are useful when multiple tags or controls need to be rendered before or after the content of the control only when the content is rendered.

Defining Render Conditions

By default, single-value controls will be rendered if they have data to display. Theme developers can further define rendering conditions, using the `DisplayConditions` and `ControlIdsToHideWhenNotVisible` properties.

DisplayConditions

The `DisplayConditions` property can be used to define a set of conditions that must evaluate to true in order to display the control. If defined, the control will only be rendered if `DisplayConditions` evaluates to true. For example,

```
<CSControl:UserData Property="DisplayName" runat="server">
   <DisplayConditions>
      <CSControl:QueryStringPropertyValueComparision QueryStringProperty="showname"
Operator="IsSetOrTrue" runat="server" />
   </DisplayConditions>
</CSControl:UserData>
```

would render the current user's display name only if the current page's query string included a variable with the name `"showname"` and a value that is not blank.

The `DisplayConditions` property provides a way to define simple as well as complex conditions based on the Community Server API and page state. `DisplayConditions` uses Chameleon condition controls, which will be discussed later in this chapter.

ControlIdsToHideWhenNotVisible

The `ControlIdsToHideWhenNotVisible` property provides a mechanism to apply conditional rendering logic to non-Chameleon controls such as regular ASP.NET controls.

If the control is not rendered, either due to control logic or conditions defined using the `DisplayConditions` property, controls identified by the `ControlIdsToHideWhenNotVisible` property will also be set to not render.

The `ControlIdsToHideWhenNotVisible` property is a comma-separated list of control IDs. For example,

```
<CSControl:UserData Property="DisplayName" runat="server"
ControlIdsToHideWhenNotRendered="Button1,Button2" />
```

```
<asp:Button id="Button1" runat="server" />

<asp:Button id="Button2" runat="server" />
```

would hide the `Button` controls if the `UserData` control is not rendered.

Formatting API-Related Single-Value Controls

Chameleon exposes objects from the Community Server API as single-value controls. These controls provide properties to retrieve, format, link, and render object data: `Property`, `ExtendedAttribute`, `IncludeDateInTime`, `FormatString`, `Text`, `ResourceName`, `ResourceFile`, `TruncateAt`, `TruncateEllipsisText`, `TruncateEllipsisResourceName`, `TruncateEllipsisResourceFile`, `ContentTemplate`, `LinkTo`, `LinkQueryStringModification`, `LinkQueryStringTargetLocationModification`, `LinkCssClass`, `LinkRel`, `LinkTarget`, `LinkTitleText`, `LinkTitleResourceName`, and `LinkTitleResourceFile`.

Property

The `Property` property is the name of the public instance property of the related Community Server API object to render.

So far in this chapter, the `UserData` control has been used to render the current user's display name, such as

```
<CSControl:UserData Property="DisplayName" runat="server" />
```

The `UserData` control provides access to the `User` object in the Community Server API. The `User` object includes a public property named `DisplayName` that reports the current user's full name if display names are enabled on the site; otherwise, it reports the user's username. The `Property` property of the `UserData` control is used to identify that the `DisplayName` property of the `User` object should be rendered.

By default, the value of the API object property identified by the `Property` property is processed according to its data type and dates are automatically converted to the accessing user's local time.

If the `Property` property is specified but the related Community Server API object does not define the specified property, an exception will be thrown. If the specified property's value is null or its string representation is equal to the empty string, the control will not render.

ExtendedAttribute

If the `Property` property is not defined, the `ExtendedAttribute` property will be used to determine the value to render in the content of the control. If the related Community Server API object represented by the control supports extended attributes, the extended attribute value identified by the name specified by the `ExtendedAttribute` property will be retrieved as the content of the control.

For example,

```
<CSControl:UserData ExtendedAttribute="Theme" runat="server" />
```

would render the current user's selected theme if the user has saved a theme selection.

If the `ExtendedAttribute` property is specified but the related Community Server API object does not support extended attributes, an exception will be thrown. If the specified extended attribute's value is null or its string representation is equal to the empty string, the control will not be rendered.

IncludeTimeInDate

If the property identified by the `Property` property represents a date/time value, setting the `IncludeTimeInDate` property to true will format the date/time value with the date and time. By default, the `IncludeTimeInDate` property is false and only the date will be rendered.

If the `FormatString` property is defined, the `IncludeTimeInDate` property is ignored.

FormatString

The `FormatString` property, if specified, is used to format the value identified by the `Property` property. Any .NET format string supported by the data type of the property identified by the `Property` property can be used. For example,

```
<CSControl:UserData Property="LastLogin" FormatString="MMMM, yyyy" runat="server" />
```

would render the last login date of the current user formatted using the full month name and four-digit year, such as:

```
March, 2004
```

Text

The `Text` property identifies the text to render as the content of the control.

If the `Text` property is defined along with the `Property` property or `ExtendedAttribute` property, the formatted value of the property or extended attribute is passed as a formatting parameter to the text identified by the `Text` property. For example,

```
<CSControl:UserData Property="DisplayName" Text="Hello {0}. How are you?"
runat="server" />
```

would be rendered as:

```
Hello My Name. How are you?
```

If both the `Text` property and `ResourceName` property are defined, the `Text` property is ignored.

ResourceName and ResourceFile

The `ResourceName` and `ResourceFile` properties identify a Community Server language resource to render as the content of the control. The `ResourceName` property identifies the name of the language resource in the file identified by the `ResourceFile` property. If the `ResourceName` property is defined, but the `ResourceFile` property is not defined, the resource identified by `ResourceName` will be loaded from the default resource file.

If the `ResourceName` property is defined along with the `Property` property or `ExtendedAttribute` property, the formatted value of the property or extended attribute is passed as a formatting parameter to the resource identified by the `ResourceName` and `ResourceFile` properties. For example, if the following resource was defined in the default resource file:

```
<resource name="sample_format">Hello {0}. How are you?</resource>
```

then,

```
<CSControl:UserData Property="DisplayName" ResourceName="sample_format"
runat="server" />
```

would be rendered as:

```
Hello My Name. How are you?
```

This places the value of the `DisplayName` property into the formatting placeholder identified on the language resource named "`sample_format`."

TruncateAt

The `TruncateAt` property can be used to truncate the content of the control defined by the `Property`, `ExtendedAttribute`, `IncludeDateInTime`, `FormatString`, `Text`, `ResourceName`, and `ResourceFile` properties at a specified length. When defined and greater than zero, the final content of the listed properties is truncated at the given length.

If the content contains HTML, the HTML markup is removed before the text is truncated. The truncation occurs at the word boundary, following the position in the content identified by the value of the `TruncateAt` property.

For example,

```
<CSControl:UserData Property="DisplayName" TruncateAt="1" runat="server" />
```

would be rendered as:

```
My...
```

The code does this by truncating at the first word boundary following the character at the position of the value of the `TruncateAt` property, one.

TruncationEllipsisText, TruncationEllipsisResourceName, and TruncationEllipsisResourceFile

If the content of the control is truncated using the `TruncateAt` property, the value of the `TruncationEllipsisText` property or the language resource identified by the `TruncationEllipsisResourceName` and `TruncationEllipsisResourceFile` properties is appended to the truncated text.

If both the `TruncationEllipsisText` and `TruncationEllipsisResourceName` properties are defined, the value of the `TruncationEllipsisResourceName` property will be used and the value of the `TruncationEllipsisText` property will be ignored.

`TruncationEllipsisText` defaults to "...".

ContentTemplate

The `ContentTemplate` property can be used to completely override the content of the control with custom markup and controls. The `ContentTemplate` is data bound and supports ASP.NET data binding syntax.

Setting the `ContentTemplate` property overrides the values of the `Property`, `ExtendedAttribute`, `IncludeTimeInDate`, `FormatString`, `Text`, `ResourceName`, `ResourceFile`, `TruncateAt`, `TruncationEllipsisText`, `TruncationEllipsisResourceName`, and `TruncationEllipsisResourceFile` properties.

The `ContentTemplate` property is useful in cases where you want to perform some programmatic function on a property of a Community Server API object, for example,

```
<CSControl:UserData runat="server">
   <ContentTemplate>
      <%# Eval("DisplayName").ToString().ToUpper().Substring(0,1) %>
   </ContentTemplate>
</CSControl:UserData>
```

would render the first letter of the current user's display name in uppercase.

LinkTo

The `LinkTo` property can be set to the name of the destination to which the content of the control should be linked. Each single-value control related to a Community Server API object defines an enumeration of related links to which the `LinkTo` property can be assigned.

The link defined by the `LinkTo` property wraps the content of the control only. The wrapping tag and markup defined in the `LeaderTemplate` and `TrailerTemplate` properties will not be linked. Additionally, if the accessing user does not have access to the link defined by the `LinkTo` property, the control will not render.

LinkQueryStringModification

When the `LinkTo` property is defined, the `LinkQueryStringModification` property can be used to modify the query string of the rendered link. When defined, the value of the `LinkQueryStringModification` property is interpreted as a query string whose name and value pairs will override existing values or be appended to the URL of the link. For example, if the `LinkTo` property value's URL would normally evaluate to

```
/members/myname.aspx?PageIndex=1
```

and the `LinkQueryStringModification` property was set to

```
PageIndex=5&showfavorites=true
```

the URL of the rendered link would be:

```
/members/myname.aspx?PageIndex=5&showfavorites=true
```

LinkTargetLocationModification

When the `LinkTo` property is defined, the `LinkTargetLocationModification` property can be used to modify the target location of the rendered link. The value of the `LinkTargetLocationModifcation` property overwrites any existing target location on the link URL. For example, if the `LinkTo` property value's URL would normally evaluate to

```
/members/myname.aspx?PageIndex=1#comments
```

and the `LinkTargetLocationModification` property was set to

```
favorites
```

the URL of the rendered link would be:

```
/members/myname.aspx?PageIndex=1#favorites
```

LinkCssClass

When the `LinkTo` property is defined, the `LinkCssClass` property can be used to define the CSS class to be rendered on the `<a></a>` tag for the defined link. For example,

```
<CSControl:UserData Text="View Profile" LinkTo="Profile" LinkCssClass="highlight"
runat="server" />
```

would be rendered as:

```
<a href="/members/btiedt.aspx" class="highlight">View Profile</a>
```

LinkRel

When the `LinkTo` property is defined, the `LinkRel` property can be used to define the relationship of the link to the current page. The `LinkRel` property sets the value of the `rel` attribute that is rendered on the `<a></a>` tag for the defined link. For example,

```
<CSControl:UserData Text="View Profile" LinkTo="Profile" LinkRel="nofollow"
runat="server" />
```

would be rendered as:

```
<a href="/members/btiedt.aspx" rel="nofollow">View Profile</a>
```

LinkTarget

When the `LinkTo` property is defined, the `LinkTarget` property can be used to define the target of the link. The `LinkTarget` property sets the value of the `target` attribute that is rendered on the `<a></a>` tag for the defined link. For example,

```
<CSControl:UserData Text="View Profile" LinkTo="Profile" LinkTarget="_blank"
runat="server" />
```

would be rendered as:

```
<a href="/members/btiedt.aspx" target="_blank">View Profile</a>
```

LinkTitleText, LinkTitleResourceName, and LinkTitleResourceFile

When the `LinkTo` property is defined, the `LinkTitleText` property or the `LinkTitleResourceName` and `LinkTitleResourceFile` properties can be used to define the title of the defined link. For example,

```
<CSControl:UserData Text="View Profile" LinkTo="Profile" LinkTitleText="Click to
view my profile…" runat="server" />
```

would be rendered as:

```
<a href="/members/btiedt.aspx" title="Click to view my profile…">View Profile</a>
```

If both the `LinkTitleText` and `LinkTitleResourceName` properties are defined, the resource identified by the value of the `LinkTitleResourceName` property will be used and the value of the `LinkTitleText` property will be ignored.

When the content being linked is truncated using the `TruncateAt` property, the default link title is the full text of the content.

API-Related Single-Value Controls Naming Conventions

Single-value controls related to objects from the Community Server API are generally named using the convention `[Object]Data`, where `Object` identifies the Community Server API object on which the control reports. For example, the `WeblogPostData` control reports on data related to the `WeblogPost` object.

The control listings in Appendices B through F identify single-value controls that are available in Community Server.

List Controls

List controls provide access to lists of data from the Community Server API. Additionally, many list controls expose options to influence the implicit data binding process. For example,

```
<CSBlog:WeblogPostList runat="server">
    <QueryOverrides PageSize="10" />
```

```
    <ItemTemplate>
        <CSBlog:WeblogPostData Tag="H4" LinkTo="Post" Property="Subject" runat="server" />
    </ItemTemplate>
</CSBlog:WeblogPostList>
```

would render the newest 10 blog posts.

All list controls support the same basic properties as single-value controls — Tag, ContainerId, CssClass, LeaderTemplate, TrailerTemplate, DisplayConditions, and ControlIdsToHideWhenNotVisible. For information on these properties, please read the description of these properties from the discussion of single-value controls earlier in this chapter.

List Control Templates

All list controls in Chameleon are based on the ASP.NET Repeater control. As with the Repeater control, Chameleon list controls expose templated properties for defining the layout of the data being listed. All list controls in Chameleon support the same templated properties: LeaderTemplate, HeaderTemplate, ItemTemplate, AlternatingItemTemplate, NoneTemplate, SeparatorTemplate, RowSeparatorTemplate, AdTemplate, FooterTemplate, and TrailerTemplate.

LeaderTemplate

The LeaderTemplate property defines the markup and controls used for rendering before the content of the control and within the wrapper tag.

The content of the LeaderTemplate property is always rendered if the list control is rendered.

HeaderTemplate

The HeaderTemplate property, inherited from the ASP.NET Repeater control, represents the header for the content of the ItemTemplate, AlternateItemTemplates, and NoneTemplate properties.

The ShowHeaderFooterOnNone property of list controls identifies whether the contents of the HeaderTemplate should be rendered when the list has no items to display. This is how the HeaderTemplate property differs from the LeaderTemplate property — the contents of the LeaderTemplate property will always be rendered if the list control is rendered, whereas the contents of the HeaderTemplate property can be optionally hidden when there are no items for the list control to display. The default value for the ShowHeaderFooterOnNone property is true.

ItemTemplate

The ItemTemplate property, inherited from the ASP.NET Repeater control, defines the markup and controls to render for each item rendered by the list control. Single-value Chameleon controls can be included in the ItemTemplate to display data related to the item being listed.

AlternatingItemTemplate

The AlternatingItemTemplate property, inherited from the ASP.NET Repeater control, defines the markup and controls to render for every other item rendered by the list control.

If the `AlternatingItemTemplate` is defined, items rendered by the list control will alternately be rendered by the `ItemTemplate` and the `AlternatingItemTemplate`. If the `AlternatingItemTemplate` is not defined, the `ItemTemplate` will be used for rendering all items in the list.

NoneTemplate

The `NoneTemplate` property defines the markup and controls to render when there are no items for the list control to display.

By default, the contents of the `HeaderTemplate` and `FooterTemplate` properties will be rendered before and after the contents of the `NoneTemplate`. To hide the `HeaderTemplate` and `FooterTemplate` contents, the `ShowHeaderAndFooterOnNone` property can be set to `false`.

SeparatorTemplate

The `SeparatorTemplate` property, inherited from the ASP.NET `Repeater` control, defines the markup and controls to render between rendered items of the list.

RowSeparatorTemplate

The `RowSeparatorTemplate` property defines the markup and controls to render between rendered rows of items in the list.

The contents of this template are only rendered if the `ItemsPerRow` property is set to a value greater than zero. If the `ItemsPerRow` property is set to a value greater than zero, the `RowSeparatorTemplate` will be rendered after each set of the specified number of items has been rendered.

The `RowSeparatorTemplate` property is useful when displaying data in rows and columns — such as photos or files rendered in a grid layout.

AdTemplate

The `AdTemplate` property contains the markup and controls representing an advertisement to be rendered among the items of the list.

The placement of the contents of the `AdTemplate` property within the list is defined by the `AdPlacement` property. The `AdPlacement` property has five possible values:

❑ `PreSecond` — Specifying `PreSecond` will cause the contents of the `AdTemplate` property to be rendered between the first and second items in the list.

❑ `PreSecondAndLast` — Specifying `PreSecondAndLast` will cause the contents of the `AdTemplate` property to be rendered between the first and second items in the list and before the contents of the `FooterTemplate` are rendered.

❑ `Seperator` — Specifying `Seperator` will cause the contents of the `AdTemplate` to be rendered between each item of the list.

❑ `PreFooter` — Specifying `PreFooter` will cause the contents of the `AdTemplate` property to be rendered before the contents of the `FooterTemplate` are rendered.

❑ `None` — Specifying `None` will cause the contents of the `AdTemplate` property not to be rendered.

The contents of the `AdTemplate`, if rendered between items in the list, will always be rendered before the contents of the `SeparatorTemplate` property if the `SeparatorTemplate` property is defined. The default value for the `AdPlacement` property is `PreSecond`.

FooterTemplate

The `FooterTemplate` property, inherited from the ASP.NET `Repeater` control, represents the footer for the contents of the `ItemTemplate`, `AlternateItemTemplates`, and `NoneTemplate` properties.

The `ShowHeaderFooterOnNone` property of list controls identifies whether the contents of the `FooterTemplate` should be rendered when the list has no items to display. This is how the `FooterTemplate` property differs from the `TrailerTemplate` property — the contents of the `TrailerTemplate` property will always be rendered if the list control is rendered, whereas the contents of the `FooterTemplate` property can be optionally hidden when there are no items for the list control to display. The default value for the `ShowHeaderFooterOnNone` property is `true`.

TrailerTemplate

The `TrailerTemplate` property defines the markup and controls to render after the content of the control and within the wrapper tag.

The `TrailerTemplate` is always rendered if the list control is rendered.

Defining Query Overrides

Many list controls expose an additional property, `QueryOverrides`, which provides theme developers with a way to define or influence the default, implicit data source retrieved by the list control. For example,

```
<CSBlog:WeblogPostList runat="server">
   <QueryOverrides PageSize="5" BlogPostType="Post" SortBy="MostViewed" />
   <ItemTemplate>
      <CSBlog:WeblogPostData Tag="H4" LinkTo="Post" Property="Subject" runat="server" />
   </ItemTemplate>
</CSBlog:WeblogPostList>
```

would list the five most viewed blog posts.

The specific options exposed by the `QueryOverrides` property depend on the type of Community Server API objects being listed by the control; however, each control's `QueryOverrides` property exposes all of the options provided by the Community Server API. For details regarding the options exposed by a specific list control, please consult the Community Server controls documentation.

Most implementations of the `QueryOverrides` property expose options for defining the page size, current page index, and related pager control.

PageSize

The `PageSize` property exposed by `QueryOverrides` defines the number of items to render on a single page rendered by the list control.

If the `PagerID` property is specified, the value of the `PageSize` property represents the maximum number of items rendered for the `PageIndex` reported by the pager control. If the `PagerID` property is not specified, the value of the `PageSize` property represents the maximum number of items displayed for the value of `PageIndex` defined on `QueryOverrides`.

PageIndex

The `PageIndex` property exposed by `QueryOverrides` defines the zero-based index of the page of data displayed.

If the `PagerID` property is not specified, the list control will render items at indexes between

```
PageSize * PageIndex
```

to:

```
PageSize * (PageIndex + 1)
```

For example, if `PageSize` is set to 10 and `PageIndex` is set to 1, only the items at indices 10 to 19 will be rendered.

If the `PagerID` property is specified, the value of `PageIndex` on `QueryOverrides` is ignored and, instead, the value of the `PageIndex` property defined on the pager control identified by the `PagerID` property is used.

PagerId

The `PagerId` property exposed by `QueryOverrides` defines the ID of the pager control that should be used to select the page of data to be displayed by the list control.

When specified, the list control will attempt to locate a pager control with an ID matching the value of the `PagerId` property. If a pager control is found, the value of the `PageIndex` property on the pager control will be used instead of the `PageIndex` property on `QueryOverrides`. The list control will populate the properties of the pager control relating to the data source being rendered and the pager control will expose and/or render options for changing the currently rendered page.

Pager controls are discussed later in this chapter.

API-Related List Controls

In general, a Chameleon list control exists for each object type in the Community Server API. These API-related list controls expose the data access options implemented in the Community Server API for their type using the `QueryOverrides` property.

All of the list controls related to objects in the Community Server API have default implementations for the `HeaderTemplate`, `ItemTemplate`, `AlternatingItemTemplate`, and `FooterTemplate` to render items in an unordered list (using `<ul>` and `<li>` tags). These list controls expose additional options to customize the default rendering of the contents of the list without overriding the templated properties of the list control: `HeaderTag`, `HeaderCssClass`, `HeaderText`, `HeaderResourceName`, `HeaderResourceFile`, `ListCssClass`, `ListItemCssClass`, and `AlternateListItemCssClass`. For example,

```
<CSBlog:WeblogPostList runat="Server" HeaderText="Recent Posts" HeaderTag="H3" />
```

uses the `WeblogPostList` control, which lists `WeblogPost` objects from the Community Server API and is rendered as

```
<h3>Recent Posts</h3>
<ul>
<li><a href="/blogs/my_blog/archive/2007/06/25/post-two.aspx">Post Two</a></li>
<li><a href="/blogs/my_blog/archive/2007/06/08/post-one.aspx">Post One</a></li>
</ul>
```

with the header text and tag defined using the `HeaderText` and `HeaderTag` properties and items rendered according to the default list-based rendering of API-related list controls.

If any of the templated properties of the list control are defined, the default implementations for all templated properties are ignored and the properties related to the default unordered list implementation have no effect on the rendered list.

HeaderTag

The `HeaderTag` property defines the name of the tag in which to wrap the header of the list defined by the `HeaderText` or `HeaderResourceName` properties on the list. If the `HeaderTag` property is not specified and the header is rendered, the header will be wrapped in a `<div>...</div>` tag.

If the `HeaderText` or `HeaderResourceName` properties are not defined, the header will not be rendered.

HeaderCssClass

The `HeaderCssClass` property defines the CSS class name to apply to the header tag specified by the `HeaderTag` property.

HeaderText

The text to display as the header of the list can be defined using the `HeaderText` property.

If the `HeaderResourceName` property is specified, the value of the `HeaderText` property is ignored.

HeaderResourceName and HeaderResourceFile

The `HeaderResourceName` and `HeaderResourceFile` properties identify a Community Server language resource to render as the header of the list. The `HeaderResourceName` property identifies the name of the language resource in the file identified by the `HeaderResourceFile` property.

If the `HeaderResourceName` property is defined, but the `HeaderResourceFile` property is not defined, the resource identified by the `HeaderResourceName` property will be loaded from the default resource file.

If the `HeaderResourceName` property is defined, the value of the `HeaderText` property is ignored and the language resource identified by the `HeaderResourceName` property is rendered as the header of the list.

ListCssClass

The `ListCssClass` property defines the CSS class name to apply to the list tag (`<ul>`...`</ul>`) that wraps the items of the list.

ListItemCssClass

The `ListItemCssClass` property defines the CSS class name to apply to the first list item (`<li>`...`</li>`) and every other list item after the first that wrap each item rendered by the list.

AlternateListItemCssClass

The `AlternateListItemCssClass` property defines the CSS class name to apply to the second list item (`<li>`...`</li>`) and every list item after the second that wraps each item rendered by the list.

API-Related Single-Value Controls Naming Conventions

List controls related to objects from the Community Server API are generally named using the convention `[Object]List`, where `Object` identifies the Community Server API object that the control lists. For example, the `WeblogPostList` control lists `WeblogPost` objects.

The control listings in Appendices B through F list controls that are available in Community Server.

Pager Controls

Most Chameleon list controls support the specifying of a `PagerId` on their `QueryOverrides` property. When specified, the list will be paged using the pager control matching the specified ID. Community Server includes four pager controls: `Pager`, `PostbackPager`, `CallbackPager`, and `ScrollingPager`. Each control provides a slightly different implementation of page selection and list updating behavior. The theme developer can choose the pager control for each paged list control that implements the desired paging behavior.

Pager

The basic `Pager` control supports paging using a full-page refresh, passing the user-selected page index using a customizable URL query string property or format. For example,

```
<CSBlog:WeblogPostList runat="server">
  <QueryOverrides PageSize="10" PagerId="PostPager" SortBy="MostRecent" />
  <ItemTemplate>
     <CSBlog:WeblogPostData Tag="H4" LinkTo="Post" Property="Subject" runat="server" />
  </ItemTemplate>
</CSBlog:WeblogPostList>
<CSControl:Pager id="PostPager" runat="server" />
```

would list the most recent blog posts, paged 10 posts at a time.

The `Pager` control supports the same basic properties as single-value controls — `Tag`, `ContainerId`, `CssClass`, `LeaderTemplate`, `TrailerTemplate`, `DisplayConditions`, and `ControlIdsToHideWhenNotVisible` — as well as `TotalPager`, `PageIndex`, `PageSize`, `TotalRecords`, `Duration`, `ShowTotalSummary`, `ShowFirst`, `ShowLast`, `ShowNext`, `ShowPrevious`, `ShowPagerItems`, `ShowIndividualPages`, `CurrentPage`, `IndividualPagesDisplayedCount`, `PagerUrlFormat`, `QueryStringProperty`, `TotalSummaryTemplate`, `FirstLinkTemplate`, `PreviousLinkTemplate`, `PageLinkTemplate`, `CurrentPageLinkTemplate`, `SeparatorTemplate`, `NextLinkTemplate`, and `LastLinkTemplate`.

TotalPages

The `TotalPages` property reports the total number of pages based on the total number of items retrieved by the parent list control and the value of the parent list control's `PageSize` property.

The value of this property can be accessed via a `PagerData` control within the `TotalSummaryTemplate` to render the total number of pages to the client.

PageIndex

The `PageIndex` property reports the zero-based page number for the page currently selected by the pager control.

PageSize

The `PageSize` property reports the number of list items to be rendered on each rendered page. This value is automatically set to the parent list control's `PageSize` property.

TotalRecords

The `TotalRecords` property reports the total number of items retrieved by the parent list control.

The value of this property can be accessed via a `PagerData` control within the `TotalSummaryTemplate` to render the total number of records to the client.

Duration

The `Duration` property reports the time, in seconds, that elapsed while the parent list control loaded the items to be displayed within the current page.

The value of this property can be accessed via a `PagerData` control within the `TotalSummaryTemplate` to render the query duration to the client.

ShowTotalSummary

The `ShowTotalSummary` property identifies whether the total summary should be rendered. The default value of the `ShowTotalSummary` property is `false`.

The contents of the total summary can be overridden by specifying the value of the `TotalSummaryTemplate` property.

ShowFirst

The `ShowFirst` property identifies whether the link to the first page should be rendered. The default value of the `ShowFirst` property is `true`.

If the value of ShowFirst is true, the first link will be rendered when the value of the PageIndex property is greater than or equal to three and the value of the TotalPages property is greater than the value of the IndividualPagesDisplayedCount property.

The rendering of the first link can be customized by specifying the value of the FirstLinkTemplate property.

ShowLast

The ShowLast property identifies whether the link to the last page should be rendered. The default value of the ShowLast property is true.

If the value of ShowLast is true, the last link will be rendered when the value of the PageIndex property is less than three less than the value of the TotalPages property and the value of the TotalPages property is greater than the value of the IndividualPagesDisplayedCount property.

The rendering of the last link can be customized by specifying the value of the LastLinkTemplate property.

ShowNext

The ShowNext property identifies whether the link to the next page should be rendered. The default value of the ShowNext property is true.

If the value of ShowNext is true, the next link will be rendered when the value of the PageIndex property is less than the value of the TotalPages property.

The rendering of the next link can be customized by specifying the value of the NextLinkTemplate property.

ShowPrevious

The ShowPrevious property identifies whether the link to the previous page should be rendered. The default value of the ShowPrevious property is true.

If the value of ShowPrevious is true, the previous link will be rendered when the value of the PageIndex property is greater than zero.

The rendering of the previous link can be customized by specifying the value of the ShowPreviousTemplate property.

ShowPagerItems

The ShowPagerItems property identifies whether any pager links should be rendered. The default value of the ShowPagerItems property is true.

Setting the value of the ShowPagerItems property to false is equivalent to setting the values of the ShowFirst, ShowLast, ShowNext, ShowPrevious, and ShowIndividualPages properties to false. Doing this is useful when total summary data should be rendered but without allowing the pager control to allow the client to select a different page to render.

ShowIndividualPages

The ShowIndividualPages property identifies whether individual page links should be rendered. The default value of the ShowIndividualPages property is true.

If the value of ShowIndividualPages is true, individual pages links will be rendered for an equal number of pages before and after the current page, with a maximum number of pages displayed not to exceed the value of the IndividualPagesDisplayedCount property.

The rendering of the individual page links can be customized by specifying the value of the PageLinkTemplate property (for links changing the current page) and CurrentPageLinkTemplate property (for the current page link).

CurrentPage

The CurrentPage property reports the current one-based page number.

The value of this property can be accessed via a PagerData control within the TotalSummaryTemplate to render the current page number to the client.

IndividualPagesDisplayedCount

The IndividualPagesDisplayedCount property defines the maximum number of page links to render. The default value for the IndividualPagesDisplayedCount property is 5.

PagerUrlFormat

The PagerUrlFormat property defines the URL format for the pager control. If defined, the pager will use this format when creating page links.

The resulting URL should match an entry in the SiteUrls.config configuration file to rewrite the formatted page index value to the query string as the value of the property identified by the QueryStringProperty property.

QueryStringProperty

The QueryStringProperty property defines the name of the query string property used to store the current page number. The default value of the QueryStringProperty property is PageIndex.

If multiple Pager controls exist on a single page, the Pager controls that should support rendering to unique pages should have their QueryStringProperty property set to a unique name. If all Pager controls on a page use the same or default value for the QueryStringProperty property, all lists on the page will be paged synchronously.

TotalSummaryTemplate

The TotalSummaryTemplate property defines the markup and controls to render as the total summary, overriding the default implementation.

The contents of the TotalSummaryTemplate property are data bound and support the use of PagerData controls (or other IPager-related controls) to report on the properties of the current pager such as Duration, TotalRecords, CurrentPage, and TotalPages.

If the value of the `ShowTotalSummary` property is `true` and the `TotalSummaryTemplate` property is not defined, the total summary will be rendered as:

```
Page [CurrentPage] of [TotalPages] ([TotalRecords] items)
```

where the values of `CurrentPage`, `TotalPages`, and `TotalRecords` are populated with the values of the pager control.

FirstLinkTemplate

The `FirstLinkTemplate` property defines the markup and controls to render as the link to the first page, overriding the default implementation.

The contents of the `FirstLinkTemplate` property are data bound and support the use of the `CSLinkData` control (or other `CSLink`-related controls) to render the link to the first page.

If the value of the `ShowFirstLink` property is `true` and the `FirstLinkTemplate` property is not defined, the first link will be rendered as:

```
<< First
```

PreviousLinkTemplate

The `PreviousLinkTemplate` property defines the markup and controls to render as the link to the previous page, overriding the default implementation.

The contents of the `PreviousLinkTemplate` property are data bound and support the use of the `CSLinkData` control (or other `CSLink`-related controls) to render the link to the previous page.

If the value of the `ShowPreviousLink` property is `true` and the `PreviousLinkTemplate` property is not defined, the previous link will be rendered as:

```
< Previous
```

PageLinkTemplate

The `PageLinkTemplate` property defines the markup and controls to render for each link to individual pages other than the current page, overriding the default implementation.

The contents of the `PageLinkTemplate` property are data bound and support the use of the `CSLinkData` control (or other `CSLink`-related controls) to render the link to each page.

If the value of the `ShowIndividualPages` property is `true` and the `PageLinkTemplate` property is not defined, each page link will consist only of the page's one-based page number linked to the associated page.

CurrentPageLinkTemplate

The `CurrentLinkTemplate` property defines the markup and controls to render as the current page, overriding the default implementation.

The contents of the `CurrentPageLinkTemplate` property are data bound and support the use of the `CSLinkData` control (or other `CSLink`-related controls) to render the link to the current page.

If the value of the `ShowIndividualPages` property is `true` and the `CurrentPageLinkTemplate` property is not defined, the current link will be rendered as the textual representation of the current page's one-based page number.

SeparatorTemplate

The `SeparatorTemplate` property defines the markup and controls to render between each pager link. The `SeparatorTemplate` is not data bound and defaults to a single space.

NextLinkTemplate

The `NextLinkTemplate` property defines the markup and controls to render as the link to the next page, overriding the default implementation.

The contents of the `NextLinkTemplate` property are data bound and support the use of the `CSLinkData` control (or other `CSLink`-related controls) to render the link to the next page.

If the value of the `ShowNextLink` property is `true` and the `NextLinkTemplate` property is not defined, the next link will be rendered as:

```
Next >
```

LastLinkTemplate

The `LastLinkTemplate` property defines the markup and controls to render as the link to the last page, overriding the default implementation.

The contents of the `LastLinkTemplate` property are data bound and support the use of the `CSLinkData` control (or other `CSLink`-related controls) to render the link to the last page.

If the value of the `ShowLastLink` property is `true` and the `LastLinkTemplate` property is not defined, the last link will be rendered as:

```
Last >>
```

PostbackPager

The `PostbackPager` control behaves and renders similarly to the `Pager` control, but instead of using the query string to identify the current page, the `PostbackPager` control uses an ASP.NET postback event to change pages.

The `PostbackPager` control exposes the same properties as the `Pager` control (except the `PagerUrlFormat` and `QueryStringProperty` properties, which are related to query string-based paging) to support customization of the rendered pager.

The `PostBackPager` control can be used on pages containing form controls when the state of the form must not be lost when changing pages.

CallbackPager

The `CallbackPager` control renders similarly to the `Pager` control but uses client-side JavaScript and the JavaScript `XmlHttpRequest` object to change pages without reloading the entire page.

The `CallbackPager` control exposes the same properties as the `Pager` control (except the `PagerUrlFormat` and `QueryStringProperty` properties, which are related to query string–based paging) to support customization of the rendered pager.

Unlike the `Pager` and `PostbackPager` controls, the `CallbackPager` control must contain the content it is paging. The paged content must be defined within the `CallbackPager`'s `PagedContent` property. For example,

```
<CSControl:CallbackPager runat="server" ID="AdminPager">
  <PagedContent>
    <CSControl:UserList runat="server">
      <QueryOverrides QueryType="Search" Role="SystemAdministrator" PageSize="5"
PagerID="AdminPager" />
      <ItemTemplate>
        <CSControl:UserData runat="server" Property="DisplayName" LinkTo="Profile"
Tag="Div" />
      </ItemTemplate>
    </CSControl:UserList>
  </PagedContent>
</CSControl:CallbackPager>
```

would list members of the "`SystemAdministrator`" role, five at a time, paged using the `CallbackPager`.

When using the `CallbackPager`, the pager links are always rendered below the contents of the `PagedContent` property.

ScrollingPager

The `ScrollingPager` renders differently from the `Pager`, `PostbackPager`, and `CallbackPager` controls. The `ScrollingPager` control is a special-purpose pager that scrolls paged items horizontally, loading additional pages of data as they first become visible while scrolling.

The `ScrollingPager` control uses the JavaScript `XmlHttpRequest` object, similarly to the `CallbackPager` control, to retrieve additional items from its associated paged list.

The `ScrollingPager` control requires the use of two associated controls: `ScrollingPagerItem` and `ScrollingPagerData`.

The `ScrollingPagerItem` control is used to enclose scrollable items and identifies to which `ScrollingPager` the item belongs. An item can represent one or more items rendered by the related list control but must be consistent in its grouping.

The `ScrollingPagerData` control works similarly to other API-related single-value controls with support for the `LinkTo` property, which provides access to `ScrollingPager`-related links to the first item, last item, previous item, next item, previous page, and next page links.

Within the scope of a `ScrollingPager` control, an item represents a single `ScrollingPagerItem` control's contents and a page represents the number of complete items that can be displayed within the width of the rendered `ScrollingPager` control (with a minimum of one).

This example of the `ScrollingPager`, `ScrollingPagerItem`, and `ScrollingPagerData` controls:

```
<CSControl:ScrollingPager runat="server" ID="AdminPager" Tag="Div" style="border:
solid 1px #000; padding: 4px;">
<PagedContent>
    <CSControl:UserList runat="server">
       <QueryOverrides QueryType="Search" Role="SystemAdministrator" PageSize="5"
PagerID="AdminPager" />
       <ItemTemplate>
          <CSControl:ScrollingPagerItem runat="server" ScrollingPagerID="AdminPager">
             <CSControl:UserData runat="server" Property="DisplayName"
LinkTo="Profile" />
          </CSControl:ScrollingPagerItem>
       </ItemTemplate>
    </CSControl:UserList>
</PagedContent>
<ItemLoadingTemplate>
    (loading)
</ItemLoadingTemplate>
<PagerLoadingTemplate>
    This pager requires JavaScript.
</PagerLoadingTemplate>
</CSControl:ScrollingPager>
<CSControl:ScrollingPagerData ScrollingPagerID="AdminPager" LinkTo="PreviousItem"
Text="&lt; Previous" runat="server" />
<CSControl:ScrollingPagerData ScrollingPagerID="AdminPager" LinkTo="NextItem"
Text="Next &gt;" runat="server" />
```

would scroll the list of administrators horizontally, with links to move to the previous and next administrator rendered below the list.

The `ScrollingPager` control exposes the properties `TotalPages`, `PageIndex`, `PageSize`, `TotalRecords`, `Duration`, and `CurrentPage` similarly to the `Pager` control. Additionally, the `ScrollingPager` control exposes the following properties to control the scrolling functionality of the control: `ItemWidth`, `ItemHeight`, `GroupedItemsPerPage`, `ItemLoadingTemplate`, `PagerLoadingTemplate`, and `PagedContent`.

ItemWidth

The `ItemWidth` property defines the static width, in pixels, of each paged item, enclosed by a `ScrollingPagerItem` control. The default value of the `ItemWidth` property is `200`.

ItemHeight

The `ItemHeight` property defines the static height, in pixels, of each paged item, enclosed by a `ScrollingPagerItem` control. The default value of the `ItemHeight` property is `100`.

GroupedItemsPerPage

The `GroupItemsPerPage` property identifies the number of items in the associated list control within each `ScrollingPagerItem`. The default value of the `GroupedItemsPerPage` property is 1.

If more than one list item is displayed within each `ScrollingPagerItem` control, the `GroupItemsPerPage` property should be set to this number.

ItemLoadingTemplate

The `ItemLoadingTemplate` property contains the markup and controls to display in place of an item in the scrolling pager as the actual contents are loaded using a JavaScript `XmlHttpRequest` object.

PagerLoadingTemplate

The `PagerLoadingTemplate` property contains the markup and controls to display in place of the `ScrollingPager` control before the `ScrollingPager` control initializes.

The `PagerLoadingTemplate` property can include a message to users who may have JavaScript disabled to identify that JavaScript is required for the `ScrollingPager` to function. If JavaScript is disabled on the client's browser, the `ScrollingPager` control will not initialize and the content of the `PagerLoadingTemplate` will be the final content of the control.

PagedContent

As previously mentioned, the `PagedContent` property, as with the `CallbackPager` control, must contain the content that will be paged.

Only the content wrapped within `ScrollingPagerItem` controls will be rendered in the `ScrollingPager`. If no `ScrollingPagerItem` controls exist in the `PagedContent` property of the `ScrollingPager`, no content will be displayed in the `ScrollingPager` when it is rendered.

PagerGroup

List controls support interacting with a single pager control via the `PagerId` option of the `QueryOverrides` property of the list. In situations where a list should support paging using multiple pagers, such as situations where a pager above and below the list is useful, a `PagerGroup` control can be used.

The `PagerGroup` control supports managing the interaction between a list control and multiple pagers. To use a `PagerGroup` control, the ID of the `PagerGroup` should be specified as the `PagerId` of the list control and the `PagerIds` property of the `PagerGroup` control should be set to the list of IDs of pagers that should be used to page the list associated to the `PagerGroup` control. For example,

```
<CSControl:Pager runat="server" id="TopAdminPager" ShowTotalSumamry="true" />

<CSControl:UserList runat="server">
    <QueryOverrides QueryType="Search" Role="SystemAdministrator" PageSize="5"
PagerID="AdminPager" />
    <ItemTemplate>
        <CSControl:UserData runat="server" Property="DisplayName" LinkTo="Profile"
Tag="Div" />
```

```
        </ItemTemplate>
    </CSControl:UserList>

    <CSControl:PagerGroup runat="server" id="AdminPager"
    PagerIds="TopAdminPager,BottomAdminPager" />

    <CSControl:Pager runat="server" id="BottomAdminPager" ShowTotalSummary="true" />
```

would display the list of all users who are members of the SystemAdministrator role, displaying five users at a time, and supporting paging via both the Pager control above and the Pager control below the list.

The PagerGroup control does not render any markup to the client. Also note that the PageGroup control cannot be used with CallbackPager or ScrollingPager controls.

Form Controls

Form controls implement behaviors that initiate a process or modify data, for example: creating a forum post, editing a user's profile, or searching the site. Form controls in Chameleon define only the behavior of the form. The user interface can be completely controlled by the theme's developer.

Most Chameleon form controls support theme-defined actions related to completion events exposed by the form. For example, when a new post is created using the CreateEditForumPostForm, the theme's developer can configure the form to redirect the user to the forum in which the post was created or to the user's profile, or perform any other action.

All form controls support the same basic properties as single-value controls — Tag, ContainerId, CssClass, LeaderTemplate, TrailerTemplate, DisplayConditions, and ControlIdsToHideWhenNotVisible. For information on these properties, please read the description of these properties from the discussion of single-value controls earlier in this chapter.

Additionally, form controls expose properties that are specific to form rendering and configuration: ValidationGroup, FormTemplate, properties to register child control IDs, properties to define form-related actions, and SubFormIDs.

ValidationGroup

The ValidationGroup property defines the name of the validation group to use when validating the form. The value of the ValidationGroup property should match the value of the ValidationGroup property defined on the validation and form controls used by the form.

Specifying a unique value for the ValidationGroup property for each form on a page will allow each form to perform validation individually and will remove the need for all forms to be valid to perform an action on any form.

FormTemplate

The FormTemplate property contains the markup and controls to be rendered as the content of the form.

It is recommended that the child form input controls be defined within the `FormTemplate` property, but this is not required.

Properties for Child Control IDs

Each form control exposes a property for each form input control that can (or must) be used by the form to implement the form's behavior.

For example, the `SearchForm` exposes properties for the query text and search input controls:

```
<CSControl:SearchForm runat="server" QueryTextBoxId="Keywords"
SubmitButtonId="SearchButton">
   <FormTemplate>
      <asp:TextBox id="Keywords" runat="server" />
      <asp:Button Text="Search" id="SearchButton" runat="server" />
   </FormTemplate>
</CSControl:SearchForm>
```

The `QueryTextBoxId` property of the `SearchForm` control defines the ID of the `TextBox` control that will represent the search query text. Similarly, the `SubmitButtonId` property of the `SearchForm` defines the ID of the `Button` control that, when clicked, will execute the search. The controls referenced by the `QueryTextBoxId` and `SubmitButtonId` properties can be styled and positioned however the theme's developer sees fit — the `SearchForm` control only needs to know which controls to use for which purpose.

Each forms' properties relating to child controls are unique to the form and its purpose. The control documentation can be used to identify the available child controls and property names. In general, the property names follow the naming convention `[Purpose or Data Name][Control Type]ID`, where the control type is the type of the control expected to have the defined ID.

Two common control types, for buttons and for text, use the Community Server interfaces `IButton` and `IText`. Form controls that identify a control type of `"Button"` expect a control that can be interpreted as an `IButton`-implementing control. Chameleon Button controls explicitly implement the `IButton` interface. The ASP.NET `Button` and `LinkButton` controls (and their child controls) are interpreted by Chameleon as if they implement the `IButton` interface even though they do not. Because Chameleon forms use the `IButton` interface, any button type can be used with Chameleon forms — the theme's developer can use the control that best fits the site design. The `IText` interface is used for controls that display static text but otherwise works similarly to the `IButton` interface, supporting the ASP.NET `Literal` and `Label` controls as well as Chameleon controls that explicitly implement the interface.

Note that not all child control properties must be defined. Form controls in Chameleon are implemented to require only the minimum number of controls to perform their task. If the required control IDs are not specified (or the related controls do not exist or are of the wrong type), the form control will throw an exception explaining which control IDs are required to render the form.

For example, the `SearchForm` control requires that the `QueryTextBoxId` and `SubmitButtonId` properties reference valid controls but also exposes optional properties to attach the following controls: user filter `TextBox`, tags filter `TextBox`, sort order selection `DropDownList`, date range selection, section tree-based filter, and context-sensitive filter `DropDownList`.

Properties for Completion Actions

Many form controls perform a function and, when this function is completed, expose properties to allow the theme developer to decide what should happen next. These completion actions are exposed as properties that accept Chameleon action controls, which can be configured to implement custom behaviors.

Most form controls expose the `SuccessActions` property, whose child controls are executed when the form is successfully completed. For example, the `LoginForm` control exposes the `SuccessActions` property that is executed when the user successfully logs in:

```
<CSControl:LoginForm runat="server" UserNameTextBoxId="UserName"
PasswordTextBoxId="Password" LoginButtonId="LoginButton">
    <SuccessActions>
        <CSControl:GoToReferralUrlAction runat="server" />
        <CSControl:GoToSiteUrlAction UrlName="home" runat="server" />
    </SuccessActions>
    <FormTemplate>
        <p>Username: <asp:TextBox id="UserName" runat="server" /></p>
        <p>Password: <asp:TextBox TextMode="Password" id="Password" runat="server" /></p>
        <p><asp:LinkButton id="LoginButton" runat="server" />
    </FormTemplate>
</CSControl:LoginForm>
```

In this example, two action controls are defined: `GoToReferralUrlAction` and `GoToSiteUrlAction`. The `GoToReferralUrlAction` is listed first, so it is executed first. If a referral URL is defined on the URL of the current page, the `GoToReferralUrlAction` will redirect the client to that referral URL. If no referral URL is defined on the URL of the current page, `GoToReferralUrlAction` does not execute and, instead, `GoToSiteUrlAction` executes and redirects the client to the home page.

Some forms have more than one completion action. In these cases, an `Actions` property is exposed for each type of completion event. Similarly, if a form has no completion events or its completion event is not configurable, no `Actions` properties will be exposed.

Subform Controls

Subform controls interact with form controls to add new features and behaviors to existing forms.

When a form control supports subforms, it exposes the `SubFormIds` property. The `SubFormIds` property, included in the discussion of form controls earlier in this chapter, identifies the comma-separated list of the IDs of subforms to attach to the form control. Once attached, the form control allows the subform to participate in loading and saving actions, enabling the subform control to extend the base functionality implemented in the hosting form control.

Subforms generally expose similar properties to form controls (except completion action-related properties). Subforms, when attached, operate in the same manner as form controls, implementing a behavior by interacting with child controls within the `FormTemplate` property defined and configured by the theme's developer.

As an example, the following shows how the `EntryTagsSubForm` control is used with the `CreateEditEntryForm` control to add tags to a file gallery post:

```
<CSFile:CreateEditEntryForm runat="server"
    NoFileErrorMessageControlId="NoFileError"
    AddUpdateAttachmentModalId="UploadFile"
    EntryDescriptionTextBoxId="EntryDescription"
    EntrySubjectTextBoxId="EntryName"
    FilenameLabelId="FileName"
    SubFormIds="TagsSubForm"
    SubmitButtonId="EntrySave">
    <FormTemplate>
        File:
        <asp:Label id="FileName" runat="server" /> <
        <CSControl:Modal ModalType="Link" ID="UploadFile" Runat="server" Width="500"
Height="300" Text="Upload File" />
        <asp:Label runat="server" ID="NoFileError" ForeColor="Red">*</asp:Label>
        <br />

        Name:
        <asp:TextBox id="EntryName" Columns="70" runat="server" />
        <br />

        Description:
        <CSControl:Editor runat="Server" id="EntryDescription" columns="110" />
        <br />

        <CSFile:EntryTagsSubForm runat="server"
            ID="TagsSubForm"
            SelectTagsModalButtonId="SelectTags"
            TagsTextBoxId="Tags">
            <FormTemplate>
                Tags:
                <asp:TextBox runat="server" ID="Tags" Columns="70" />
                <CSControl:Modal ModalType="Button" Width="400" Height="350"
ID="SelectTags" Text="Select Tags" runat="server" />
                <br />
            </FormTemplate>
        </CSFile:EntryTagsSubForm>

        <asp:Button id="EntrySave" runat="server" Text="Save" />
    </FormTemplate>
</CSFile:CreateEditEntryForm>
```

Notice that the `EntryTagsSubForm` is registered with the `CreateEditEntryForm` control by setting the `CreateEditEntryForm` control's `SubFormIds` property to the ID of the `EntryTagsSubForm` control, `TagsSubForm`. Additionally, the content of the `EntryTagsSubForm` is defined within the control's `FormTemplate` property and the control IDs of the child input controls are registered with the `EntryTagSubForm` in the same manner that the host form's child input controls are registered with `CreateEditEntryForm` control.

Subform Naming Conventions and Host Form Support

Subform controls will only function if they are attached to a supporting host form. For example, if a subform expecting to work with a `Post` object is attached to a host form editing a `User` object, the subform will not be able to function and will not be rendered.

To identify the object expected by the subform control and to identify the subform's behavior, subform controls are generally named using the convention `[Object][Behavior]SubForm`, where `Object` identifies the Community Server API object on which the subform is designed to perform its behavior and `Behavior` is a short name identifying the behavior implemented by the subform.

For example, the `EntryTagsSubForm` control used in the example earlier in this chapter operates on `Entry` objects and provides support for editing `Tags`.

The control listings in Appendices B through F identify subform controls that are available in Community Server.

Condition Controls

Condition controls are the building blocks for defining custom conditional behavior, such as whether to display a control.

Condition controls are generally used by other single-value controls, list controls, form controls, and subform controls to define conditions under which they should be rendered. As discussed earlier in this chapter, rendering conditions are defined using the `DisplayConditions` property of supporting Chameleon controls.

Chameleon includes a set of general-purpose condition controls. Included condition controls include: `Conditions`, property/value comparison controls, property comparison controls, `ControlVisibilityCondition`, `UserInRoleCondition`, `SectionPermissionCondition`, `CurrentSiteUrlCondition`, `CurrentUserIsAccessingUserCondition`, and `CustomCondition`.

Conditions

The `Conditions` control provides support for comparing the results of one or more nested condition controls. For example,

```
<CSControl:PlaceHolder runat="server">
    <DisplayConditions>
        <CSControl:Conditions Operator="And" runat="server">
            <CSControl:PostPropertyValueComparison runat="server"
ComparisonProperty="HasVideo" Operator="IsSetOrTrue" />
            <CSControl:PostPropertyValueComparison runat="server"
ComparisonProperty="IsApproved" Operator="IsSetOrTrue" />
        </CSControl:Conditions>
    </DisplayConditions>
```

```
      <ContentTemplate>
         This post has a video and is approved.
      </ContentTemplate>
   </CSControl:PlaceHolder>
```

would display the message "This post has a video and is approved." only if the current Post object has a video and is approved.

The Conditions control exposes the Operator property, which is used to define the method used to compare the nested condition controls. The Conditions control supports the following values for the Operator property:

❑ And — All nested condition controls must evaluate to true for the Conditions control to evaluate to true.

❑ Or — At least one nested condition control must evaluate to true for the Conditions control to evaluate to true.

❑ Not — None of the nested condition controls can evaluate to true for the Conditions control to evaluate to true.

❑ ExclusiveOr — One and only one nested condition control must evaluate to true for the Conditions control to evaluate to true.

Conditions controls can contain other Conditions controls. Nesting Conditions controls is useful when implementing complex conditions. For example,

```
   <CSControl:PlaceHolder runat="server">
      <DisplayConditions>
         <CSControl:Conditions Operator="And" runat="server">
            <CSControl:Conditions Operator="Not" runat="server">
               <CSControl:PostPropertyValueComparison runat="server"
ComparisonProperty="HasVideo" Operator="IsSetOrTrue" />
            </CSControl:Conditions>
            <CSControl:PostPropertyValueComparison runat="server"
ComparisonProperty="IsApproved" Operator="IsSetOrTrue" />
         </CSControl:Conditions>
      </DisplayConditions>
      <ContentTemplate>
         This post doesn't have a video but is approved.
      </ContentTemplate>
   </CSControl:PlaceHolder>
```

would render the message "This post doesn't have a video but is approved." if the current post does not have a video but is approved. This example is the same as the earlier example, but wraps the check of the HasVideo property of the current Post object in another Conditions control, whose Operator property is set to Not to negate the result of the check of the HasVideo property.

The DisplayConditions property exposed by single-value controls, list controls, form controls, and sub-form controls is actually a Conditions control. The previous example would normally be condensed to:

```
   <CSControl:PlaceHolder runat="server">
      <DisplayConditions Operator="And">
```

```
    <CSControl:Conditions Operator="Not" runat="server">
        <CSControl:PostPropertyValueComparison runat="server"
ComparisonProperty="HasVideo" Operator="IsSetOrTrue" />
      </CSControl:Conditions>
      <CSControl:PostPropertyValueComparison runat="server"
ComparisonProperty="IsApproved" Operator="IsSetOrTrue" />
    </DisplayConditions>
    <ContentTemplate>
        This post doesn't have a video but is approved.
    </ContentTemplate>
</CSControl:PlaceHolder>
```

which simply sets the `Operator` property of the `Conditions` control exposed as the `DisplayConditions` property of the `PlaceHolder` control, removing the need for one of the nested `Conditions` controls.

Property and Value Comparison Condition

For each object in the Community Server API, comparison condition control exists in Chameleon for comparing a property of the object to a static value. For example,

```
<CSControl:PostPropertyValueComparison runat="server" ComparisonProperty="PostDate"
ComparisonValue="6/25/2005" Operator="GreaterThan" />
```

would evaluate to true only if the current `Post` object's `PostDate` property is greater than the date 6/25/2005.

Property and value comparison conditions related to objects from the Community Server API are generally named using the convention `[Object]PropertyValueComparison` where `Object` identifies the Community Server API object on which the control performs comparisons. For example, the `WeblogPostPropertyValueComparison` control compares data related to the `WeblogPost` object.

The control listings in Appendices B through F identify property and value comparison condition controls that are available in Community Server.

All property and value comparison controls expose the same set of properties: `ComparisonProperty`, `ComparisonValue`, `ComparisonValueAdjustment`, `ComparisonValueAdjustmentUnit`, and `Operator`.

ComparisonProperty

The `ComparisonProperty` property defines the name of the property on the associated object from the Community Server API whose value will be compared using the defined `Operator` against the `ComparisonValue` property value.

ComparisonValue

The `ComparisonValue` property defines the static value to compare to the value of the property identified by the `ComparisonProperty` property of the associated object from the Community Server API.

If the property identified by the `ComparisonProperty` property represents a `DateTime` type, the `ComparisonValue` property can be set to `"today"` or `"now"` to specify the current date or date and time.

To specify dates offset from today, such as yesterday or last week, the `ComparisonValueAdjustment` and `ComparisonValueUnit` properties can be used.

ComparisonValueAdjustment

The `ComparisonValueAdjustment` property defines a number to be used to adjust the `ComparisonValue`. This property is useful when specifying `"today"` or `"now"` for the value of the `ComparisonValue` property, in which case the specified number of `ComparisonValueAdjustmentUnits` are added to `"today"` or `"now"` before processing the condition.

The value of `ComparisonValueAdjustment` is processed only when the property identified by the `ComparisonProperty` property is a `DateTime`, `int`, or `double` type.

ComparisonValueAdjustmentUnit

When the `ComparisonValueAdjustment` property is specified, the `ComparisonValueAdjustmentUnit` property identifies the unit of the adjustment value. Supported values for `ComparisonValueAdjustment` are:

❑   `Minute` — Adds the number of minutes specified by the `ComparisonValueAdjustment` property value to the `ComparisonValue`.

❑   `Hour` — Adds the number of hours specified by the `ComparisonValueAdjustment` property value to the `ComparisonValue`.

❑   `Day` — Adds the number of days specified by the `ComparisonValueAdjustment` property value to the `ComparisonValue`.

❑   `Month` — Adds the number of months specified by the `ComparisonValueAdjustment` property value to the `ComparisonValue`.

❑   `Year` — Adds the number of years specified by the `ComparisonValueAdjustment` property value to the `ComparisonValue`.

❑   `Default` — If the `ComparisonProperty` property's value identifies a property on the associated Community Server API object of type `DateTime`, the number of days specified by the `ComparisonValueAdjustment` property's value is added to the `ComparisonValue`. If the `ComparisonProperty` property's value identifies a property on the associated Community Server API object of type `int` or `double`, the number specified by the `ComparisonValueAdjustment` property's value is simply added to the `ComparisonValue`.

The `Minute`, `Hour`, `Day`, `Month`, and `Year` values for `ComparisonValueAdjustmentUnit` are only valid if the `ComparisonProperty` property's value identifies a property on the associated Community Server API object of type `DateTime`. The `ComparisonValueAdjustmentUnit`'s value is completely ignored if the `ComparisonProperty` property's value identifies a property that is not of type `DateTime`, `int`, or `double`.

To check to see if the current `Post` object was posted within the last 24 hours, the following condition could be defined:

```
<CSControl:PostPropertyValueComparison runat="server" ComparisonProperty="PostDate"
Operator="GreaterThan" ComparisonValue="now" ComparisonValueAdjustment="-24"
ComparisonValueAdjustmentUnit="Hour" />
```

Operator

The `Operator` property defines the method by which the value of the property identified by the `ComparisonProperty` property on the associated object from the Community Server API is compared to the static value identified by the `ComparisonValue` property.

Valid values for the `Operator` property are:

- ❏ `Contains` — Evaluates to true if the string representation of the value identified by the `ComparisonProperty` property contains the value of the `ComparisonValue` property

- ❏ `EndsWith` — Evaluates to `true` if the string representation of the value identified by the `ComparisonProperty` property ends with the value of the `ComparisonValue` property

- ❏ `EqualTo` — Evaluates to true if the value identified by the `ComparisonProperty` property equals the value of the `ComparisonValue` property

- ❏ `GreaterThan` — Evaluates to `true` if the value identified by the `ComparisonProperty` property is greater than the value of the `ComparisonValue` property

- ❏ `GreaterThanOrEqualTo` — Evaluates to `true` if the value identified by the `ComparisonProperty` property is greater than or equal to the value of the `ComparisonValue` property

- ❏ `LessThan` — Evaluates to `true` if the value identified by the `ComparisonProperty` property is less than the value of the `ComparisonValue` property

- ❏ `LessThanOrEqualTo` — Evaluates to `true` if the value identified by the `ComparisonProperty` property is less than or equal to the value of the `ComparisonValue` property

- ❏ `StartsWith` — Evaluates to `true` if the string representation of the value identified by the `ComparisonProperty` property starts with the value of the `ComparisonValue` property

- ❏ `IsSetOrTrue` — Evaluates to `true` if the value identified by the `ComparisonProperty` property is set (non-null and not the default value) or true (if the value is of type `bool`)

Unless otherwise noted, comparisons are performed using the type of the value identified by the `ComparisonProperty` property. For example, if the `ComparisionProperty` property identified a `DateTime` value, the value of the `ComparisonValue` property would be interpreted as a `DateTime` value before the comparison is performed.

When the `Operator` property is set to `IsSetOrTrue`, the value of the `ComparisonValue` property is ignored.

Property Comparison Condition

Similarly to property and value controls, a property comparison control is defined for each object in the Community Server API. Property comparison controls provide a way to implement conditions based on the comparison of two properties of an object. For example,

```
<CSControl:PostPropertyComparison runat="server" ComparisonProperty1="Views"
ComparisonProperty2="Replies" Operator="EqualTo" />
```

would evaluate to true if the current `Post`'s number of views is equal to its number of replies.

Property comparison conditions related to objects from the Community Server API are generally named using the convention `[Object]PropertyComparison`, where `Object` identifies the Community Server API object on which the control performs comparisons. For example, the `WeblogPostPropertyComparison` control compares property values on `WeblogPost` objects.

The control listings in Appendices B through F identify property comparison condition controls that are available in Community Server.

All property comparison controls expose the same set of properties: `ComparisonProperty1`, `ComparisonProperty2`, and `Operator`.

ComparisonProperty1

The `ComparisonProperty1` property defines the name of the property on the associated object from the Community Server API whose value will be compared using the defined `Operator` against the value of the property defined by the `ComparisonProperty2` property.

ComparisonProperty2

The `ComparisonProperty2` property defines the name of the property on the associated object from the Community Server API whose value will be compared using the defined `Operator` against the value of the property defined by the `ComparisonProperty1` property.

Operator

The `Operator` property defines the method by which the values of the properties identified by the `ComparisonProperty1` and `ComparisonProperty2` are compared.

Valid values for the `Operator` property are:

- ❑ `Contains` — Evaluates to `true` if the string representation of the value identified by the `ComparisonProperty1` property contains the string representation of the value identified by the `ComparisonProperty2` property

- ❑ `EndsWith` — Evaluates to `true` if the string representation of the value identified by the `ComparisonProperty1` property ends with the value identified by the `ComparisonProperty2` property

- ❑ `EqualTo` — Evaluates to `true` if the value identified by the `ComparisonProperty1` property equals the value identified by the `ComparisonProperty2` property

- ❑ `GreaterThan` — Evaluates to `true` if the value identified by the `ComparisonProperty1` property is greater than the value identified by the `ComparisonProperty2` property

- ❑ `GreaterThanOrEqualTo` — Evaluates to `true` if the value identified by the `ComparisonProperty1` property is greater than or equal to the value identified by the `ComparisonProperty2` property

- ❑ `LessThan` — Evaluates to `true` if the value identified by the `ComparisonProperty1` property is less than the value identified by the `ComparisonProperty2` property

- ❑ `LessThanOrEqualTo` — Evaluates to `true` if the value identified by the `ComparisonProperty1` property is less than or equal to the value identified by the `ComparisonProperty2` property

❑ StartsWith — Evaluates to true if the string representation of the value identified by the ComparisonProperty1 property starts with the value identified by the ComparisonProperty2 property

❑ IsSetOrTrue — Evaluates to true if the value identified by the ComparisonProperty1 property is set (non-null and not the default value) or true (if the value is of type bool)

When the Operator property is set to IsSetOrTrue, the value identified by the ComparisonProperty2 property is ignored.

ControlVisibilityCondition

The ControlVisibilityCondition control provides a way to define conditions based on the visibility of a control on the current page.

The ControlVisibilityCondition control is useful in situations where an ASP.NET input control may be made invisible and associated content also needs to be hidden. For example,

```
<CSControl:PlaceHolder runat="server">
   <DisplayConditions><CSControl:ControlVisibilityCondition runat="server"
ControlId="LoginName" ControlVisibilityEquals="true" /></DisplayConditions>
   <ContentTemplate>
      Login Name:
      <asp:TextBox id="LoginName" runat="server" />
   </ContentTemplate>
</CSControl:PlaceHolder>
```

would not render the "Login Name:" text whenever the TextBox control with the ID "LoginName" is not visible.

The ControlVisibilityCondition control defines only two configuration properties: ControlId and ControlVisibilityEquals.

ControlId

The ControlId property identifies the ID of the control on the current page whose visibility will be compared.

ControlVisibilityEquals

The ControlVisibilityEquals property sets the visibility value required of the control identified by the ControlId property for this condition to evaluate to true.

For example,

```
<CSControl:ControlVisibilityCondition ControlId="Header" ControlVisibilityEquals="true"
runat="server" />
```

would evaluate to true only if the control with an ID of "Header" is visible.

UserInRoleCondition

The `UserInRoleCondition` control provides a way to define conditions based on a user's membership in a specific role. This control exposes two configuration properties: `Role` and `UseAccessingUser`.

Role

The `Role` property identifies the name of the role of which the user must be a member for this condition to evaluate to `true`.

UseAccessingUser

The `UseAccessingUser` property identifies whether the user accessing the site should be used when checking role membership. If true, the accessing user is used. If false, the current user according to the controls context is used.

SectionPermissionCondition

The `SectionPermissionCondition` control provides a way to define conditions based on a user's permissions to the current `Section`.

This control exposes only one configuration property: `Permission`.

Permission

The `Permission` property defines the name of the permission (`View`, `Read`, `Post`, `Reply`, `Edit`, `Delete`, `LocalAttachment`, `Vote`, `MarkAsAnswer`, `RemoteAttachment`, `Video`, `Ink`, `CreatePoll`, `Sticky`, `Announcement`, `EditOthers`, `Moderate`, `Administer`, or `SystemAdmin`) required by the user accessing the page for the `SectionPermissionCondition` to evaluate to `true`.

If the user accessing the page has the specified permission for the current section (or section and post), the `SectionPermissionCondition` control evaluates to `true`, otherwise `false`.

CurrentSiteUrlCondition

The `CurrentSiteUrlCondition` control provides a way to define conditions based on the URL record from the `SiteUrls.config` configuration file that was processed to render the current page. This control exposes only one configuration property: `SiteUrlName`.

SiteUrlName

The `SiteUrlName` property identifies the name of the URL from the `SiteUrls.config` configuration file that should be matched. If the current page is accessed via the URL defined by the `SiteUrlName` property, the `CurrentSiteUrlCondition` control evaluates to `true`. This control is useful in situations where multiple URLs in the `SiteUrls.config` configuration file are rendered using a single ASPX page or use a common ASCX user control but require minor variations depending on the specific URL being accessed. The `SiteUrlName` control can also be useful in customized navigation lists to detect the currently selected navigation item.

CurrentUserIsAccessingUserCondition

The CurrentUserIsAccessingUserCondition control provides a way to detect if the current user in the context of the control is the same user who is accessing the site. The control exposes no configuration properties and simply evaluates to true if the current user is the accessing user, otherwise false.

CustomCondition

The CustomCondition control provides support for custom code-based conditions. The CustomCondition control exposes a single property: CustomResult.

CustomResult

The CustomResult property defines whether the CustomCondition control should evaluate to true or false. The CustomResult property can be set to the result of custom code, for example,

```
<CSControl:CustomCondition runat="server" CustomResult='<%# DateTime.Now.Hour == 6 %>' />
```

would evaluate to true only if the server time's hour is 6 AM.

Action Controls

Action controls are the building blocks for defining custom actions related to events initiated by other Chameleon controls. Each Action control defines a single function or behavior that can be invoked by other Chameleon controls as configured by the theme developer.

Action controls can be used with Chameleon form controls to define the actions to perform when the form completes its function. For example,

```
<CSControl:LoginForm runat="server" UserNameTextBoxId="UserName"
PasswordTextBoxId="Password" LoginButtonId="LoginButton">
   <SuccessActions>
      <CSControl:GoToReferralUrlAction runat="server" />
      <CSControl:GoToSiteUrlAction UrlName="home" runat="server" />
   </SuccessActions>
   <FormTemplate>
      <p>Username: <asp:TextBox id="UserName" runat="server" /></p>
      <p>Password: <asp:TextBox TextMode="Password" id="Password" runat="server" /></p>
      <p><asp:LinkButton id="LoginButton" runat="server" />
   </FormTemplate>
</CSControl:LoginForm>
```

shows the LoginForm control, which exposes the SuccessActions property, which is used to define actions to perform when the user is successfully logged in. In this case, the GoToReferralUrlAction will be executed, which redirects the user to the page that referred the user to the current page. If the referral URL is not defined, the GoToSiteUrlAction will be executed, which will redirect the user to the home page.

Community Server includes many general-purpose action controls: ExecuteScriptAction, GoToCurrentContentAction, GoToCurrentPostAction, GoToModifiedUrlAction, GoToReferralUrlAction, GoToSiteUrlAction, SetVisibilityAction, CustomAction, and Actions.

ExecuteScriptAction

The `ExecuteScriptAction` control, when executed, will cause a client-side JavaScript script to be executed when the page refreshes. For example,

```
<CSControl:LoginForm runat="server" UserNameTextBoxId="UserName"
PasswordTextBoxId="Password" LoginButtonId="LoginButton">
    <SuccessActions>
        <CSControl:ExecuteScriptAction runat="server" Script="alert('You are now
logged in'); window.location = '/';" />
    </SuccessActions>
    <FormTemplate>
        <p>Username: <asp:TextBox id="UserName" runat="server" /></p>
        <p>Password: <asp:TextBox TextMode="Password" id="Password" runat="server" /></p>
        <p><asp:LinkButton id="LoginButton" runat="server" />
    </FormTemplate>
</CSControl:LoginForm>
```

would execute the defined script that displays the alert message "You are now logged in." and redirect the user to the root of the site when the user successfully logs in using the `LoginForm` control.

This control exposes only one property: `Script`.

Script

The `Script` property defines the JavaScript script to execute when the `ExecuteScriptAction` control is executed.

GoToCurrentContentAction

The `GoToCurrentContentAction` control, when executed, redirects the client to view the current `Content` object, if a `Content` object exists in context of the control. The `GoToCurrentContentAction` control exposes no configuration properties.

GoToCurrentPostAction

The `GoToCurrentPostAction` control, when executed, redirects the client to view the current `Post` object, if a `Post` object exists in the context of the control. The `GoToCurrentPostAction` control exposes no configuration properties.

The Forums application within Community Server defines its own version of the `GoToCurrentPostAction` control that can be used to navigate to the permalink of the current `ForumPost` object.

GoToModifiedUrlAction

The `GoToModifiedUrlAction` control, when executed, redirects the client to a modified version of the current page's URL. The `GoToModifiedUrlAction` control defines the following configuration properties: `QueryStringModification` and `TargetLocationModification`.

QueryStringModification

The `QueryStringModification` property can be used to modify the query string of the current URL before the client is redirected by the `GoToModifiedUrlAction` control. When defined, the value of the `QueryStringModification` property is interpreted as a query string whose name and value pairs will override existing values or be appended to the current page's URL. For example, if the current page's URL is currently

```
/members/myname.aspx?PageIndex=1&PostID=5
```

and the `QueryStringModification` property was set to

```
PageIndex=5&showfavorites=true
```

the URL client would be redirected to

```
/members/myname.aspx?PageIndex=5&PostID=5&showfavorites=true
```

when the `QueryStringModificationAction` is executed.

TargetLocationModification

The `TargetLocationModification` property can be used to modify the target location of the current URL before the client is redirected by the `GoToModifiedUrlAction` control. The value of the `TargetLocationModifcation` property overwrites any existing target location on the current page's URL. For example, if current page's URL is currently

```
/members/myname.aspx?PageIndex=1#comments
```

and the `TargetLocationModification` property is set to

```
favorites
```

the client would be redirected to

```
/members/myname.aspx?PageIndex=1#favorites
```

when the `GoToModifiedUrlAction` control is executed.

GoToReferralUrlAction

The `GoToReferralUrlAction` control, when executed, redirects the client to the URL identified by the value of the `ReturnUrl` property of the query string of the current page's URL.

The `GoToReferralUrlAction` will not perform any redirection if the `ReturnUrl` property of the current query string is not defined or if the `ReturnUrl` property is set to a URL that shows an error, logs the user out, changes the user's password, or sends the user's password via email.

GoToSiteUrlAction

The GoToSiteUrlAction control, when executed, redirects the user to a URL defined in the SiteUrls .config configuration file. The control exposes the following configuration properties: UrlName and parameter properties.

UrlName

The UrlName property identifies the name of the URL defined in the SiteUrls.config file to which the client should be redirected when the GoToSiteUrlAction control is executed.

Parameter Properties

The GoToSiteUrlAction control also exposes parameter properties, Parameter1 through Parameter9, which can be used to define required parameters for the URL defined by the UrlName property.

SetVisibilityAction

The SetVisibilityAction control, when executed, sets the Visible property of one or more controls on the page. The SetVisibilityAction control exposes the following properties: ControlIdsToShow and ControlIdsToHide.

ControlIdsToShow

The ControlIdsToShow property defines a comma-separated list of the IDs of controls on the current page that should be shown (have their Visible property set to true) when the SetVisibilityAction is executed.

ControlIdsToHide

The ControlIdsToHide property defines a comma-separated list of the IDs of controls on the current page that should be hidden (have their Visible property set to false) when the SetVisibilityAction is executed.

CustomAction

The CustomAction control, when executed, fires an event which can be handled by custom code on the page. The CustomAction control adds support for custom actions that are not handled by existing actions controls. The control exposes only one property: CustomEvent.

CustomEvent

The CustomEvent event property is executed when the CustomAction control is executed. Custom code can attach to the CustomEvent event property to be notified when the CustomAction control is executed. Custom code attached to the CustomEvent event property is sent a reference to the control executing the CustomAction control as well as the parent control's parameter (which is control-specific). For example:

```
<script runat="server" language="C#">
protected void MyCustomEventHandler(System.Web.UI.Control sender, object parameter)
{
```

```
        // custom code here
    }
    </script>

    <CSControl:LoginForm runat="server" UserNameTextBoxId="UserName"
    PasswordTextBoxId="Password" LoginButtonId="LoginButton">
        <SuccessActions>
            <CSControl:CustomAction runat="server" CustomEvent="MyCustomEventHandler" />
        </SuccessActions>
        <FormTemplate>
            <p>Username: <asp:TextBox id="UserName" runat="server" /></p>
            <p>Password: <asp:TextBox TextMode="Password" id="Password" runat="server" /></p>
            <p><asp:LinkButton id="LoginButton" runat="server" />
        </FormTemplate>
    </CSControl:LoginForm>
```

would execute the custom code within the `MyCustomEventHandler` method defined on the page when the user successfully logs in using the `LoginForm` control.

Actions

The `Actions` control, when executed, simply executes a set of subactions. The `Actions` control can contain one or more action controls that are executed in the order in which they are defined.

The completion event properties defined on form controls is an `Actions` control. This control is generally only used by other controls to define properties that support executing theme-defined actions.

Utility Controls

Chameleon provides a set of utility controls that make common theming tasks easier for theme developers, including: `ConditionAction`, `ConditionalContent`, `ModifiedUrl`, `PlaceHolder`, `ThemeImage`, `ThemeScript`, `ThemeStyle`, and `SiteUrl`.

ConditionalAction

The `ConditionalAction` control provides a simple way to execute Chameleon action controls based on a condition defined by using Chameleon condition controls. For example,

```
<CSControl:ConditionalAction runat="server">
    <Conditions>
        <CSControl:UserPropertyValueComparison runat="server"
ComparisonProperty="IsAnonymous" Operator="IsSetOrTrue" UseAccessingUser="true" />
    </Conditions>
    <Actions>
        <CSControl:GoToSiteUrlAction runat="server" UrlName="login_clean" />
    </Actions>
</CSControl:ConditionalAction>
```

would redirect anonymous users to the login page.

The `ConditionalAction` control defines two properties: `Conditions` and `Actions`.

Conditions

The `Conditions` property defines the conditions which must be satisfied to execute the actions defined by the `Actions` property. The `Conditions` property is a `Conditions` control (discussed earlier in this chapter).

Actions

The `Actions` property defines the actions to execute when the conditions of the control are satisfied.

ConditionalContent

The `ConditionalContent` control is the Chameleon equivalent to an `IF-ELSE` programming statement. For example,

```
<CSControl:ConditionalContent runat="server">
    <ContentConditions>
        <CSControl:UserPropertyValueComparison runat="server"
ComparisonProperty="IsAnonymous" Operator="IsSetOrTrue" UseAccessingUser="true" />
    </ContentConditions>
    <TrueContentTemplate>You are anonymous.</TrueContentTemplate>
    <FalseContentTemplate>You are not anonymous.</FalseContentTemplate>
</CSControl:ConditionalContent>
```

would tell the user if he or she is currently anonymous or not.

The `ConditionalContent` control is a single-value control that supports the standard single-value control properties and three more: `ContentCondition`, `TrueContentTemplate`, and `FalseContentTemplate`.

ContentCondition

The `ContentCondition` property defines the conditions that must be satisfied to render the contents of the `TrueContentTemplate`. If the conditions defined within the `ContentCondition` property evaluate to `false`, the `FalseContentTemplate` will be rendered.

Note that the `ConditionalContent` control supports the `DisplayCondition` property as well, allowing theme developers to also define whether the control should be rendered at all.

TrueContentTemplate

The `TrueContentTemplate` defines the markup and controls that should be rendered if the conditions defined within the `ContentCondition` property evaluate to `true`.

FalseContentTemplate

The `FalseContentTemplate` defines the markup and controls that should be rendered if the conditions defined within the `ContentCondition` property evaluate to `false`.

ModifiedUrl

The `ModifiedUrl` control links its content to a modified version of the current page's URL.

The `ModifiedUrl` control is a single-value control supporting the standard single-value control properties, which can be used to define the content of the control. The control has two more properties: `QueryStringModification` and `TargetLocationModification`. These additional properties function similarly to the similarly named properties on the `GoToModifiedUrlAction` control described earlier in this chapter.

PlaceHolder

The `PlaceHolder` control is the Chameleon equivalent to the ASP.NET `PlaceHolder` control. The `PlaceHolder` control has no default content or additional properties, but, instead exposes the basic single-value control properties for general-purpose use.

`PlaceHolder` controls are useful when `DisplayConditions` need to be applied to non-Chameleon controls or when many Chameleon controls will be affected by the same `DisplayConditions`. Wrapping any number or type of controls within a `PlaceHolder` control and defining its `DisplayConditions` ensures that all of the controls in its `ContentTemplate` will be rendered appropriately. For example,

```
<CSControl:PlaceHolder runat="server" Tag="Div" ContainerId="LoginNote">
    <DisplayConditions Operator="Not">
       <CSControl:UserPropertyValueComparison runat="server"
ComparisonProperty="IsAnonymous" Operator="IsSetOrTrue" UseAccessingUser="true" />
    </DisplayConditions>
    <ContentTemplate>
       Welcome back, <CSControl:UserData Property="DisplayName" runat="server" /><br />
       <asp:Button runat="server" Text="Go To Members Only Area" />
    </ContentTemplate>
</CSControl:PlaceHolder>
```

would only render the message and ASP.NET button if the user is currently logged in (not anonymous).

ThemeImage

The `ThemeImage` control functions exactly the same as the ASP.NET `Image` control except that it processes the leading "~" in the `ImageUrl` and `DescriptionUrl` properties as being the root folder of the accessing user's selected theme instead of the root folder of the application.

`ThemeImage` controls are useful when including images defined within the theme's folder.

The `ThemeImage` control is defined in two namespaces: `CommunityServer.Controls` and `CommunityServer.Blogs.Controls`. The `CommunityServer.Controls.ThemeImage` control interprets "~" as the root folder of the accessing user's site theme, and the `CommunityServer.Blogs.Controls.ThemeImage` control interprets "~" as the root folder of the current blog's theme. The controls can be accessed as `<CSControl:ThemeImage />` and `<CSBlog:ThemeImage />`, respectively.

ThemeScript

The `ThemeScript` control is used to include a script file and interprets a leading "~" in its `Url` property's value as being the root folder of the accessing user's theme.

Similarly to the `ThemeImage` control, a `ThemeScript` control is defined both for the accessing user's site theme (`<CSControl:ThemeScript />`) and the current blog's theme (`<CSBlog:ThemeScript />`).

ThemeStyle

The `ThemeStyle` control is used to include a cascading stylesheet file and interprets a leading "~" in its `Href` property's value as being the root folder of the accessing user's theme.

The `ThemeStyle` control renders as a `<link />` tag and should be placed within the `<head></head>` tag for the page.

Similarly to the `ThemeImage` control, a `ThemeStyle` control is defined both for the accessing user's site theme (`<CSControl:ThemeStyle />`) and the current blog's theme (`<CSBlog:ThemeStyle />`).

SiteUrl

The `SiteUrl` control links its content to a URL defined in the `SiteUrls.config` configuration file. The `SiteUrl` control is useful when static or data-less links are required in a theme.

The `SiteUrl` control is a single-value control supporting the standard single-value control properties which can be used to define the content of the control. The control adds the following properties: `UrlName`, `Parameter` properties, `UrlQueryStringModification` and `UrlTargetLocationModification`.

UrlName

The `UrlName` property identifies the name of the URL defined in the SiteUrls.config file to which the content of the `SiteUrl` control should be linked.

Parameter Properties

The `SiteUrl` control exposes parameter properties, `Parameter1` through `Parameter9`, which can be used to define required parameters for the URL defined by the `UrlName` property.

UrlQueryStringModification

The `UrlQueryStringModification` property can be used to modify the query string of the URL identified by the `UrlName` property. When defined, the value of the `UrlQueryStringModification` property is interpreted as a query string whose name and value pairs will override existing values or be appended to the URL identified by the `UrlName` property.

UrlTargetLocationModification

The `UrlTargetLocationModification` property can be used to modify the target location of the URL identified by the `UrlName` property. The value of the `UrlTargetLocationModification` property overwrites any existing target location on the URL identified by the `UrlName` property.

Page Controls

Chameleon controls require that the ASPX page on which they are hosted inherit from a Chameleon page control. Chameleon page controls provide access to objects from the Community Server API that are defined by the current page's URL, provide utility methods to set the current page's title, register auto-discoverable RSS feed URLs, register the accessing user's current location for tracking online users, and perform other background and utility functions.

A Chameleon page control is defined for each Community Server application. Each application-specific implementation of the page control exposes application-specific Community Server API object properties, providing easy access to application-specific data defined on the current page's URL.

For example, on a file gallery page inheriting from the CSThemePage page control,

```
<%@ Page Language="C#" AutoEventWireup="true"
Inherits="CommunityServer.Controls.CSThemePage" %>
<script runat="server">
    void Page_Load()
    {
        if (CurrentEntry != null)
            SetTitle(CurrentEntry.Subject, true);
    }
</script>
```

would set the page title to the current Entry's subject if a current Entry exists. The CurrentEntry property and SetTitle method are both defined on the CSFileThemePage. For more information on the properties and controls exposed by a specific Chameleon page control, consult the Community Server controls documentation.

Summary

Chameleon consists of a set of general-purpose ASP.NET server controls that use implicit data binding along with overridable query logic to enable theme developers to form data from Community Server into the markup required to render custom theme designs. The Chameleon control types define the standard properties and behaviors that theme developers can expect when interacting with specific Chameleon controls, providing a consistent development experience.

The next two chapters will provide specific examples of implementing pages using Chameleon controls to develop a custom blog and site theme.

6

Implementing Blog Themes

In the previous chapter, you learned about the many different Chameleon controls. In this chapter, you will take that knowledge and apply it by creating an actual blog theme. To help ease into developing an entire site theme, it is helpful to start small with a blog theme. During this process, you will learn about the various files that are required to create a blog theme. Additionally, this chapter presents an example of a blog theme that you can create. By the end of the chapter, you should be comfortable enough to create a blog theme on your own.

Blog Theme Files

Perhaps one of the most amazing things about a blog theme is that it only needs to contain seven page files. In addition to the page files, it also needs a single theme.config file. The `theme.config` file will be discussed in Chapters 9 and 10 in much greater detail.

You should store your blog theme in a folder under the `Themes\Blogs` directory. The folder name that you use to contain your theme files should be the name of your theme. For example, if your blog theme is called "Delux," then your theme files will be located in `Themes\Blogs\Delux`.

The blog pages that your themes should contain are presented below. Keep in mind, though, that you can have more pages than what is listed by adding new URL entries to your `SiteUrls.config`. Adding new pages to the `SiteUrls.config` was discussed in detail in Chapter 4. Also, the following description for each page is only a common example of what content each of these pages could contain. You are not required to make each page contain the specific content listed; you are free to have them present whatever content you desire. However, your blog theme should contain all of the following page files.

❑ **About.aspx** — Contains the content for the page that is presented whenever "about the blog" is enabled.

❑ **Contact.aspx** — Contains the content for the contact page; this page allows for visitors to find contact information or contact the blog owner(s) directly.

- ❑ **Linklist.aspx** — Contains the links that are created from the blog part of the Control Panel under the link list menu. This is useful for allowing people to easily define custom links for a blog.

- ❑ **Post.aspx** — Contains the content for a complete blog post. Usually this page also contains controls to allow users to post comments and rate a post.

- ❑ **Postlist.aspx** — Contains a paged list for blog posts, usually each post on this page displays an excerpt of the complete content.

- ❑ **Search.aspx** — Contains the search results content whenever a user searches a blog.

- ❑ **Taglist.aspx** — Contains a list of blog posts that relate to a specific tag that was selected.

Aside from these pages, a blog theme will generally also have image files and stylesheet files. However, you are not limited to just these types of files. You can always add Flash and JavaScript files to your blog theme and simply reference them from your blog theme pages as well. These extra files can be referenced just as you would do in any other web page.

Another file that is often used is the `theme.Master` file. This is used to set up a general template for the presentation of your blog. It is strongly recommended that you use a master page to create a common presentation for your theme. Later in the site theme chapter, Chapter 7, you will see how these master pages can be used to create a consistent look in other areas of your site.

In the next section, you will see an example of a blog theme that uses all of the pages described above as well as a custom stylesheet and image files. This example should serve as a general reference for how these various files can be used.

Creating a Custom Blog Theme

To begin creating your blog theme, first make a new directory to contain all of your theme files. In this example, you will be creating a theme called Infusion. Therefore, create a folder called "Infusion" inside the `\Themes\Blogs` parent directory. After you do this, you should have a folder structure that looks like: `\Themes\Blogs\Infusion`.

It is a good idea to have a design for your blog theme before adding any files to the theme folder. However, for the purposes of this example, you don't need to have a preset design that you are trying to create; instead the example will simply be a way to get your feet wet. That being said, keep in mind that these steps can be used as a template for future themes when going through the example. The same files will need to be created in future themes, so you can use this process as a reference.

Creating a Basic theme.config File

Before you create any pages, first create a `theme.config` file. This will be used to select your new theme inside the blog dashboard. At this point, this theme.config file does not need to be very complicated. It just needs to provide the name of the theme.

Please realize that the theme.config file can do some pretty amazing things once you combine it with a dynamic stylesheet page and theme pages. This topic will be discussed in much greater detail in Chapters 9 and 10. If you are interested in adding more advanced options to this file, you should consult these chapters. For the time being, and for the straightforwardness of this example, create a file named `theme.config` in the root of your Infusion directory and place the following code in it.

```
<?xml version="1.0" encoding="utf-8" ?>
<Theme previewText="A nice looking blog theme.">
    <DynamicConfiguration>
        <propertyGroup id="cssOverrides" text="Custom Styles (Advanced)">
        <property id="cssOverrides" text="CSS Overrides" dataType="string"
            controlType="
            Telligent.DynamicConfiguration.Controls.MultilineStringControl,
            Telligent.DynamicConfiguration" descriptionText="Enter any CSS
            overrides to the default stylesheets." />
        </propertyGroup>
    </DynamicConfiguration>
</Theme>
```

Once you save the above file, you can go into your blog's dashboard and you will be able to select the `Infusion` blog theme. The theme configuration at this point will allow you to define custom stylesheet properties and preview the theme. This is a good starting point for creating your new blog theme. However, you should realize that your site theme is not fully functioning at this point as all of the page files required by a blog theme are not implemented.

Creating a Master Page

Create a master page in the `Infusion` folder that you created previously. This master page can be named `theme.Master`, as the other blog themes master pages are named. You can create multiple master pages for your blog theme, but one is usually more than enough to ease into the process of creating a blog theme. You should also be using Visual Studio 2005 or later to create this master page file. Once you have the file created, add the following code, or similar code. This page is going to be used as a general template for your blog theme. Meaning that it will contain the header and footer as well as any sidebar controls that you would like to have on each of the pages that use this master page.

Another possible approach is to create a master page for each of the main areas of your site, since master pages can rely on other master pages. You can have a `theme.Master` and perhaps a `header.Master` or `footer.Master` page that the pages in your theme rely on.

The code example below was shortened slightly to show you the basic idea of how the master page can be formatted. The doctype on the page, some ID attributes, and `Meta` tags were removed for example. Another item that was removed was all of the `runat="server"` attribute from the server controls that are obviously going to be server controls. One thing to notice are the different `ContentPlaceHolder` controls that will be used by pages that use the master page. Also, you should notice that this is a standard ASP.NET 2.0 master page and is not proprietary to Community Server.

```
<%@ Master Language="C#" AutoEventWireup="true" %>
<%@ Register TagPrefix="CSUserControl" TagName="UserWelcome"
    Src="~/Themes/default/Common/UserWelcome.ascx" %>
<html xmlns="http://www.w3.org/1999/xhtml" xml:lang="en" lang="en">
<head runat="server">
<CSControl:Head>
    <CSBlog:ThemeStyle Href="~/style/style.css" Media="screen" />
    <CSControl:SectionThemeConfigurationDataStyle
        StyleUrlProperty="secondaryCssUrl" Media="screen" />
```

```
            <CSBlog:ThemeStyle Href="~/style/DynamicStyle.aspx" Media="screen"
                EnsureNotCachedOnPreview="true" />
    </CSControl:Head>
    </head>
    <body>
        <form id="form1" runat="server">
        <TWC:Modal CssClasses="Modal" TitleCssClasses="ModalTitle"
            CloseCssClasses="ModalClose" ContentCssClasses="ModalContent"
            FooterCssClasses="ModalFooter" ResizeCssClasses="ModalResize"
            MaskCssClasses="ModalMask" LoadingUrl="~/utility/loading.htm"
        />
        <div id="outer_container">
            <div id="container">
                <div id="top_container">
                <CSBlog:WeblogData Property="Name" Tag="H2" LinkTo="HomePage" />
                <CSBlog:WeblogData Property="Description" Tag="P"
                    ContainerId="tagline" />
            <CSBlog:SearchForm QueryTextBoxId="SearchBox"
                    SubmitButtonId="SearchButton" Tag="div" CssClass="search">
                    <FormTemplate>
                    <CSControl:DefaultButtonTextBox Button="SearchButton"
                        CssClass="searchbox" id="SearchBox" />
                    <CSControl:ResourceLinkButton Text="Search" id="SearchButton"
                        CausesValidation="false" />
                    </FormTemplate>
                </CSBlog:SearchForm>
                </div>

                <CSControl:NavigationList ContainerId="nav_container" />

                <div id="main_container">
                    <div id="content_container">
                        <asp:ContentPlaceHolder ID = "Main" />
                    </div>

                <asp:ContentPlaceHolder ID="SideBar">
                <div class="sidebar_item">
                    <h3>Common Links</h3>
                        <ul class="sidelist">
                        <CSBlog:WeblogData ResourceName="Weblog_Link_Home"
                            LinkTo="HomePage" Tag="Li" />
                        <CSBlog:WeblogData ResourceName="Weblog_Link_Contact"
                            LinkTo="ContactForm" Tag="Li" />
                        <CSBlog:WeblogData ResourceName="Weblog_Link_AboutAuthor"
                            LinkTo="About" Tag="Li" />
                        <CSControl:LinkCategoryList />
                        </ul>
                    </div>

                    <div class="sidebar_item">
                    <h3>
                        <CSControl:ResourceControl
                            ResourceName="Weblog_Subscriptions" />
                        </h3>
```

```
                    <ul>
                        <CSBlog:WeblogData ResourceName="Weblog_Link_Rss"
                            LinkTo="RSS" Tag="Li" />
                        <CSBlog:WeblogData ResourceName="Weblog_Link_Atom"
                            LinkTo="Atom" Tag="Li" />
                    <CSBlog:WeblogData
                            ResourceName="Weblog_Link_Rss_AllComments"
                            LinkTo="RssComments"
                            ContainerId="RssComments" Tag="Li" />
                        </ul>
            </div>

            <div class="sidebar_item">
                <CSBlog:TagCloud
                        TagCssClasses="Tag6,Tag5,Tag4,Tag3,Tag2,Tag1"
                        IgnoreFilterTags="true" ContainerId="TagSideBar"
                        TagCloudCssClass="SidebarTagCloud">
                    <LeaderTemplate>
                        <CSControl:ResourceControl
                            ResourceName="Weblog_TagsTitle" Tag="H3" />
                    </LeaderTemplate>
                    </CSBlog:TagCloud>
            </div>

            <div class="sidebar_item">
                <CSBlog:ArchiveDataItemList
                        HeaderResourceName="Weblog_Archive"
                        ContainerId="ArchiveSideBar" HeaderTag="H3" />
            </div>
                </asp:ContentPlaceHolder>
            </div>

            <div id="footer_container">
                <asp:ContentPlaceHolder id="BodyFooterRegion">
        <CSControl:SiteSettingsData Property="Copyright" Tag="Div"
                CssClass="Copyright" />
                </asp:ContentPlaceHolder>
            </div>
        </div>
    </div>
    </form>
</body>
</html>
```

If you created a page at this point that uses the above master page, you will see a fairly useful unstyled blog page. This master page includes links to the other pages that can exist on a blog, such as a search box or a tag cloud, as well as links to syndication pages. As a result, any blog page that uses this master page will have all of these features.

Generally, the master page also contains an image in the footer or a common location that indicates the type of license that a Community Server site is using. In addition, there can be extra links to some Control Panel pages, such as creating a new blog post. These Control Panel links are often only visible to blog owners by using specific DisplayConditions. Another nice feature that can be added is the email subscription form, which allows for users to subscribe to a blog anonymously. You can look at the other blog themes that ship with Community Server, as each includes these extra features in their master pages.

Another nice feature of the master page included here is that you can have a blog page fill the `SideBar` `ContentPlaceHolder` with additional links and other content. This allows you to still use the master page on a page that has a different sidebar look than other blog pages. Furthermore, if you want to have more definable content areas, you can place them wherever you like inside of the master page and then choose to use them on your pages that use this master page.

Creating Postlist.aspx

It is helpful to see how your theme looks as you are creating it. This will help you gage how far along you are as well as identify any additional tweaks that need to be made before the theme is complete. The first page that I like to create is the `Postlist.aspx` page, as it presents a good amount of content on the blog. Remember that the `Postlist` page is used to display a list of all of the posts on a blog. Therefore, it should, by its very nature, feature the most content on a single page, with the exception of a post with a large number of comments.

Begin by creating a new page in Visual Studio 2005 called `Postlist.aspx` and place it in your `Infusion` root folder, in the same place that you have the `theme.Master` file. For the purposes of this example, add the following code to this file. The `postlist.aspx` page can be viewed by visiting the homepage of your blog. You will notice that this page will use the previously created `theme.Master` file for its master page. Also, like the previous example, this code has some of the nonessential items omitted, such as the `runat="server"` attributes, which you can add back in where needed.

```
<%@ Page Language="C#" AutoEventWireup="true" EnableViewState="false"
    MasterPageFile="theme.Master"
    Inherits="CommunityServer.Blogs.Controls.CSBlogThemePage" %>
<script runat="Server">
    void Page_Load(object sender, EventArgs e)
    {
        BindData(EntryItems, a, pager);
    }
</script>
<asp:Content ContentPlaceHolderID="Main" runat="Server">

    <CSControl:WrappedLiteral ID="a" Tag="h2" CssClass="pageTitle" />
    <CSBlog:WeblogPostList id="EntryItems">
        <ItemTemplate>
        <dl class="entrylist">
            <dt>
                <CSBlog:WeblogPostData Property="Subject" LinkTo="Post"
                    Tag="span" CssClass="entrylistheader" />
                <br />
                created
                <span class="entrylistheadersub">
                    <CSControl:ResourceControl
                        ResourceName="Weblog_EntryList_By" />
                    <CSBlog:WeblogPostData Property="DisplayName"
                        LinkTo="AuthorUrl" />
                </span>
```

```
            on
            <CSBlog:WeblogPostData Property="UserTime" LinkTo="Post"
                FormatString="f" Tag="span"
                CssClass="entrylistheadersub" />
        </dt>
        <dd>

            <CSBlog:WeblogPostData Property="FormattedBody" />

            <div class="entrylistfooter">
            <CSControl:PlaceHolder runat="server">
                <DisplayConditions Operator="Not">
                <CSBlog:WeblogPostPropertyValueComparison
                ComparisonProperty="IsExternal" Operator="IsSetOrTrue"/>
                </DisplayConditions>
                <ContentTemplate>
                    <CSBlog:WeblogPostData Text="{0} comment(s)"
                        Property="Replies" LinkTo="PostComments"
                        LinkCssClass="commentslink">
                    <DisplayConditions>
                        <CSBlog:WeblogPostPropertyValueComparison
                        ComparisonProperty="Replies"
                        ComparisonValue="0"
                        Operator="GreaterThan" />
                    </DisplayConditions>
                    </CSBlog:WeblogPostData>
                    <CSBlog:WeblogPostData Text="no comments"
                        Property="Replies" LinkTo="PostComments"
                        LinkCssClass="commentslink">
                    <LeaderTemplate>with </LeaderTemplate>
                    <DisplayConditions>
                        <CSBlog:WeblogPostPropertyValueComparison
                            ComparisonProperty="Replies"
                            ComparisonValue="0"
                            Operator="LessThanOrEqualTo" />
                    </DisplayConditions>
                    </CSBlog:WeblogPostData>
                </ContentTemplate>
            </CSControl:PlaceHolder>
            <CSBlog:WeblogPostRating RatingCssClass="CommonRateControl"
                RatingReadOnlyCssClass="CommonRateControlReadOnly"
                RatingActiveCssClass="CommonRateControlActive"
                ImagesBaseUrl="~/Themes/default/images/common/" />
            <CSBlog:WeblogPostData LinkTo="PostEditor"
                ResourceName="Weblog_Link_EditPost" />
            <CSBlog:WeblogPostTagEditableList id="InlineTagEditorPanel"
                EditorLinkCssClass="TextButton"
                EditorCssClass="InlineTagEditor" Tag="Div"
                CssClass="filedunder" />
            </div>
        </dd>
    </dl>
    </ItemTemplate>
</CSBlog:WeblogPostList>
```

```
              <CSControl:SinglePager id="pager" />

    </asp:Content>
```

As you can see, most of the content that is displayed in the `postlist` page are from various properties in the `WeblogPost`. This data is displayed by using the `WeblogPostData` control and selecting the property to display. Other than this control, the `WeblogPostRating` and `WeblogPostTagEditableList` are the only other weblog-specific controls that are used on the page. The fact that only a handful of different controls are needed to render this page helps demonstrate the power of Chameleon controls.

Also notice that the page is organized with normal HTML tags and that some of the controls are using the `Tag` property that is available on many chameleon controls. Remember from the previous chapter that this surrounds the rendered control with the tag that is used. These tags and their respective style classes or IDs are useful whenever you apply a stylesheet to the page.

Creating a Stylesheet

In order to make your blog theme look appealing, you need to create a stylesheet. The stylesheet is used to alter the various elements of your theme so that it looks exactly how you want it to look. This is also the location where you connect many of the images that you will use with the theme itself.

If you are not currently familiar with stylesheets and you want to create a blog theme, you should really take the time to learn more about them. It will greatly help make the presentation of your theme all the more impressive as well as make you a more skilled developer. There are many resources online that can help you become better at creating custom styles. Also, you can always look at the source of a page to find out how something was accomplished. In addition to the online resources, there are also numerous books that have been published on the topic of cascading stylesheets. *Beginning CSS: Cascading Style Sheets for Web Design, 2nd Edition* by Richard York is a good beginner's reference on the topic.

In this example, you will be putting into place a stylesheet that will be used by the `theme.Master` page above. This means that this particular stylesheet will be used to create the presentation of all of the pages in the blog theme. Also, it is important to note that there are custom images that are used in this theme. The images are not necessary but will be included in the stylesheet to help demonstrate how images can be used exclusively from a stylesheet.

To begin, you should create a new folder called "`style`" inside of your new Infusion directory. Even though this example has a single stylesheet file, you should still get in the habit of placing your stylesheet in a specific directory to help keep them organized and separated from other files. Likewise, you should also try to place your images in an organized location, such as under a folder called `images`. After you have created the style directory create a new file called `style.css` with Visual Studio 2005 or any other editor of your choosing. You should place the following lines of code inside the `style.css` file and save the file. The following stylesheet code is compatible with FireFox and Internet Explorer 6 and later.

```
html, body
{
    height: 100%;
    padding-bottom: 10px;
    margin: 0px;
    background-image: url(../Images/background.gif);
```

```css
        background-repeat: repeat-x;
        background-color: #405a7c;
}

#outer_container
{
    width: 958px;
    text-align: left;
    top: 15px;
    margin: auto;
    border: 1px solid #333333;
    padding: 6px;
    position: relative;
    background-color: #cccccc;
}

#container
{
    width: 956px;
    background-color: #ececec;
    font-size: 9pt;
    border:1px solid #999999;
}

#top_container
{
    height: 105px;
    background: #fff url(../Images/header-rt.jpg) top right no-repeat;
    float: left;
    width: 100%;
}

#top_container h2
{
    margin-left: 30px;
    margin-top: 20px;
    float: left;
    background: url(../Images/logo.jpg) no-repeat;
    height: 70px;
    display: block;
    padding-left: 64px;
    padding-top: 20px;
}

#top_container h2 a
{
    text-decoration: none;
    color: #12325D;
    font-size: 1.3em;
    padding: 3px;
    padding-left: 10px;
}
```

```
#nav_container
{
    margin: 0px;
    text-align: left;
    float: left;
    width: 100%;
}

#nav_container ul
{
    list-style: none;
    margin: 0px;
    background: #CCCCCC url(../Images/navbar-bg.gif) repeat-x top left;
    height: 30px;
    padding-left: 10px;
}

#nav_container ul li
{
    padding: 3px;
    text-align: left;
    float: left;
    margin: 0px;
}

#nav_container ul li a
{
    display: block;
    margin-right:20px;
    text-decoration: none;
    color: #12325D;
    font-size: 1.2em;
    font-weight: bold;
    padding: 3px;
}

#main_container
{
    float: left;
    background-color: #EBEBEB;
}

#content_container
{
    padding: 10px;
    padding-top: 5px;
    margin: 5px;
    border: solid 1px #CCCCCC;
    background: #fff url(../Images/content-topleft.gif) top left no-repeat;
    float: left;
    width: 745px;
    overflow: hidden;
}
```

```
.sidebar_item
{
    float: right;
    width: 140px;
    border: solid 1px #CCCCCC;
    margin: 5px;
    margin-left: 3px;
    background: #fff url(../Images/content-topleft.gif) top left no-repeat;
    padding: 10px;
}

.sidebar_item h3
{
    font-size: 1.3em;
    color: #405A7C;
    margin: 0px;
    margin-bottom: 3px;
    border-bottom: solid 1px #E6EFFA;
    padding: 0px;
}

.sidebar_item ul
{
    list-style: none;
    margin: 0px;
    padding: 0px;
}

.sidebar_item ul li
{
    margin: 0px;
    text-align: left;
    padding: 2px;
}

.sidebar_item a
{
    text-decoration: none;
    color: #078FDD;
    font-weight: bold;
}

a
{
    text-decoration: none;
    color: #078FDD;
}

#footer_container
{
    background-color: #f2f2f2;
    margin-top: 10px;
    padding: 5px;
```

```
        clear: both;
        text-align: center;
}

.entrylistheader a
{
        text-decoration: none;
        color: #12325D;
        font-size: 1.3em;
        font-weight: bold;
        border-bottom: 1px solid #12325D;
}

.entrylistheadersub a, .entrylistfooter a
{
        margin-bottom: 5px;
        color: #405A7C;
}

.entrylist dd p
{
        font-family: Courier, Helvetica, sans-serif;
        background: url(../Images/content-p-bg.gif);
        font-size: 1.1em;
        border-right: 1px solid #F0F0F0;
        border-left: 1px solid #F0F0F0;
        padding: 2px;
}
```

Notice that the class names in the stylesheet can also be found in the `theme.Master` or `postlist.aspx` pages. This is because the stylesheet controls how each of these different elements is presented to the user.

The stylesheet above can be expanded to support other pages on your site. Also, you can always reuse many of the existing styles, as they are contained in classes. For example, if you want to have a link use the `entrylistheader` style, you can simply add the `entrylistheader` as a class in a tag surrounding the link you want to change.

As a result of applying the above stylesheet in conjunction with the `postlist.aspx` and `theme.Master` pages you should get a blog that has a look similar to Figures 6-1 and 6-2. Figure 6-1 shows the navigation as well as the `postlist` items. In Figure 6-1, the sidebar is presented and shows how the search area also looks when the theme is complete. When you later add other pages to this theme, you can use this same stylesheet and master page to control the presentation of the page.

Once you have the `postlist` page tweaked so that it looks how you would like, you can begin creating the other pages in your theme. One approach that many people take for creating these remaining files is to make copies of the same files in another theme and place them inside your directory. This is helpful for pages such as the Contact and About pages that generally do not change dramatically from theme to theme. Otherwise, you can create the remaining files from scratch and tweak them as you create them.

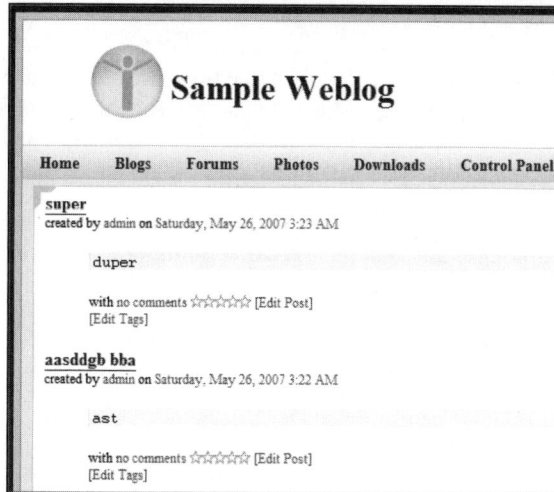

Figure 6-1: Blog Theme Example

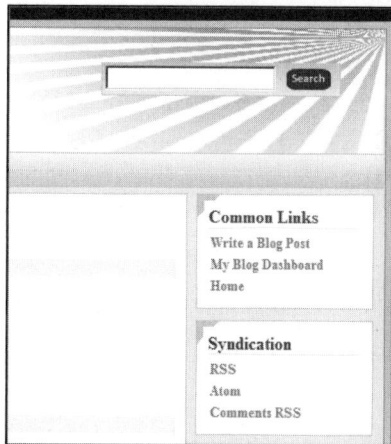

Figure 6-2: Blog Theme Example Presentation

Remember that there are really only six more pages that would need to be created in order to make this a complete theme. Once you have all of the pages together you can package the files and distribute them as a blog theme. Generally, people will simply zip the blog theme folder and distribute the resulting Zip file. More information regarding packaging and distributing your themes is available in Chapter 8.

Summary

In this chapter, you learned about the various files that make up a blog theme. In addition, you saw an example of how many of these files can look to create a simple blog theme. From this example, you now have a template that you can use to start creating a blog theme. Furthermore, you learned some basic information on how you can package and distribute your themes.

In the next chapter, you will learn about site themes and the various files that they are comprised of. In addition, you will see, similar to this chapter, a starting point for creating a basic site theme.

7

Implementing Site Themes

In the previous chapter, you learned how to create blog themes. You can apply many of the same principles that you learned in the previous chapter to create a site theme. By the end of this chapter, you will be able to create and extend a site theme for Community Server 2007 and later. Furthermore, you will be familiar with the following areas of a site theme:

❑   Site theme files
❑   Extending existing themes
❑   Creating a site master page
❑   Creating theme pages

Site Theme Files

One of the nice things about a site theme is that it only has to contain the theme pages that you need. This means that you are able to omit some of the theme pages that you find in the default or leanandgreen themes. Additionally, if you would like to add more pages to your site theme, you are able to do so.

That being said, there is still a set of standard page files that your theme should contain. Looking at the SiteUrls.config file, you will find a complete list of all of the URLs on a site. Below is a list of the pages, and their parent folder, that are contained in the default theme, as well as the pages that your site can contain. If you would like to create a theme that involves fewer pages, you should consult the basic theme or only create those pages that are used by your theme.

❑   **Common\error-notfound.aspx** — Whenever the datastore is not found, this is the page that is displayed.

❑   **Common\home.aspx** — The homepage for a site.

❑ **Common\login.aspx** — The page that accepts a username and password to identify a user on a site.

❑ **Common\logout.aspx** — Handles logging out a user so that they are anonymous.

❑ **Content\content.aspx** — Used to edit the content part, this is a modal page.

❑ **Msgs\message.aspx** — Page used to view a private message.

❑ **Msgs\modalmessage.aspx** — Modal page that is used to send a message to another user.

❑ **Search\indexpostlist.aspx** — The search results page.

❑ **Search\searchform.aspx** — The advanced search options.

❑ **Tags\tagslist.aspx** — A list of tags available on a site.

❑ **User\acceptinvitation.aspx** — Page used to handle a user accepting another user's invitation to join a site.

❑ **User\banneduser.aspx** — The page to display when a user is banned and tries to access a site.

❑ **User\changepassword.aspx** — The page that allows users to change their password.

❑ **User\createuser.aspx** — The page that allows a user to enter user information required to join a site.

❑ **User\edituser.aspx** — The Edit User Profile page; it allows a user to change their details after they have joined a site.

❑ **User\forgottenpassword.aspx** — Page used to recover a password.

❑ **User\inviteuser.aspx** — Page for users to invite people they know to join a site.

❑ **User\privatemessagelist.aspx** — Page used to display all private messages for a user.

❑ **User\sendemail.aspx** — Modal page for sending an email to another user on a site.

❑ **User\userlist.aspx** — A list of users on a site; generally this is a paged list that allows searching to occur.

❑ **User\useronlinelist.aspx** — A list of users currently logged in to a site.

❑ **User\userprofile.aspx** — The public profile page for each user.

❑ **Utility\editad.aspx** — A modal page that allows an administrator to edit the content of an ad.

❑ **Utility\editarticle.aspx** — A modal page that allows an administrator to edit an article.

❑ **Utility\editcontent.aspx** — A modal page that allows for an administrator to edit the content of a `contentpart`.

❑ **Utility\ratinglist.aspx** — A list of rated posts on your site.

❑ **Utility\selectcontent.aspx** — Modal page that allows for browsable lists to be used and selected; generally, this does not need to be themed.

❑ **Utility\selecttags.aspx** — Modal page that allows for tags to be selected and assigned to various content on a site.

Please note that the above list does not include any of the application-specific pages. This means that the above list is only a starting point, and if you plan to support specific applications, such as blogging, you want to include the pages found in the blogs folder of the default theme, for example.

Furthermore, you should note that while Community Server allows you to customize the presentation of each of the modal pages, in general you will not need to. For example, the `selectcontent.aspx` page displays the `browseablelists`. Generally, this presentation will not need to be altered. Therefore, you are usually fine to copy these pages from existing themes and leave them intact. That being said, you are always free to alter the presentation of all of the pages on your Community Server site.

Another important point to consider is that all of the above pages do not always need to exist on your site. For example, if you omit links to tag pages on your site and do not include their presentation, then you can also remove the `tagslist.aspx` page from your theme. This allows for a theme to be as basic or sophisticated as requirements demand it to be.

Blog-Specific Theme Files

The weblog application allows for each blog to use a different theme than the site theme. The files that are required for these blog themes and how to create them were covered in the previous chapter. Aside from the blog themes, you can have a couple of site blog pages. These basically allow for a high-level overview of the content provided by the blogs on a site. All of these pages are contained in the `Blogs` folder inside of a site theme and include the following:

- ❑ **Blogs\bloglist.aspx** — A listing of the different blogs that exist on a site
- ❑ **Blogs\postlist.aspx** — A listing of the content from the various blogs on a site

Forum-Specific Theme Files

Unlike the blogs, the forums cannot be themed separately from a selected site theme. That being said, there are still several forum pages that can be themed and can always look different from the site theme that is selected. This means that if the default site theme is selected, the forum pages inside the default theme folder will be used for forums.

There are many more pages that exist for a forum on a site theme level. This is due to the fact that they are not themeable separate from a site theme. The various forum theme pages are contained in the `Forums` folder inside of a site theme and include the following:

- ❑ **Forums\createeditpost.aspx** — The page used to create and edit a forum post.
- ❑ **Forums\deletepost.aspx** — Page used to delete a forum post.
- ❑ **Forums\emailinformation.aspx** — Page used to display information about posting to a forum through email whenever the `MailGateway` is enabled.
- ❑ **Forums\filteredthreadlist.aspx** — Page used to display a list of threads after certain filtering criteria was specified.
- ❑ **Forums\forumsubscriptions.aspx** — Page used to display a list of forums that a user is currently subscribed to. Usually it allows for a user to both subscribe and unsubscribe to forums. When a user is subscribed to a forum they can be emailed whenever content in the forum changes.
- ❑ **Forums\grouplist.aspx** — The top-level page that displays what forum groups exist and usually what forums exist under each group.
- ❑ **Forums\nntpinformation.aspx** — Whenever the NNTP module is enabled, this page provides information to users explaining how to configure their NNTP clients.

❑ **Forums\post.aspx** — An individual forum post view page. `ForumPostData` is available on this page for the particular post that is being displayed.

❑ **Forums\postmoderatedinformation.aspx** — Page used to display information about a post after it was moderated. Usually, this is the page that is navigated to as a `SuccessAction` after a post is moderated.

❑ **Forums\post-threadedview.aspx** — If you allow for users to view a forum in a threaded view, then this is the page that is displayed when a user views a post and he or she has threaded view enabled. It is similar to the `post.aspx` page, except that it usually allows other posts to be easily navigated to in a threaded fashion. For an example, enable threaded view as your default view in your profile on the default theme and navigate to a forum post.

❑ **Forums\quickreply.aspx** — When you allow users to click a Quick Reply button on a forum post, this is the page that you can present them with. It should be a slimmed-down version of what they see when they click Reply.

❑ **Forums\reportabuse.aspx** — Page that allows for a post to be reported to an administrator. When a post is made from this page some reporting action should occur, such as filing the reason for the abuse in the reporting forum.

❑ **Forums\thread.aspx** — Page that displays the post content for a thread.

❑ **Forums\threadlist.aspx** — Page that displays a list of threads that exist in a parent forum.

❑ **Forums\uploadpostattachment.aspx** — If you allow for users to attach files to a forum post, this is the page that they will be presented with when they click to upload an attachment.

Photo Gallery–Specific Files

In Community Server 2007, Photo Galleries can no longer be themed separately from a site theme. Previously, you were able to create individual gallery themes just as you would a blog theme. This ability was not widely used and so the process was simplified to integrating the gallery theme into the site theme. The theme files for a Photo Gallery are now contained to the Galleries folder of the parent theme. Here is a listing of the various files that can exist in the gallery-specific portion of a site theme.

❑ **Galleries\about.aspx** — Page that displays information about a particular gallery. The content of this page is controlled from the gallery dashboard.

❑ **Galleries\category.aspx** — Whenever a gallery has albums enabled, this is the page that is displayed whenever a particular album is selected.

❑ **Galleries\emailsubscriptions.aspx** — Just as you are able to subscribe to a forum and receive email updates whenever content changes or is added, you can do the same for galleries. This is the page that displays the current email subscriptions for galleries on a site.

❑ **Galleries\exif.aspx** — Page that displays EXIF data about a selected picture.

❑ **Galleries\gallery.aspx** — Page used to display all of the pictures contained in a gallery. This is the homepage for a gallery.

❑ **Galleries\gallerylist.aspx** — Page used to display a list of the different galleries on a site and potentially some of the pictures in each gallery.

❑ **Galleries\gallerypost.aspx** — Page used to display a picture in a gallery.

❑ **Galleries\grouplist.aspx** — Galleries can be grouped like other applications; this page displays the various groups that exist in the gallery application for a site.

❑ **Galleries\orderprints.aspx** — You can allow users to order prints of selected pictures. This is the page that handles the ordering of the prints.

❑ **Galleries\slideshow.aspx** — One of the nice features of a gallery is that it can display a slideshow of the pictures inside it. This page is used to display this slideshow.

❑ **Galleries\slideshowpro.aspx** — This is essentially the same as the `slideshow.aspx` page. It is the page that the user is directed to whenever a slideshow is requested.

❑ **Galleries\taglist.aspx** — Page to display the available tags on a site.

File Gallery–Specific Theme Files

The File Gallery is similar to the forum and gallery applications in that it, too, cannot be themed apart from a site theme. Therefore, the theme that is specified in the File Gallery theme pages will be used whenever a specific site theme is selected. The File Gallery theme page files are contained in the `Files` folder of a site theme and are:

❑ **Files\createeditentry.aspx** — Page used to upload a new file to or edit an existing file in the File Gallery.

❑ **Files\deleteentry.aspx** — Page is used to allow an administrator to delete a file from the File Gallery without having to visit the Control Panel.

❑ **Files\downloadentry.aspx** — Page that displays any user agreement information before allowing a user to download a file.

❑ **Files\entry.aspx** — Page used to present a user with a download link to a file as well as provide any helpful information about the requested file.

❑ **Files\entrylist.aspx** — Page that displays a list of files in a parent folder.

❑ **Files\folderlist.aspx** — Page that displays the available folders and possibly files in a parent folder.

❑ **Files\grouplist.aspx** — Page that displays the top-level groups of folders and possibly the files or folders in the groups.

❑ **Files\taglist.aspx** — This page displays the available tags for the File Galleries.

❑ **Files\uploadattachment.aspx** — Modal page that allows a user to link to a file or upload it.

Extending Existing Themes

Perhaps the easiest way to begin making a custom theme is to start with an existing site theme and extend it. There are a few different themes that you can start with. If you are interested in creating a theme that has all of the bells and whistles with all of the available pages already created for you, you can start with the default or `leanandgreen` theme. Otherwise, if you want a barebones theme, you should consider downloading and starting with the basic site theme.

In the following example, you will be extending the basic site theme. This is available for download from http://communityserver.org. Once you have downloaded a theme, you should begin by making a copy of its root folder in a new folder with the name of the theme you are creating. For example, if you are creating a theme called oxygen, you can copy the files and folders contained in the basic theme folder into a new folder called oxygen.

After you have the parent folder with the same name as your theme, you should alter the theme.config file so that it has the same name as your theme. In this example where you are using the basic theme, you should edit the theme.config so that its contents are the same as those shown below. Please note that the only thing that was changed from the basic theme is the title and previewText.

```
<?xml version="1.0" encoding="utf-8" ?>
<Theme title="oxygen" previewText="This is the oxygen site theme.">
</Theme>
```

Once you have changed the theme.config file inside the oxygen folder, you can begin altering the pages. In this example, you are using the basic theme as a starting point; therefore, chances are that you will need to add extra controls, depending on the site's requirements. For this example, you will add a sidebar column to the basic theme and add an extra content placeholder. Because you want this column to be available across the site, you should edit the Common\master.Master page file. Change this file so that after the bodyContent placeholder and after the CommonContentArea-enclosing div tag, there is a new placeholder that looks like the following:

```
<div id="CommonSidebarArea">
    <asp:ContentPlaceHolder ID="sidebarContent" runat="server" />
</div>
```

After this is done, you can edit your pages and add items that will go in this sidebar. Open the Common\ home.aspx page, and add the following code after the bodyContent ASP.NET Content control:

```
<asp:Content ContentPlaceHolderID="sidebarContent" runat="server">
    <CSControl:ContentPart ContentName="welcome-default" runat="server"
            ContentCssClass="CommonContentPartBorderOff"
            ContentHoverCssClass="CommonContentPartBorderOn">
        <DefaultContentTemplate>
            <h2>Sidebar</h2>
            This is the content that is in your sidebar.
        </DefaultContentTemplate>
    </CSControl:ContentPart>
</asp:Content>
```

After this is done, change to your site theme in the Control Panel so that the site loads your theme. When you view the homepage, you should see the sidebar displayed at the bottom of the page. To fix this, you will need to edit the stylesheet that is used for the basic theme called screen.css. Open this file, and add the following code to the end of the file:

```
#CommonSidebarArea
{
    float: left;
    border: 1px solid #000;
    background: #fff;
}
```

```
#CommonContentArea
{
    float: left;
}
```

Whenever you save the changes to the stylesheet and reload your homepage, you should see the sidebar float up to the right part of your page. On computers with small resolutions, the sidebar will automatically be positioned below the main body content area. However, if your resolution is wide enough, you should see the sidebar on the right side of the screen, and it will look similar to Figure 7-1.

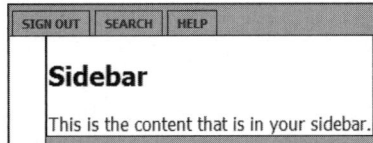

Figure 7-1: New sidebar in modified basic theme

As you can see from the above example, it is easy to begin modifying an existing theme to create your own custom theme. Whenever you begin this process, you can take ownership of the theme and make some useful changes to it. Remember to give credit to the creators of the theme that you are modifying, and always ask for approval to use the theme. When working with the themes that ship with Community Server you are free to tweak and make changes.

One of the next steps that you can try when modifying a theme is to alter the stylesheet file as much as possible before altering the markup. You are usually safe to make a site theme look the way you would like to without even touching page files.

Creating a Site theme.config File

Whenever you are creating a site theme from scratch, one of the first steps that you should take is to create the theme.config file for your theme. This file is what will be read and used to offer the option to select your theme in the theme configuration portion of the Control Panel. Additionally, this file is used to provide dynamic configuration options. If you are interested in learning more about this file and its many capabilities, consult Chapters 9 and 10.

In this example, you will be creating a theme that is super-simple and will be named Simplest. Begin creating this new theme by making a folder called Simplest that is located in your Themes folder. After you have done this, create a file inside of the Simplest folder, using Notepad or a similar text editor, that is named theme.config. Inside of theme.config add the following contents:

```
<?xml version="1.0" encoding="utf-8" ?>
<Theme title="Simplest" previewText="This is the simplest site theme." />
```

Once you have saved the theme.config file, you can choose to use it as your site theme. Do this by navigating to the Theme Options page inside of the Control Panel and selecting the Simplest theme from the dropdown. After you have done this, you are ready to being creating site pages for your theme.

Creating a Site Master Page

The purpose of master pages was covered in the previous chapter on creating a custom blog theme. If you are not familiar with what they are used for, first consult the section in Chapter 6 on master pages. For the Simplest site theme, you will create a master page that shows the site title and provides the navigation links to navigate through your site.

Create a new file called master.Master, and place it in a folder called Common inside your Simplest theme folder. This is how other site themes are structured, and it is a good idea to maintain this structure for consistency. Inside your newly created master.Master file, add the following contents:

```
<%@ Master Language="C#" AutoEventWireup="true" %>

<!DOCTYPE html PUBLIC "-//W3C//DTD XHTML 1.0 Transitional//EN"
"http://www.w3.org/TR/xhtml1/DTD/xhtml1-transitional.dtd">
<html xmlns="http://www.w3.org/1999/xhtml" xml:lang="en" lang="en">
    <head runat="server">
    <CSControl:Head runat="Server" >
        <meta http-equiv="Content-Type" content="text/html; charset=UTF-8" />
        <CSControl:ThemeStyle runat="server" Href="~/style/screen.css"
                media="screen" />
    </CSControl:Head>
    </head>
    <body>
        <form runat="server">

            <CSControl:SiteSettingsData Tag="H1" Property="SiteName"
                    runat="server"  />
            <CSControl:NavigationList runat="server" />

            <asp:ContentPlaceHolder ID="bodyContent" runat="server" />

        </form>
    </body>
</html>
```

A stylesheet called screen.css is included in the above master page. Additionally, a content placeholder is included that allows for content to be placed below the navigation on a site. This is the potion of the master.Master page file that will be used by pages on your site.

Creating the Site Homepage

Your site's homepage must be located in the Common directory that you created in the previous section. Begin by creating a page file called home.aspx, and place it in the Common folder. Because there is not really any content that needs to be displayed on the homepage of the Simplest theme, the homepage will simply output the markup generated by the main site master page. Therefore, the contents of the home.aspx page should look like this:

```
<%@ Page EnableViewState="false" Language="C#" AutoEventWireup="true"
    Inherits="CommunityServer.Controls.CSThemePage"
    MasterPageFile="master.Master"
%>
```

Whenever you load your new homepage, you should see a page that looks like Figure 7-2. At this point, it is very simple and provides a starting point for navigating to different parts of a site. To help make the site look a little more interesting, you can create a stylesheet called `screen.css` and place it in a new folder from the root of your `Simplest` theme folder called `Style`.

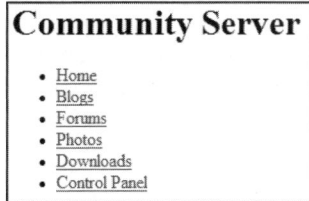

Community Server

- Home
- Blogs
- Forums
- Photos
- Downloads
- Control Panel

Figure 7-2: Simplest site theme without CSS

Inside the `screen.css` file, add the following styles to give your site theme a little color and organization. Also, if you are curious about how the themes were derived, you can look at the markup generated by the homepage.

```
html, body
{
    background-color: black;
    color: white;
    font-family: Arial, Helvetica;
    margin: 0;
    padding: 0;
}

a:link, a:visited
{
    color: red;
    text-decoration: none;
}

a:active, a:hover
{
    color: black;
    background-color: white;
    text-decoration: none;
}

LI
{
    float: left;
    padding-right: 10px;
    list-style-type: none;
}
```

Once you have saved the above changes, your homepage should look like Figure 7-3. Note that the home link has the mouse hovering over it. As you can see, it was rather easy to add a little color to your site theme. Furthermore, you did not have to create any extra markup to do so; this is part of the power of CSS.

Community Server

Home Blogs Forums Photos Downloads Control Panel

Figure 7-3: Styled site theme with minimal markup

At this point, you are able to easily add the other page files for your site, just as you did the homepage. Only, whenever you would like to add custom content, which should be on every page, you need to add a `Content` control to occupy the `ContentPlaceHolder` specified in the master page. An example of this exists in all the other site themes. Just know that you will need the following lines to wrap the content on the pages you create:

```
<asp:Content ContentPlaceHolderID="bodyContent" runat="server">

</asp:Content>
```

A straightforward approach to creating these new pages is to do them one at a time and check that they are accurate before continuing. To finish creating your site theme, start at the homepage and click each link; whenever the page for the link is missing you should add it. This is a sure way to create a theme that only contains the pages that are required by your site theme.

Summary

In this chapter, you learned the basics of creating a site theme. You learned about all of the pages that you can create for your theme, as well as what each of them is used for. Then you saw an example of how to extend an existing site theme with minor tweaks. After this, you learned the starting steps to create your own custom site theme from the ground up.

In the next chapter, you will learn about some nice features that you can add to your themes to make them more robust. You will learn how to add AJAX controls as well as Silverlight functionality to a theme.

8

Theme Considerations

In the previous two chapters, you learned how to create a new blog and site theme. With this knowledge, you should now feel comfortable with the files that are involved in creating a theme in either situation. In this chapter, you will expand this knowledge and learn about some advanced options you can add to your theme. By the end of this chapter, you will be more knowledgeable in the following areas:

- ❑   Interaction with ASP.NET AJAX
- ❑   Interaction with external scripts
- ❑   Interaction with Silverlight
- ❑   Packaging your theme for distribution

Interaction with ASP.NET AJAX

One of the more powerful abilities of chameleon controls in Community Server is that they are able to work inside of ASP.NET AJAX controls. This allows you to more easily create a rich user experience. Furthermore, all of the ASP.NET AJAX control toolkit controls work with Community Server. As a result, you are able to use some more advanced controls, such the slideshow control, inside of your Community Server site.

It is important to realize that the ASP.NET AJAX control extender controls do not necessarily work directly with chameleon controls. Instead, you need to wrap the chameleon controls with a containing ASP.NET `Panel` control. This is not anything to be concerned about, as a `Panel` simply renders a `div` tag, and also serves as a container for the part of the page that you want to force the AJAX control to work with.

Installing ASP.NET AJAX

In order to begin doing ASP.NET AJAX development with Community Server, you need to install the ASP.NET AJAX assemblies on your server. In addition, you will most likely want to add the control toolkit assemblies to the Community Server web project `bin` directory. After you have added the assemblies, update your `web.config` so that you can use ASP.NET AJAX and easily access these new controls.

You can acquire the ASP.NET AJAX installer from `http://ajax.asp.net` in the downloads section of the site. You need to download both the ASP.NET 2.0 AJAX Extensions as well as the ASP.NET AJAX Control Toolkit. Inside the folder that was created when you extract the Control Toolkit you will find an example of a `web.config` file that has been updated to work with the ASP.NET AJAX assemblies.

ASP.NET AJAX is a new technology that seems to change continually. At the time of this writing, the setup is as described below; however it could be different as you are reading this. Consult the AJAX toolkit docs for up-to-date information.

One of the main changes that you need to make to your `web.config` file is to add the AJAX controls and the AJAX control toolkit as a tag prefix that is accessible on all of your ASP.NET pages. To do this, you should add the following two lines to the controls node in the `web.config`. The controls node is found as a child to the pages node inside the parent node `system.web`. The two lines that you need to add are shown below. One thing to double-check is that the fully qualified namespace value is the same as that presented here. A trick that is useful for identifying the namespace value is to use the tool called Reflector. You can load the assembly inside Reflector, and it will tell you the fully qualified namespace, which you can enter in the namespace value.

```
<add tagPrefix="ajax" namespace="System.Web.UI"
    assembly="System.Web.Extensions, Version=1.0.61025.0, Culture=neutral,
    PublicKeyToken=31bf3856ad364e35"/>
<add tagPrefix="ajax" namespace="AjaxControlToolkit"
    assembly="AjaxControlToolkit, Version=1.0.10301.0, Culture=neutral,
    PublicKeyToken=28f01b0e84b6d53e" />
```

After you have added the `tagPrefix` entries above and set up ASP.NET AJAX inside the Community Server web project, you can begin adding ASP.NET AJAX controls to your site. If you are adding ASP.NET AJAX to an existing site that you do not have a web project set up for, you can do one of two things to set up the AJAX toolkit. Your first option is to open the site using Visual Studio 2005 as an existing website. Once you have done this, you can follow the steps above and add the assemblies as references. The second option is to manually copy the assemblies into your `bin` folder on your website and edit the `web.config` file with the above changes.

ASP.NET AJAX Example

Now that you have your site set up to host ASP.NET AJAX controls, you should begin adding AJAX functionality. For this example, you will be adding a very simple AJAX control that allows a site to always show how many members are currently signed into your site. In addition to this information, when a user is viewing their profile they will also be able to see their post count and user rank.

The information that you are presenting will always be visible across a site and will also be unobtrusive. Because the content will exist across a site, the controls will be added to the themes `\Common\master .Master` page. This is the page that all public-facing pages outside of blogs use. Also, because this content should always be visible, you will use the ASP.NET AJAX control called `AlwaysVisibleControlExtender`.

Once you are ready, add the following code to your `master.Master` page before the footer area. The content will float to the lower-right side of the page and will stay positioned in this area even while a user is scrolling through a page. However, because the `AlwaysVisibleControlExtender` code example below sets the `ScrollEffectDuration` to .1, the content will have a slight delay when scrolling occurs and the content is repositioning itself to the bottom.

Another thing to take note of in the following code example is that the `ScriptManager` control is used. This is required for the ASP.NET AJAX controls to function correctly, so it is important to make sure that your pages have a `ScriptManager` server control on them. This control appears before the ASP.NET AJAX controls, which is also necessary. To make things easy, you could potentially add the control to the `master.Master` page before any of the content areas. This would allow for any pages that use the `master.Master` page not to have a `ScriptManager` control defined on the page file itself.

```
<ajax:ScriptManager runat="server" EnablePartialRendering="true" />

<asp:Panel runat="server" ID="userDataPanel">
    <CSControl:PlaceHolder ID="userData" runat="server" style="border: solid
        1px blue;">
        <ContentTemplate>

        <CSControl:UserData runat="server" Property="TotalPosts"
                LinkTo="PostsSearch">
            <DisplayConditions>
            <CSControl:UserPropertyValueComparison runat="server"
                    UseAccessingUser="true" Operator="GreaterThan"
                    ComparisonValue="0" ComparisonProperty="TotalPosts" />
            </DisplayConditions>
            <LeaderTemplate>
            <CSControl:ResourceControl runat="server"
                    ResourceName="ViewUserProfile_TotalPosts" />
            </LeaderTemplate>
        </CSControl:UserData>

        <CSControl:UserData runat="server" Property="PostRank">
            <DisplayConditions>
            <CSControl:UserPropertyValueComparison runat="server"
                    UseAccessingUser="true" Operator="GreaterThan"
                    ComparisonValue="0" ComparisonProperty="TotalPosts" />
            </DisplayConditions>
            <LeaderTemplate>
            <CSControl:ResourceControl runat="server"
                    ResourceName="ViewUserProfile_PostRank" />
            </LeaderTemplate>
        </CSControl:UserData>

        <CSControl:UsersOnlineData runat="server" Property="MemberCount"
                ResourceName="WhoIsOnlineView_UsersOnlineCount">
            <LeaderTemplate><br/></LeaderTemplate>
        </CSControl:UsersOnlineData>
        </ContentTemplate>
    </CSControl:PlaceHolder>

</asp:Panel>
```

```
<ajax:AlwaysVisibleControlExtender runat="server"
        TargetControlID="userDataPanel"
        VerticalSide="Bottom"
        VerticalOffset="30"
        HorizontalSide="Right"
        HorizontalOffset="30"
        ScrollEffectDuration=".1" />
```

Something that is very important to realize at this point is that the `AlwaysVisibleControlExtender` would not work correctly if it was applied to the Community Server `PlaceHolder` control. Instead, you should use this and other extender controls on ASP.NET `Panel` controls. Another thing to notice is that the `AlwaysVisibleControlExtender` has a property for the `TargetControlID`, which is the ID of the panel surrounding the Community Server user content.

Whenever you have the above code added to the default theme's `master.Master` page file, you will get a little box in the lower-right part of the screen that contains the currently logged-in user's post count and the number of members that are currently accessing the site. Figure 8-1 shows an example of what the code above looks like when it is rendered.

Total Posts: 19 Post Rank: 1
There are 1 member(s) online.

Figure 8-1: Rendered AlwaysVisibleControlExtender

To make the area look more appealing you can add another AJAX toolkit control to the panel to give it a drop shadow. This control extender is called the `DropShadowExtender` and can be added in conjunction with the `AlwaysVisibleControlExtender`. It is interesting, though, that the naming is not completely consistent, as one says that it is a `ControlExtender` and the other is simply an `Extender`, but they both do extend controls. Add the following code after the `AlwaysVisibleControlExtender` in the `master.Master` page file:

```
<ajax:DropShadowExtender runat="server"
        BehaviorID="DropShadowBehavior1"
        TargetControlID="userDataPanel"
        Rounded="true"
        Radius="10"
        Opacity=".35"
        TrackPosition="true" />
```

To help give the panel a cleaner look, also change the `Panel` and `PlaceHolder` controls so that they look like the following code. This will remove the border and provide some spacing between the inner text and the gray container.

```
<asp:Panel runat="server" ID="userDataPanel" style="padding-left: 10px;">
<CSControl:PlaceHolder ID="userData" runat="server">
```

After you have added the `DropShadowExtender` and changed the `Panel` and `PlaceHolder` controls, as demonstrated above, your rendered controls should look like Figure 8-2. As you can see, the containing box now has rounded corners.

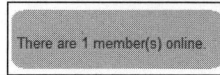

Figure 8-2: Rounded Corners with DropShadowExtender

Adding these nice little effects is quite easy to do with the ASP.NET AJAX controls. Notice that you are able to use the other controls as well as any custom ones that you create with Community Server. In the following section, you will learn how to create rounded corners on an area using a JavaScript library.

You can take the same approach above to add any other ASP.NET AJAX controls. You should remember to include the `ScriptManager` at the beginning of your page. Also, you may want to consider using some of the existing AJAX-enabled Community Server controls. For example, there is an AJAX `Pager` control that can be useful for paging through lists of items, such as the lists of threads in a forum.

Interaction with External Scripts

Inside of the themes that ship with Community Server are some examples of how to interact with an external JavaScript file. One that produces a similar result to the `DropShadowExtender` ASP.NET AJAX control can be found in the Riviera blog theme. Inside this theme is an example of how to give a container a drop shadow and rounded corners, using the `RuzeeBorder` JavaScript.

Whenever you are adding scripts to your theme, you will generally want to place them inside of a scripts subfolder. In the Riviera blog theme, the `RuzeeBorders.js` file is found inside a scripts folder. This is useful, as it helps to keep your scripts organized and separate from other types of files.

Another important thing to take note of is that you should include your JavaScript files just as you would do on any other page. There is also a nice control that is available to help include your script files, called the `ThemeScript` control, which is available in the `Blogs` assembly. To include a file located in a scripts folder, with the scripts folder being in the root location of your theme directory, you can add the following control inside of a `Head` server control:

```
<CSBlog:ThemeScript Src="~/scripts/YourScript.js" runat="server" />
```

In the case of the `RuzeeBorders` JavaScript, you should have the following entry in your `Head` server control. Also, you should realize that this head control occurs only in the master page file for your pages. For example, in the case of the Riviera blog theme, the `theme.Master` file contains the HTML head markup, which includes the `RuzeeBorders.js` file. This file will then be accessible in all of the pages in the blog theme that rely on the `theme.Master` master page file.

```
<CSBlog:ThemeScript Src="~/scripts/ruzeeborders.js" runat="server" />
```

After you have your JavaScript file included, you can use it as you would normally. Also, you should realize that the SRC can have the value of an external JavaScript file, on a different server, if you would like it to. Looking again at the Riviera theme, the `theme.Master` page gives a couple of the HTML elements rounded corners with the following code inside of the head tag:

```
<script type="text/javascript" type="text/javascript">
// <![CDATA[
```

```
    RUZEE.Borders.add({
        '#header': { borderType:'simple', cornerRadius:10 },
        '#container': { borderType:'shadow', cornerRadius:10, shadowWidth: 10 }
    });

    window.onload=function(){
        RUZEE.Borders.render();
    };

// ]]>
</script>
```

As a result of the above code, the container- and header-identified tags will have rounded corners, as shown in Figure 8-3. You can reuse this script in your own theme by including the RuzeeBorders.js and license.txt files in your scripts folder. If you would like to know more about how to use RuzeeBorders, you can visit the website dedicated to it at www.ruzee.com.

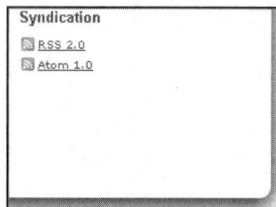

Figure 8-3: Riviera Rounded Corners

Interaction with Silverlight

Silverlight is a new technology that enables you to have managed code running inside of all major browsers. It allows you to easily create rich interactive application experiences that perform extremely well. If you would like to learn more about Silverlight in general, you can consult www.silverlight.net.

Throughout this section, you will learn how to create a simple Silverlight application and then integrate it with a Community Server site. In order for this to work correctly, you will need to have the following tools installed:

❑   Microsoft Visual Studio codename "Orcas" Beta 1 or later

❑   Microsoft Silverlight

❑   Microsoft Expression Blend 2

❑   Microsoft Silverlight tools for Visual Studio codename "Orcas"

Once you have these items installed on your machine you're ready to begin creating a Silverlight application. For this example, you will create a very simple "Hello Community Server" application that features a minor animation. Begin by opening Orcas and going to file and selecting create new project. Inside of your new project window, you should see an option for a new Silverlight project that looks like Figure 8-4. Create a new Silverlight Project, and call it SilverlightProjectTest.

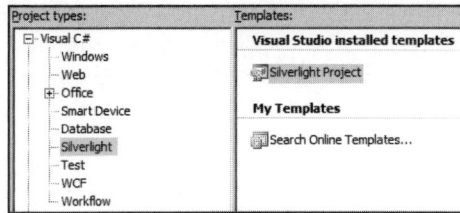

Figure 8-4: New Silverlight Project Window

In Orcas there is an option to link a Silverlight project to an existing project. You will be using this feature to bring the Silverlight project files into your Community Server site. To make it easy to keep your files organized, you should structure the files in the Silverlight project in the same way that they will be organized on your Community Server site. Therefore, you should create a new folder called `Themes` and then a subfolder called `default`. Under the default folder, you can create a folder called `Scripts` and one called `XAML`. After you are done, you should move the Silverlight project files into the appropriate folders, as illustrated in Figure 8-5.

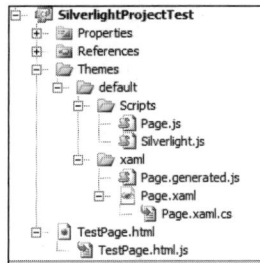

Figure 8-5: Silverlight Project Folder Structure

When you build your Silverlight project, it will create an assembly that can be downloaded by a browser running Silverlight. You can go ahead and build the project to make sure that it still builds after moving these files around. After you have built the project, you should add the Community Server website to your solution. You can do this by going to the File menu and selecting the Add Existing Website option. Then you can navigate to any Community Server site that is running 2007 or a later version. The Community Server 2007 release can be opened with Visual Studio 2005 and later as an existing web site. This is especially useful for theme developers because it means that you do not have to have the entire SDK downloaded to run your site from Visual Studio.

After you have added an existing Community Server website to your solution, you can link the existing Silverlight project to your website. To do this, you should have the Solution Explorer open in Visual Studio Orcas and right-click on the Community Server website. In the context menu, you should now see an option to link a Silverlight project, which looks like Figure 8-6. Whenever you select this option, a new window will appear with all of the Silverlight projects in the solution available to select. You should select the `SilverlightProjectTest` project and click OK.

Figure 8-6: Add Silverlight Link Menu Option

Once your Silverlight project is linked to your Community Server website your Silverlight files will automatically be copied into your website whenever you build the `SilverlightProjectTest` project. Go ahead and build this project and notice how your files are copied into the appropriate location in Community Server. You should now have a file structure similar to Figures 8-7 and 8-8 inside of your Community Server website.

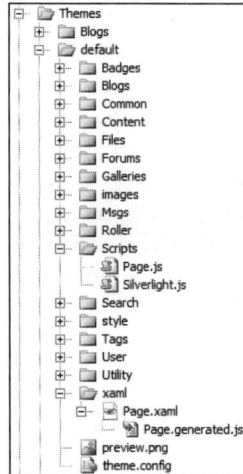

Figure 8-7: Community Server Silverlight Linked Project Folder Structure

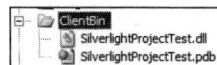

Figure 8-8: Community Server Silverlight Assemblies in the Newly Created ClientBin Folder

As a result of the above steps, you now have a Community Server site that has Silverlight assemblies and files inside it. However, it is not that useful at this point because the presentation of the site does not include any Silverlight features. Now that you have these projects linked up, you can begin editing the Silverlight files in the original `SilverlightProjectTest` project so that something actually happens. After you edit these files with the appropriate code that is shown below, you can add the XAML page content to an existing Community Server page. Begin by editing the original `Page.xaml` file and changing it so that it looks like the following code:

```
<Canvas
    xmlns="http://schemas.microsoft.com/client/2007"
    xmlns:x="http://schemas.microsoft.com/winfx/2006/xaml"
    x:Name="parentCanvas"
    Loaded="Page_Loaded"
    x:Class="SilverlightProjectTest.Page;
        assembly=/theme/ClientBin/SilverlightProjectTest.dll"
    Background="White"
    Width="136" Height="84"
    >
```

```
    <Canvas.Triggers>
        <EventTrigger RoutedEvent="Canvas.Loaded">
            <BeginStoryboard>
                <Storyboard x:Name="Timeline1">
        <DoubleAnimationUsingKeyFrames BeginTime="00:00:00"
                    Storyboard.TargetName="textBlock"
                    Storyboard.TargetProperty="
                    (UIElement.RenderTransform).(TransformGroup.Children)[2].
                    (RotateTransform.Angle)">
                <SplineDoubleKeyFrame KeyTime="00:00:00.5000000"
                    Value="180.805"/>
                <SplineDoubleKeyFrame KeyTime="00:00:02" Value="360.234"/>
                </DoubleAnimationUsingKeyFrames>
                </Storyboard>
            </BeginStoryboard>
        </EventTrigger>
    </Canvas.Triggers>
    <TextBlock Name="tbHelloCS" RenderTransformOrigin="0.5,0.5"
        x:Name="textBlock" Width="132.687" Height="82.537" Canvas.Top="-2.537">
        <TextBlock.RenderTransform>
        <TransformGroup>
            <ScaleTransform ScaleX="1" ScaleY="1"/>
            <SkewTransform AngleX="0" AngleY="0"/>
            <RotateTransform Angle="0"/>
            <TranslateTransform X="0" Y="0"/>
        </TransformGroup>
    </TextBlock.RenderTransform>
    Hello<LineBreak/>COMMUNITY<LineBreak/>Server</TextBlock>
</Canvas>
```

The above code was generated using Microsoft Expression Blend 2. You can use this tool to open the Page.xaml file in the Silverlight project and edit it. If you would like to create a different effect, this is a great tool to do so. The above code will create an animation that spins the text "Hello COMMUNITY Server." Something that you should notice with the above code is that the path to the assembly is fully qualified with the name of the virtual directory is called "theme." If you have your Community Server running at a different location, you should change this path. In future versions of Silverlight, there are plans to make this path something that you will not have to concern yourself with.

Next, you should open the Page.js file, which is what will be used to create the Silverlight object. You should only have to make a minor tweak to this file so that the path to Page.xaml is fully qualified. Remember that in this example the Community Server site is running in the virtual directory called "theme" on the default website in IIS. Therefore, if your site has a different name, you should update this part of the source value in the code below.

```
function createSilverlight()
/{
    Sys.Silverlight.createObjectEx({
        source: "/theme/themes/default/xaml/Page.xaml",
        parentElement: document.getElementById("SilverlightControlHost"),
        id: "SilverlightControl",
        properties: {
            width: "100%",
            height: "100%",
```

```
            version: "0.95",
            enableHtmlAccess: true
        },
        events: {}
    });
}
```

After you have made the above changes, you are ready to build your `SilverlightProjectTest` project so that the correct files are updated in your Community Server website. Once you have built the project and the files are copied, you are ready to edit the `master.Master` page in the default theme and add the new Silverlight functionality. You will need to include the Silverlight JavaScript file that handles the installation of Silverlight if it is not currently installed in the user's browser. In addition, you will need to include the `Page.js` file that will be used to instantiate the Silverlight control. Therefore, you should add the following controls inside of the head server control in the common `master.Master` page file.

```
<CSControl:Script runat ="server" Src="../Scripts/Silverlight.js" />
<CSControl:Script ID="Script1" runat="server" Src="../Scripts/Page.js" />
```

Once you have included the appropriate JavaScript files above, you can add a container for your Silverlight control. In this example, it is added to the `CommonHeaderUserWelcome div` element so that it looks like the following code:

```
<div id="CommonHeaderUserWelcome">
    <CSUserControl:UserWelcome runat="server" />
    <div id="SilverlightControlHost" >
        <script type="text/javascript">
            createSilverlight();
        </script>
    </div>
</div>
```

As you can see in the above code, the `createSilverlight` function that exists in the `Page.js` file is called. This then creates the `SilverlightControl` inside the `SilverlightControlHost div` element. As a result of the above code, when you access your Community Server site, in the header of your pages you will see a white area that has text that spins. The rendered Silverlight control should look like Figure 8-9.

Figure 8-9: Rendered Silverlight Control Inside a Community Server Site

One of the nice things about this example is that it does not require you to build the Community Server website project. Instead, the only project that you need to build is the `SilverlightProjectTest` project. In addition, these steps provide a starting point for adding additional Silverlight controls to a site, which can provide a much richer user experience.

You can now easily add C# code to your `Page.xaml.cs` file that responds to events triggered in the Silverlight control. For example, you can add the following code to your `Page.xaml.cs` file to respond to the `Timeline1` completed event that causes it to start again. As a result of this code, you will cause the animation to never stop, and the text will continuously swing back and forth.

```
public void Page_Loaded(object o, EventArgs e)
{
    // Required to initialize variables
    InitializeComponent();
    this.Timeline1.Completed += new EventHandler (Timeline1_Completed);
}

void Timeline1_Completed(object sender, EventArgs e)
{
    this.Timeline1.Begin();
}
```

Something that you may be wondering is how you can access Community Server–specific data from a Silverlight control. There are several different ways that you access this data, which include calling an AJAX-enabled method or using a web service. To learn more on how to do either task, you should view the example videos and code on the `www.silverlight.net` website.

Silverlight allows you to do some pretty amazing things inside of a Community Server site. If you are interested in making Silverlight controls that you can combine inside an assembly without the need for separate XAML pages inside of your site, you should explore the Silverlight Control Project type. This essentially is a way to create custom Silverlight controls that you can embed inside of parent XAML pages.

Another feature that Silverlight allows you to more easily add to an existing Community Server site is to mash up external services inside your site. Because Silverlight is able to run managed code inside a browser, you can create subapplication widgets inside of your Community Server site with Silverlight. For example, if you want to allow for your users to display their Facebook friends inside of their profile, you can easily do so with a custom Silverlight application. This application could call to the Facebook service and retrieve a member's friends list. Again, one of the especially nice things about this is that it runs in the users' browser so that it does not require any extra processing by the web server running your Community Server site.

Packaging Your Theme for Distribution

Once you have a theme in a place that is stable enough for distribution, there are a few easy steps that you can follow to allow others to use it. However, to make sure that your theme is indeed stable, you should test it. One of the easiest ways to test a theme is to access a site running your theme with different popular browsers. In general, you should try out the theme with Internet Explorer 6 and 7, Firefox 1.5 and 2.0, Opera, and Safari. If your theme works well in the majority of these browsers, then you are most likely at a point to begin packaging your theme.

If all of your theme files are contained inside of the themes folder on your site, packaging it will be very easy. However, if you have files that are required, such as additional assemblies, then the packaging process can be more involved. Perhaps one of the most straightforward approaches to packaging a theme is to create a new folder and begin putting folders and files in it that are required for your theme to function.

Therefore, if you have a couple of assemblies that are required, you should create a `bin` folder and place only these two required assemblies in it. Likewise, you should create a `Themes` folder and place your specific theme inside this folder.

Once you are done creating this structure, you should be able to simply select all of the items in this new folder and copy them into an existing site to install your theme. Before you actually package your theme, you should try performing this task. Install a fresh Community Server site and copy the files from your new folder into this site. When you are done, you should be able to select your theme from the Control Panel and have it function correctly.

After you have tested installing your theme in a fresh Community Server site, you can simply compress these same files into a new archive package. You should use either a `.zip` or `.rar` format to compress these files. This is an easy format for people to understand and use to extract your theme files into their site.

Another consideration for your theme package is a `readme` file that explains the main advantages to using your theme. It is usually helpful to include this information for your theme, such as the fact that it has been tested with specific browsers so that the end user will be confident enough to try it out. Also, you may add contact information so that users can contact you with any suggestions or bug issues. In addition, the readme should contain basic steps for how to install your theme, such as simply copying the extracted folder structure into an existing Community Server site.

One last item to consider adding to your theme package is a license file. If you have any specific restrictions on the usage and distribution of your theme, you can communicate these in a license file. If you need any examples of license files, you should consult the `http://sourceforge.org` website.

Whenever your theme is packaged it is ready to distribute. Most often people will post a theme package into their blog for people to download. This is a good way to distribute the theme if you have any amount of readership. Another approach is to post your theme as an attachment to a forum post on `http://communityserver.org`. This ensures that Community Server administrators are able to find your theme and discuss its various qualities.

Summary

In this chapter, you learned about several ideas for how you can improve your Community Server themes. You learned about how you can add ASP.NET AJAX support into your theme. This allows you to achieve useful functionality with a seamless user experience. Then you were provided with an example of how you can use external JavaScript libraries to add additional features and control the presentation of your theme. You also learned how to improve the end user experience of your theme by leveraging the new Silverlight technology. In this section, you were presented with the basic steps to start adding Silverlight controls to your Community Server site. Finally, you learned about how you can package your theme so that other Community Server sites are able to install it and use it.

In the next chapter, you will learn about other ways that you can improve your theme. In the next chapter, you will explore some of the basic options available to you inside of the theme configuration files. You will experience how the combination of all of these ideas allows you to create extremely powerful themes that are also portable.

9

Basics of Dynamic Configuration Options

Community Server includes support for defining configuration options for each site and blog theme, to allow theme developers to quickly and easily support exposing theme configuration options to end users. Dynamic configuration options can be used within a theme to hide content, change interface styles, select images or other files, or perform any other behavior based on data entered by a user.

Dynamic configuration options are defined within each theme's `theme.config` file. Community Server has built-in support for rendering dynamically generated configuration forms supporting many common data types and allows custom data, custom configuration controls, and custom rules to be defined to further extend and tailor the configuration options and form for each theme.

This chapter outlines the support for dynamic configuration options in Community Server, providing the information required to define and utilize user-configurable options in custom themes.

Theme Configuration Pages

The theme configuration pages expose the visible configuration options of themes to end users. A theme configuration page exists for blogs in the My Blogs area of the Community Server Control Panel, in the Global Settings section under the Change How My Blog Looks menu item. For site themes, the Administration area of the Control Panel provides access to the Theme Configuration menu item in the Settings section.

Both of these theme configuration pages support rendering the configuration form representing the configuration options of a custom theme, previewing changes, saving changes, exporting the current configuration, importing a saved configuration, and reverting to the default configuration values for the current theme.

Configuration Form

The configuration form on the theme configuration pages (see Figure 9-1) is automatically generated based on the selected theme's `theme.config` file.

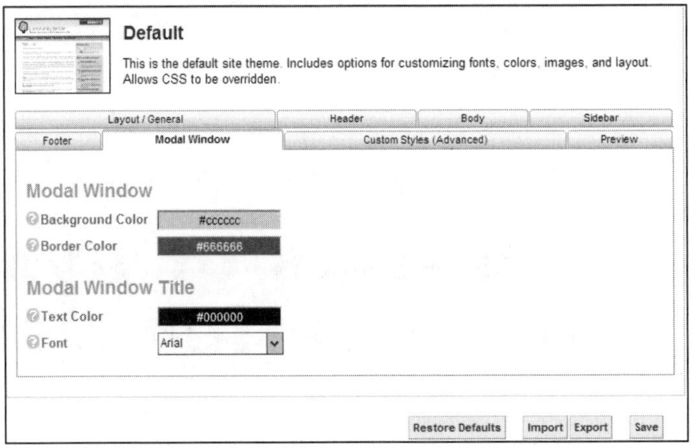

Figure 9-1: Theme Configuration Form

Community Server dynamically generates the tabs, headers, properties, tooltips, and input controls based on the configuration options defined within the `theme.config` file. The format of the `theme.config` file is discussed later in this chapter.

Preview

All theme configuration pages allow the end user to preview their changes to the current theme's configuration before committing.

The Preview tab on each theme configuration page (see Figure 9-2) provides the preview options.

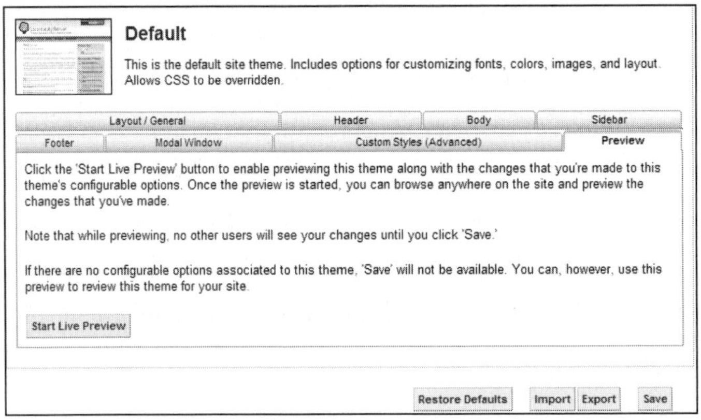

Figure 9-2: Configuration Preview Tab

When previewing (see Figure 9-3), a cookie is saved within the user's browser session that notifies Community Server to load the preview configuration data when the user is viewing pages within the site or blog being previewed. Only the user with this cookie will see the uncommitted changes.

The live preview allows the user to view any page within the site exactly as it will be rendered when the configuration changes are committed.

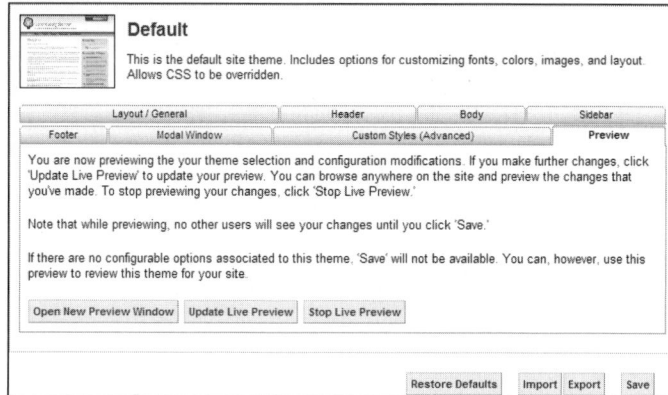

Figure 9-3: Previewing a Configuration

If users make changes to the theme configuration form while previewing the site, they can click the Update Live Preview button to update the preview configuration data associated with their preview cookie. The live preview is ended when a user clicks the Stop Live Preview button, saves the configuration form, or closes his or her browser.

Save

The Save button on the theme configuration page commits the changes to the database. In a single web server configuration, the changes should affect the site or blog immediately. In a web farm, each server will update its cache with the latest theme configuration changes within 30 minutes.

Export

The currently committed theme configuration can be exported into an XML file and backed up or shared. Clicking the Export button will cause the export XML file to be generated and sent to the client. The export file simply identifies values for each property within the theme's configuration.

The contents of a sample theme configuration export are shown in this code example:

```
<theme name="default">
  <dynamicConfiguration>
    <properties>
      <property id="columns" dataType="Int">
        <value>2</value>
      </property>
```

```
          <property id="width" dataType="Unit">
            <value>960px</value>
          </property>
          <property id="textColor" dataType="Color">
            <value>#333333</value>
          </property>
          <property id="textFont" dataType="String">
            <value>Arial, Helvetica</value>
          </property>
          <property id="linkColor" dataType="Color">
            <value>#000000</value>
          </property>
          <property id="visitedLinkColor" dataType="Color">
            <value>#666666</value>
          </property>
          <property id="activeLinkColor" dataType="Color">
            <value>#000000</value>
          </property>
        </properties>
      </dynamicConfiguration>
    </theme>
```

When a property of type Url references a file stored within the Community Server Site Files or Blog Files file store, the exported configuration file will include the contents of the referenced file.

Import

Theme configuration export files, as generated by the Export button, can be imported into the currently selected theme, overwriting the current configuration with the values from the imported file.

Clicking the Import button displays the Import Theme Configuration modal window (see Figure 9-4). On this form, you can select the configuration export file. When the Import button is clicked, the selected file is imported and a message will display identifying the number of property values that were imported.

File contents within XML export files for properties of type Url will be saved within the Site Files or Blog Files file store and the associated URLs will be updated to reference the newly saved files.

It is not necessary to import a configuration export file generated from the same theme. Export files from other themes can be imported as well. When importing a configuration export file, only properties that match by both id and data type will be imported. If the current theme does not define a property identified within the theme configuration export file being imported, the property's value will not be imported. Imported configuration values are immediately committed.

Restore Defaults

The theme configuration page also supports restoring the default values of all of the properties of the currently selected theme. When you click the Restore Defaults button, all property values revert to the default values identified in the theme's theme.config file.

Note that when restoring defaults, clicking the Restore Defaults button only applies the default values to the configuration form. It does not commit those changes. To commit the default values, you still must click the Save button.

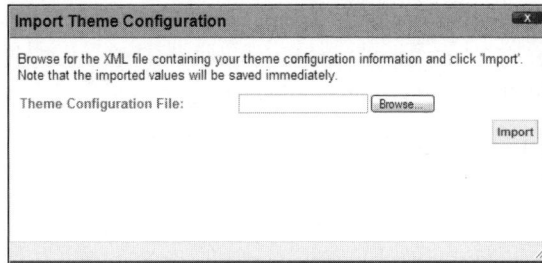

Figure 9-4: Import Theme Configuration Modal Window

The theme.config File

The theme.config file, located in the root folder of blog and site themes, identifies folders containing themes and defines configuration information for use by Community Server.

Every theme in Community Server is required to have a theme.config file in its root folder. As mentioned previously, site themes are located in the themes folder and blog themes are located in the themes/blogs folder in Community Server. Only subfolders within these theme folders containing theme.config files will be made available as theme selections through the Control Panel.

A sample theme.config file is shown here:

```xml
<?xml version="1.0" encoding="utf-8" ?>
<Theme title="Default" previewImageUrl="~/themes/default/preview.png"
previewText="This is the default site theme.">
  <DynamicConfiguration>
  </DynamicConfiguration>
</Theme>
```

This sample includes two nodes: Theme and DynamicConfiguration.

Theme node

The Theme node identifies optional information used to identify the theme. It supports the title, previewImageUrl, and previewText attributes.

Title attribute

The title attribute of the Theme node identifies the displayed name for the theme. If specified, the value of the title attribute will be displayed wherever themes are selected within Community Server. If it is not specified, themes will be identified by their folder name.

previewImageUrl attribute

The previewImageUrl attribute can be used to identify a preview image for the theme. When specified, the preview image will be shown when selecting and configuring themes.

A "~" in the value of the previewImageUrl attribute is interpreted as the root folder of Community Server.

121

previewText attribute

The `previewText` attribute can be used to further describe the theme. The `previewText` will be shown in the same locations that the preview image is displayed.

DynamicConfiguration node

The `DynamicConfiguration` node, located within the `Theme` node, contains the definition of dynamic configuration options. This is discussed throughout the remainder of this chapter.

A sample `theme.config` file containing a single configuration property is shown here:

```
<?xml version="1.0" encoding="utf-8" ?>
<Theme title="Default" previewImageUrl="~/themes/blogs/default/preview.png"
previewText="This is the default blog theme and inherits styles from the default
site theme. Also allows CSS to be overridden.">
  <DynamicConfiguration>
    <propertyGroup id="cssOverrides" text="Custom Styles (Advanced)">
      <property id="cssOverrides" text="CSS Overrides" dataType="string"
defaultValue=""
controlType="Telligent.DynamicConfiguration.Controls.MultilineStringControl,
Telligent.DynamicConfiguration" />
    </propertyGroup>
  </DynamicConfiguration>
</Theme>
```

The following nodes are used to identify and organize dynamic configuration options within the `DynamicConfiguration` node: `propertyGroup`, `propertySubGroup`, `property`, `propertyValue`, and `propertyRule`.

Property Groups

Property groups, identified by `propertyGroup` nodes, are defined within the `DynamicConfiguration` node of `theme.config`. Property groups group the properties defined within them and are rendered as tabs on the theme configuration pages within Community Server. For example,

```
<propertyGroup text="Theme Options" descriptionText="Select the options for this
theme.">
  <property id="showHeader" dataType="Bool" text="Show Header" />
</propertyGroup>
```

would be rendered on the theme configuration pages as in Figure 9-5.

Figure 9-5: Rendered Property Group with a Single Property

Property groups expose the following attributes: id, resourceName, resourceFile, text, descriptionResourceName, descriptionResourceFile, descriptionText, orderNumber, visible, and unrecognized attributes.

id

The id attribute of property groups is used to identify the property group for programmatic access. The value of the id attribute should be unique among all property groups defined for the theme: however, the id attribute is not required for property groups.

resourceName, resourceFile, and text

The resourceName, resourceFile, and text attributes identify the name of the property group. This name is displayed on the tab representing the group on the theme configuration page.

The value of the resourceName attribute identifies the language resource within the file identified by the value of the resourceFile attribute to render as the name of the property group. If the resourceName attribute is defined, the value of the text attribute is ignored.

descriptionResourceName, descriptionResourceFile, and descriptionText

The descriptionResourceName, descriptionResourceFile, and descriptionText attributes identify the text to render as the description of the property group. This name is displayed at the top of the content of the tab representing the property group.

The value of the descriptionResourceName attribute identifies the language resource within the file identified by the value of the descriptionResourceFile attribute to render as the description of the property group. If the descriptionResourceName attribute is defined, the value of the descriptionText attribute is ignored.

The descriptionResourceName, descriptionResourceFile, and descriptionText attributes are all optional.

orderNumber

The orderNumber attribute identifies an optional order number for the property group. If it is defined, property groups will be sorted by their order numbers before being rendered on the theme configuration pages.

Property groups without order numbers will be rendered after the property groups with order numbers in the order that they are defined within the theme.config file.

visible

The visible attribute identifies whether the property group should be displayed to the user on the theme configuration pages. Only property groups that contain visible properties will be rendered, regardless of the value of the visible attribute of the property group.

If this is set to true, the property group will be displayed on the theme configuration page. If it is set to false, the property group will not be displayed.

If the visible attribute is not defined, the property group will be displayed.

Unrecognized Attributes

Property groups support storing unrecognized attributes for use by custom property controls and rules.

The documentation for the specific property control or property rule should identify which additional attributes are supported on property groups.

Property Subgroups

Property subgroups, identified by propertySubGroup nodes, are defined within propertyGroup nodes of the theme.config file. Property subgroups group the properties defined within them and are rendered as headings within tabs on the theme configuration pages within Community Server. For example:

```
<propertySubGroup text="Header Options">
    <property id="showHeader" dataType="Bool" text="Show Header" />
</propertySubGroup>
```

This would be rendered on the theme configuration pages as in Figure 9-6.

> **Header Options**
> Show Header   ☐

Figure 9-6: Rendered Property Subgroup

Property subgroups are optional and only exist to provide subgroupings of properties within a single property group.

Property subgroups expose the following attributes: id, resourceName, resourceFile, text, descriptionResourceName, descriptionResourceFile, descriptionText, orderNumber, visible, and unrecognized attributes.

id

The id attribute of property subgroups is used to identify the property subgroup for programmatic access. The value of the id attribute should be unique among all property subgroups defined for the theme: however, the id attribute is not required.

resourceName, resourceFile, and text

The `resourceName`, `resourceFile` and `text` attributes identify the name of the property subgroup. This name is displayed as a heading within the content of tabs on the theme configuration page.

The value of the `resourceName` attribute identifies the language resource within the file identified by the value of the `resourceFile` attribute to render as the name of the property subgroup. If the `resourceName` attribute is defined, the value of the `text` attribute is ignored.

descriptionResourceName, descriptionResourceFile, and descriptionText

The `descriptionResourceName`, `descriptionResourceFile`, and `descriptionText` attributes identify the text to render as the description of the property subgroup. This name is displayed below the heading representing the property subgroup.

The value of the `descriptionResourceName` attribute identifies the language resource within the file identified by the value of the `descriptionResourceFile` attribute to render as the description of the property subgroup. If the `descriptionResourceName` attribute is defined, the value of the `descriptionText` attribute is ignored.

The `descriptionResourceName`, `descriptionResourceFile`, and `descriptionText` attributes are all optional.

orderNumber

The `orderNumber` attribute identifies an optional order number for the property subgroup. If defined, property subgroups will be sorted by their order numbers before being rendered on the theme configuration pages.

Property subgroups without order numbers will be rendered after the property subgroups with order numbers within the same property group in the order that they are defined within the `theme.config` file.

visible

The `visible` attribute identifies whether the property subgroup should be displayed to the user on the theme configuration pages. Only property subgroups that contain visible properties will be rendered, regardless of the value of the `visible` attribute of the property subgroup.

If this is set to `true`, the property subgroup will be displayed on the theme configuration page. If it is set to `false`, the property subgroup will not be displayed.

If the `visible` attribute is not defined, the property subgroup will be displayed.

Unrecognized Attributes

Property subgroups support storing unrecognized attributes for use by custom property controls and rules.

The documentation for the specific property control or property rule should identify which additional attributes are supported on property subgroups.

Properties

Properties, identified by `property` nodes, define configuration options related to a theme. Each property represents a single value that can be used by the theme to control styles, include images, conditionally display content, or provide any other configurable function supported by the theme.

For example,

```
<property id="sidebarWidth" text="Width" dataType="Unit" descriptionText="Select
the width of the sidebars." defaultValue="174px" />
```

This would define a property in which the width of sidebars would be stored for use by the theme and would be rendered as shown in Figure 9-7.

Figure 9-7: Rendered Property

Properties can be defined within `propertyGroup` or `propertySubGroup` nodes in the `theme.config` file.

The `property` node exposes the following attributes: `id`, `resourceName`, `resourceFile`, `text`, `descriptionResourceName`, `descriptionResourceFile`, `descriptionText`, `descriptionImageUrl`, `orderNumber`, `dataType`, `defaultValue`, `editable`, `visible`, `controlType`, and unrecognized attributes.

id

The `id` attribute of properties is used to identify the property for programmatic access. The value of the `id` attribute should be unique among all properties defined for the theme.

When retrieving values from a theme's configuration within a theme, property values are referenced by their `id`s.

resourceName, resourceFile, and text

The `resourceName`, `resourceFile`, and `text` attributes identify the name of the property. This name is displayed as the label for the property's value on the theme configuration page.

The value of the `resourceName` attribute identifies the language resource within the file identified by the value of the `resourceFile` attribute to render as the name of the property. If the `resourceName` attribute is defined, the value of the `text` attribute is ignored.

descriptionResourceName, descriptionResourceFile, and descriptionText

The descriptionResourceName, descriptionResourceFile, and descriptionText attributes identify the text to render as the description of the property. This name is displayed in the help tooltip next to the label identifying the property's value.

The value of the descriptionResourceName attribute identifies the language resource within the file identified by the value of the descriptionResourceFile attribute to render as the description of the property. If the descriptionResourceName attribute is defined, the value of the descriptionText attribute is ignored.

The descriptionResourceName, descriptionResourceFile, and descriptionText attributes are all optional.

descriptionImageUrl

The descriptionImageUrl attribute identifies the URL of an image to display within the help tooltip next to the label identifying the property's value.

If specified, the image identified by the URL will be rendered above the property's description (identified by the descriptionResourceName or descriptionText attributes) in the help tooltip.

orderNumber

The orderNumber attribute identifies an optional order number for the property. If defined, properties will be sorted by their order numbers before being rendered on the theme configuration pages.

Properties without order numbers will be rendered after the properties with order numbers within the same property group or property subgroup in the order that they are defined within the theme.config file.

dataType

The dataType attribute identifies the type of the value the property should store.

If the property is editable (see the editable attribute), the dataType is also used to identify the default control used to allow its associated value to be edited on the theme configuration pages. All data types have a default control type (which can be overridden using the controlType attribute) except the Custom data type.

Supported values are: Custom, Bool, Int, Double, String, Date, Time, DateTime, Guid, Color, Unit, and Url.

Custom

The Custom data type should be used only when a custom controlType is specified for the property that will store data in a nonstandard format; that is, a format that is not supported by one of the other possible data types. The Custom data type can be used to store any serializable data for use with custom property and rendering controls.

There is no default property control associated to the Custom data type.

Bool

The Bool data type stores a true or false value. The default control type for Bool properties is a checkbox, as shown in Figure 9-8.

☑

Figure 9-8: Rendered Bool Property

Int

The Int data type stores an integer value. The default control type for Int properties is a validated textbox as shown in Figure 9-9.

234234

Figure 9-9: Rendered Int Property

Double

The Double data type stores a double-precision floating point value. The default control type for Double properties is a validated textbox, as shown in Figure 9-10.

1234.123412

Figure 9-10: Rendered Double Property

String

The String data type stores a text string value. The default control type for String properties is a single-line textbox as shown in Figure 9-11.

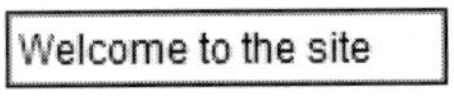

Welcome to the site

Figure 9-11: Rendered String Property

Date

The Date data type stores a date value. The default control for Date properties is a date selector control, allowing the month, day, and year to be typed or selected from a pop-up calendar, as shown in Figure 9-12.

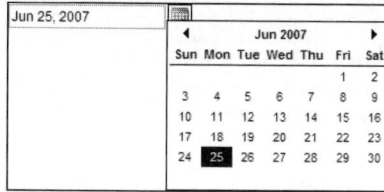

Figure 9-12: Rendered Date Property

Time

The Time data type stores a time value. The default control for Time properties is a date selector control, allowing the hour, minute, and AM/PM designator to be specified, as shown in Figure 9-13.

Figure 9-13: Rendered Time Property

DateTime

The DateTime data type stores a date and time value. The default control for DateTime properties is a date selector control, allowing the month, day, year, hour, minute, and AM/PM designator to be specified, as shown in Figure 9-14. The default control also provides a pop-up calendar for selecting the month, day, and year.

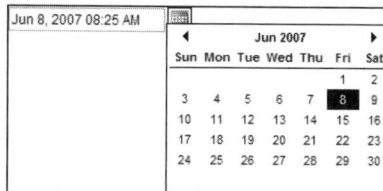

Figure 9-14: Rendered DateTime Property

Guid

The Guid data type stores a guaranteed unique identifier value. The default control for Guid properties is a validated textbox, as shown in Figure 9-15.

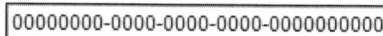

Figure 9-15: Rendered Guid Property

Color

The `Color` data type stores a color value. The default control for `Color` properties is a color selector control, which allows colors to be entered using the `#rrggbb` format or by selecting the color using an adjustable color palette, as shown in Figure 9-16.

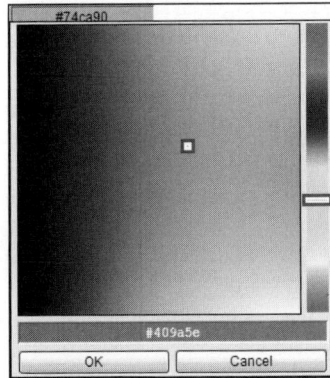

Figure 9-16: Rendered Color Property

Unit

The `Unit` data type stores a CSS-compliant unit value. The default control for `Unit` properties is a unit selector, which allows the value and unit to be entered as shown in Figure 9-17. Supported values range from `0` to `1600` and supported units are `px`, `pt`, `%`, `pc`, `in`, `mm`, `cm`, `em`, and `ex`.

Figure 9-17: Rendered Unit Property

Url

The `Url` data type stores a relative or absolute URL value. The default control for `Url` properties is a validated textbox, as shown in Figure 9-18.

Figure 9-18: Rendered Url Property

defaultValue

The `defaultValue` attribute identifies the default value of the property.

When no value has been selected or when the Restore Defaults option on the theme configuration pages is clicked, the value identified by the `defaultValue` attribute will be used as the value of the property.

editable

The `editable` attribute identifies whether this property can be edited on the dynamic configuration pages.

If the `editable` attribute is set to `true`, the property will be displayed on the theme configuration pages using the default control or the control identified by the `controlType` attribute (if specified). If the `editable` attribute is set to `false`, the property's value will be displayed in a noneditable format on the theme configuration pages.

If the `editable` attribute is not defined, the property will be editable.

visible

The `visible` attribute identifies whether the property should be displayed to the user on the theme configuration pages.

If set to `true`, the property will be displayed on the theme configuration page. If this is set to `false`, the property will not be displayed.

If the `visible` attribute is not defined, the property will be displayed.

controlType

The `controlType` attribute identifies the type of control to load and use when rendering the property if the property is editable. The control class identified by the `controlType` attribute must implement the `Telligent.DynamicConfiguration.Components.IPropertyControl` interface.

Specifying the `controlType` for the property overrides the default property control for the property's data type.

Values of the `controlType` attribute should be type descriptors, including the assembly name, for example,

```
<property id="cssOverrides" text="CSS Overrides" dataType="string" defaultValue=""
controlType="Telligent.DynamicConfiguration.Controls.MultilineStringControl,
Telligent.DynamicConfiguration" />
```

specifies the control type as:

```
Telligent.DynamicConfiguration.Controls.MultilineStringControl,
Telligent.DynamicConfiguration
```

where `Telligent.DynamicConfiguration.Controls.MultilineStringControl` is the full class name of the control and `Telligent.DynamicConfiguration` is the name of the assembly in which the control is defined.

Unrecognized Attributes

Properties support storing unrecognized attributes for use by custom property controls and rules.

The documentation for the specific property control or property rule should identify which additional attributes are supported on properties.

Property Values

Property values, identified by `propertyValue` nodes, define selectable values for a property within a theme. Each property value represents a single value that can be selected as the value of the property in which it is defined.

For example,

```
<property id="titleFontSize" text="Font Size" dataType="string" defaultValue="180%" >
    <propertyValue value="140%" text="Smallest" />
    <propertyValue value="160%" text="Smaller" />
    <propertyValue value="180%" text="Medium" />
    <propertyValue value="210%" text="Larger" />
    <propertyValue value="240%" text="Largest" />
</property>
```

would provide users with options for "Smallest," "Smaller," "Medium," "Larger," and "Largest" font sizes on the theme configuration page when selecting a value for the Font Size property and would be rendered as shown in Figure 9-19.

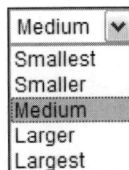

Figure 9-19: Rendered Property Values

Property values can be defined within `property` nodes in the `theme.config` file. When a property contains property values, the default control for the property, when editable, becomes a dropdown list, allowing the user to select a single property value on the theme configuration pages.

The `propertyValue` node exposes the following attributes: `value`, `resourceName`, `resourceFile`, `text`, `orderNumber`, and unrecognized attributes.

value

The value attribute identifies the selectable value represented by the `propertyValue` node. This value should be in a format that can be interpreted as a value in the type identified by the property's `dataType` attribute.

resourceName, resourceFile, and text

The `resourceName`, `resourceFile`, and `text` attributes identify the name of the property value. This name is displayed as the name of the value displayed in the dropdown list on the theme configuration page.

The value of the `resourceName` attribute identifies the language resource within the file identified by the value of the `resourceFile` attribute to render as the name of the property. If the `resourceName` attribute is defined, the value of the `text` attribute is ignored.

orderNumber

The `orderNumber` attribute identifies an optional order number for the property value. If this is defined, property values will be sorted by their order numbers before being rendered on the theme configuration pages.

Property values without order numbers will be rendered after the property values with order numbers within the same property in the order they are defined within the `theme.config` file.

Unrecognized Attributes

Property values support storing unrecognized attributes for use by custom property controls and rules.

The documentation for the specific property control or property rule should identify which additional attributes are supported on property values.

Property Rules

Property rules, identified by `propertyRule` nodes, define rules that should be processed whenever the value of a property changes.

For example,

```
<property id="secondaryCssUrl" text="Variation" dataType="url" defaultValue="">
  <propertyValue value="" text="Blue" />
  <propertyValue value="~/themes/blogs/marvin3/style/brown.css" text="Brown" />
  <propertyValue value="~/themes/blogs/marvin3/style/green.css" text="Green" />
  <propertyRule type="Telligent.DynamicConfiguration.Rules.ValueAutomationRule,
Telligent.DynamicConfiguration" processImmediately="true">
    <checkValue value="">
      <setValue id="siteBackgroundColor" value="#ffffff" />
      <setValue id="linkColor" value="#00F" />
      <setValue id="visitedLinkColor" value="#00F" />
    </checkValue>
```

```
            <checkValue value="~/themes/blogs/marvin3/style/brown.css">
              <setValue id="siteBackgroundColor" value="#ddc" />
              <setValue id="linkColor" value="#700" />
              <setValue id="visitedLinkColor" value="#700" />
            </checkValue>
            <checkValue value="~/themes/blogs/marvin3/style/green.css">
              <setValue id="siteBackgroundColor" value="#ffffff" />
              <setValue id="linkColor" value="#093" />
              <setValue id="visitedLinkColor" value="#093" />
            </checkValue>
          </propertyRule>
        </property>
```

This defines a rule that sets the values of other properties in the theme when the "Variation" property's value changes.

Property rules can be defined within `property` nodes in the theme.config file.

The `propertyRule` node exposes the following attributes: `type`, `processImmediately`, and unrecognized attributes.

type

The `type` attribute identifies the type of rule to load and execute when the value of the property is changed. The rule class identified by the `type` attribute must implement the `Telligent.DynamicConfiguration` `.Components.IPropertyRule` interface.

processImmediately

The `processImmediately` attribute identifies whether the rule should be executed immediately after the value changes.

If the `processImmediately` attribute is set to `true`, the rule will be executed immediately, causing the theme configuration pages to refresh by performing a postback. If the `processImmediately` attribute is set to `false`, the rule will execute when the property's value is saved.

If the `processImmediately` attribute is not specified, the rule will be executed when the property's value is saved.

Unrecognized Attributes

Property rules support storing unrecognized attributes for use by custom property controls and rules.

The documentation for the specific property control or property rule should identify which additional attributes are supported on property rules.

Built-In Property Controls

Community Server includes a few general-purpose property controls, which can be used to enhance the presentation of some common types of properties. These property controls can be used instead of the default property controls within custom themes by specifying the `controlType` attribute on the `property` node for which the control should be used.

Included property control overrides include: `CssValueSelectionControl`, `HtmlTextSelectionControl`, `ImageSelectionControl`, `MultilineStringControl`, `HtmlEditorStringControl`, `SiteFileUrlControl`, and `BlogFileUrlControl`.

CssValueSelectionControl

The `CssValueSelectionControl` renders a property with defined selectable values (using `propertyValue` nodes). The control supports previewing the value of each selection as the value of a CSS property, allowing users to preview the effect of the selection.

To use this control, specify:

```
Telligent.DynamicConfiguration.Controls.CssValueSelectionControl,
Telligent.DynamicConfiguration
```

as the value of the `controlType` attribute of the `property` node for which this control should be used. For example,

```
<property id="siteTitleFontSize" text="Font Size" dataType="string"
defaultValue="140%"
controlType="Telligent.DynamicConfiguration.Controls.CssValueSelectionControl,
Telligent.DynamicConfiguration" cssPropertyName="font-size" width="200px"
showStyleWhenSelected="false">
    <propertyValue value="100%" text="Smallest" />
    <propertyValue value="120%" text="Smaller" />
    <propertyValue value="140%" text="Medium" />
    <propertyValue value="160%" text="Larger" />
    <propertyValue value="180%" text="Largest" />
</property>
```

This would render as in Figure 9-20 and provides a way to preview the different font selections.

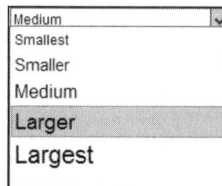

Figure 9-20: Rendered Property Values using the CssValueSelectionControl

The `CssValueSelectionControl` supports the following extended attributes on the `property` node: `cssPropertyName`, `width`, `height`, `selectListHeight`, `selectListWidth`, and `showStyleWhenSelected`.

cssPropertyName

The `cssPropertyName` attribute should be set to the CSS property to which the value of each property value should be applied when previewing values within this control. For example, `font-family`.

width

The `width` attribute can be used to specify the width of the select box, in pixels. If not specified, the width will be automatically determined.

height

The `height` attribute can be used to specify the height of the select box, in pixels. If not specified, the height will be automatically determined.

selectListHeight

The `selectListHeight` attribute can be used to specify the height of the select list, in pixels. If not specified, the height will automatically be determined.

selectListWidth

The `selectListWidth` attribute can be used to specify the width of the select list, in pixels. If not specified, the width will automatically be determined.

showStyleWhenSelected

The `showStyleWhenSelected` attribute can be used to specify whether the selected value should preview the CSS change represented by the property. By default, `showStyleWhenSelected` is set to `true`.

HtmlTextSelectionControl

The `HtmlTextSelectionControl` renders a property with defined selectable values (using `propertyValue` nodes). The control supports rendering the name of each value as HTML, adding support for HTML markup in the name (using the `text` or `resourceName`) of each selectable value.

To use this control, specify

```
Telligent.DynamicConfiguration.Controls.HtmlTextSelectionControl,
Telligent.DynamicConfiguration
```

as the value of the `controlType` attribute of the `property` node for which this control should be used. For example,

```
<property id="titleStyle" text="Title Style" dataType="string" defaultValue="2"
controlType="Telligent.DynamicConfiguration.Controls.HtmlTextSelectionControl,
Telligent.DynamicConfiguration">
```

```
        <propertyValue value="bold" text="&lt;b&gt;Bold&lt;/b&gt;" />
        <propertyValue value="italic" text="&lt;i&gt;Italic&lt;/i&gt;" />
        <propertyValue value="underline" text="&lt;u&gt;Underline&lt;/u&gt;" />
    </property>
```

would be rendered as shown in Figure 9-21 and providing a preview of the "Title Style" options.

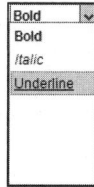

Figure 9-21: Rendered Property Values using the HtmlTextSelectionControl

The HtmlTextSelectionControl supports the following extended attributes on the property node: width, height, selectListHeight, selectListWidth, and showHtmlWhenSelected.

width

The width attribute can be used to specify the width of the select box, in pixels. If not specified, the width will be automatically determined.

height

The height attribute can be used to specify the height of the select box, in pixels. If not specified, the height will be automatically determined.

selectListHeight

The selectListHeight attribute can be used to specify the height of the select list, in pixels. If not specified, the height will automatically be determined.

selectListWidth

The selectListWidth attribute can be used to specify the width of the select list, in pixels. If it is not specified, the width will automatically be determined.

showHtmlWhenSelected

The showHtmlWhenSelected attribute can be used to specify whether the selected value should render HTML in its name. By default, showHtmlWhenSelected is set to true. When set to false, HTML in the selected value's name will be removed when rendered as the selected value.

ImageSelectionControl

The `ImageSelectionControl` renders a property with defined selectable values (using `propertyValue` nodes). The control supports rendering an image with each value, adding support for providing visual previews of complex property effects.

To use this control, specify,

```
Telligent.DynamicConfiguration.Controls.ImageSelectionControl,
Telligent.DynamicConfiguration
```

as the value of the `controlType` attribute of the property node for which this control should be used. For example,

```
<property id="columns" text="Columns" dataType="int" defaultValue="2"
controlType="Telligent.DynamicConfiguration.Controls.ImageSelectionControl,
Telligent.DynamicConfiguration" selectListWidth="440" selectListHeight="400"
showImageWhenSelected="false" >
    <propertyValue value="-1" text="Two Columns (sidebar on left)"
imageUrl="~/themes/default/images/preview-2columns-left.png" imageWidth="200px"
imageHeight="150px" />
    <propertyValue value="1" text="Two Columns (sidebar on right)"
imageUrl="~/themes/default/images/preview-2columns-right.png" imageWidth="200px"
imageHeight="150px" />
    <propertyValue value="2" text="Three Columns (sidebar on left and/or right)"
imageUrl="~/themes/default/images/preview-3columns.png" imageWidth="200px"
imageHeight="150px" />
</property>
```

This would be rendered as shown in Figure 9-22 and provides a visual representation of each of the available options for the `Columns` property.

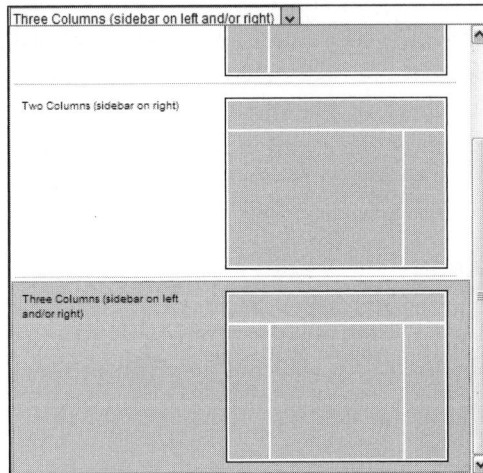

Figure 9-22: Rendered Property Values using the ImageSelectionControl

The `ImageSelectionControl` supports the following extended attributes on the `property` node: `includeTextWithImage`, `width`, `height`, `selectListHeight`, `selectListWidth`, and `showHtmlWhenSelected`.

Additionally, the `ImageSelectionControl` supports the following extended attributes on each `propertyValue` node: `imageWidth`, `imageHeight`, and `imageUrl`.

includeTextWithImage

The `includeTextWithImage` attribute can be specified to identify whether the name (using the `text` or `resourceName` attribute) of each selectable value is rendered aside the preview image. By default, `includeTextWithImage` is set to `true`.

width

The `width` attribute can be used to specify the width of the select box, in pixels. If not specified, the width will be automatically determined.

height

The `height` attribute can be used to specify the height of the select box, in pixels. If not specified, the height will be automatically determined.

selectListHeight

The `selectListHeight` attribute can be used to specify the height of the select list, in pixels. If not specified, the height will automatically be determined.

selectListWidth

The `selectListWidth` attribute can be used to specify the width of the select list, in pixels. If not specified, the width will automatically be determined.

showImageWhenSelected

The `showImageWhenSelected` attribute can be used to specify whether the selected value should render the associated image.

When `showImageWhenSelected` is set to `true`, the rendered selected value will include the related image. When `showImageWhenSelected` is set to `false`

By default, `showImageWhenSelected` is set to `true`.

imageWidth

The `imageWidth` attribute, set on each `propertyValue` node, can be used to specify the width of the associated image, in a valid CSS unit format. By default, `imageWidth` is set to `200px`.

imageHeight

The `imageHeight` attribute, set on each `propertyValue` node, can be used to specify the height of the associated image, in a valid CSS unit format. By default, `imageHeight` is set to `150px`.

imageUrl

The `imageUrl` attribute, set on each `propertyValue` node, identifies the URL of the image associated to the value.

MultilineStringControl

The `MultilineStringControl` adds support for entering multiple lines of text into a property of type `String`.

To use this control, specify:

```
Telligent.DynamicConfiguration.Controls.MultilineStringControl,
Telligent.DynamicConfiguration
```

as the value of the `controlType` attribute of the `property` node for which this control should be used. For example,

```
<property id="cssOverrides" text="CSS Overrides" dataType="string" defaultValue=""
controlType="Telligent.DynamicConfiguration.Controls.MultilineStringControl,
Telligent.DynamicConfiguration" columns="70" />
```

This would be rendered as shown in Figure 9-23.

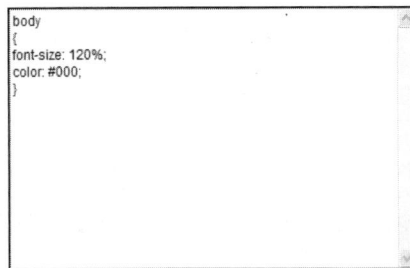

```
body
{
font-size: 120%;
color: #000;
}
```

Figure 9-23: Rendered Property using the MultilineStringControl

The `MultilineStringControl` supports the following extended attributes on the `property` node: `rows` and `columns`.

rows

The `rows` attribute specifies the number of rows of text to support when editing the value of the property. By default, `rows` is set to `15`.

columns

The `columns` attribute specifies the number of columns of text to support when editing the value of the property. By default, `columns` is set to `60`.

HtmlEditorStringControl

The `HtmlEditorStringControl` adds support for using the current user's selected HTML editor to edit a property of type `String`, adding support for easily specifying formatted text as the value of a property.

To use this control, specify

```
CommunityServer.Controls.HtmlEditorStringControl, CommunityServer.Controls
```

as the value of the `controlType` attribute of the `property` node for which this control should be used. For example,

```
<property id="footerHtml" text="Footer Content" dataType="string" defaultValue=""
controlType="CommunityServer.Controls.HtmlEditorStringControl,
CommunityServer.Controls" />
```

would render as in Figure 9-24.

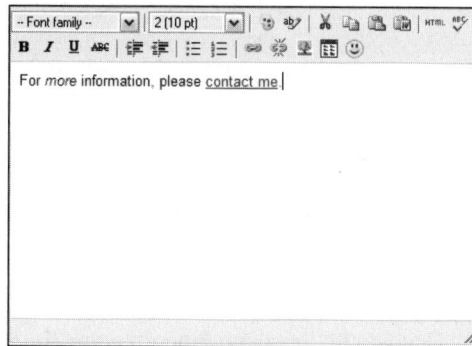

Figure 9-24: Rendered Property using the HtmlEditorStringControl

The `HtmlEditorStringControl` supports the following extended attributes on the property node: `width`, `height`, and `enableHtmlScrubbing`.

width

The `width` attribute can be used to specify the width of the HTML editor, in a valid CSS unit format. By default, `width` is set to `300px`.

height

The `height` attribute can be used to specify the height of the HTML editor, in a valid CSS unit format. By default, `height` is set to `250px`.

enableHtmlScrubbing

The `enableHtmlScrubbing` attribute specifies whether the HTML entered as the value of the property should be scrubbed according to the rules of the Community Server HTML scrubber before being saved as the value of the property. By default, `enableHtmlScrubbing` is set to `true`.

SiteFileUrlControl

The `SiteFileUrlControl` adds support for uploading and selecting files from the Community Server Site Files data store for properties of type `Url`, adding support for easily uploading and selecting files in site themes.

To use this control, specify:

```
CommunityServer.Controls.SiteFileUrlControl, CommunityServer.Controls
```

as the value of the `controlType` attribute of the `property` node for which this control should be used. For example,

```
<property id="siteTitleBackgroundImage" text="Background Image URL" dataType="Url"
controlType="CommunityServer.Controls.SiteFileUrlControl, CommunityServer.Controls" />
```

would render as in Figure 9-25 and allow the selection of files from the "Site Files" file store.

Figure 9-25: Rendered Property using the SiteFileUrlControl

BlogFileUrlControl

The `BlogFileUrlControl` adds support for uploading and selecting files from the Community Server blog files data store for the current blog for properties of type `Url`, adding support for easily uploading and selecting files in blog themes.

To use this control, specify

```
CommunityServer.Blogs.Controls.BlogFileUrlControl, CommunityServer.Blogs
```

as the value of the `controlType` attribute of the `property` node for which this control should be used. For example,

```
<property id="blogTitleBackgroundImage" text="Background Image URL" dataType="Url"
controlType="CommunityServer.Blogs.Controls.BlogFileUrlControl, CommunityServer.Blogs" />
```

would be rendered as in Figure 9-26 and allow the selection of files from the Blog Files file store for the current blog.

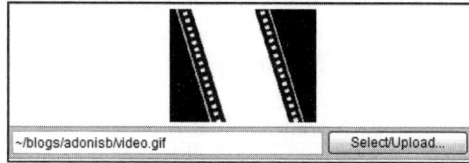

Figure 9-26: Rendered Property using the BlogFileUrlControl

Built-In Property Rules

Community Server includes a single general-purpose property rule, which can be used to automate property value selections. This rule is the ValueAutomationRule.

ValueAutomationRule

The ValueAutomationRule provides support for automating the specification of values for many properties based on the selection of a value for a single property.

To use this control, specify

```
Telligent.DynamicConfiguration.Rules.ValueAutomationRule, Telligent.DynamicConfiguration
```

as the value of the type attribute of the propertyRule node within the property node of the property to which this rule should be applied.

The ValueAutomationRule uses an additional XML-based configuration to identify the actionable values on the current property and the actions related to each actionable value. For example,

```xml
<property id="secondaryCssUrl" text="Variation" dataType="url" defaultValue="">
    <propertyValue value="" text="Normal" />
    <propertyValue value="~/themes/blogs/hover/style/ms.css" text="Microsoft Style" />
    <propertyRule type="Telligent.DynamicConfiguration.Rules.ValueAutomationRule,
Telligent.DynamicConfiguration" processImmediately="true">
        <checkValue value="">
            <setValue id="linkColor" value="#066" />
            <setValue id="visitedLinkColor" value="#066" />
            <setValue id="activeLinkColor" value="#933" />
        </checkValue>
        <checkValue value="~/themes/blogs/hover/style/ms.css">
            <setValue id="linkColor" value="#039" />
            <setValue id="visitedLinkColor" value="#039" />
            <setValue id="activeLinkColor" value="#f30" />
        </checkValue>
    </propertyRule>
</property>
```

defines a property, `secondaryCssUrl`, with two selectable values and a `ValueAutomationRule`. The `ValueAutomationRule` will set the values of the `linkColor`, `visitedLinkColor`, and `activeLinkColor` properties based on the value of the `secondaryCssUrl` property.

In the example, the `ValueAutomationRule`'s configuration nodes are shown: `checkValue` and `setValue`. When the value of the property on which the `ValueAutomationRule` is applied changes, the new value is compared against each `checkValue` nodes' `value` attribute value. When a match is found, each `setValue` node is processed within the matching `checkValue`, applying the specified value (identified by the `value` attribute of the `setValue` node) to the specified property (identified by the `id` attribute of the `setValue` node).

Additionally, the `ValueAutomationRule` provides a single configuration option: `forceSetValues`.

forceSetValues

The `forceSetValues` attribute, defined on the `propertyRule` node when using the `ValueAutomationRule`, specifies whether `setValue` nodes should always be processed. By default, when processing the `setValue` nodes for a matching `checkValue` node, automated property values are only applied if the automated property's current value is set to an automated value; that is, a value that is specified in a `setValue` node defined within this rule. This behavior ensures that user-initiated customizations made to automated properties are not overridden. To force all `setValue` nodes to always be processed, the `forceSetValues` attribute can be set to `true`.

Using Theme Configuration Data

Theme configuration options are only as good as their purpose. To implement each property's purpose, Community Server provides both Chameleon controls for and direct code access to the values of properties identified by the theme's `theme.config` file.

Using Theme Configuration Controls

Community Server includes a set of Chameleon controls to access theme configuration property values and use them to render markup or implement custom conditions.

SiteThemeConfigurationData and SectionThemeConfigurationData

The `SiteThemeConfigurationData` and `SectionThemeConfigurationData` controls are single value Chameleon controls supporting theme configuration data. For example,

```
<CSControl:SiteThemeConfigurationData Property="footerHtml" runat="server" />
```

would render the value of the `footerHtml` theme configuration property for the site.

Each control's `Property` property identifies the `id` of the property from the current theme's `theme.config` file whose value should be rendered. Additionally, instead of the `LinkTo` property exposed by other single value controls, these controls support a `LinkToProperty` property, which identifies the `id` of the property whose value identifies the URL to which the content of the control should be linked.

The `SiteThemeConfigurationData` control accesses properties from the site theme's configuration, whereas the `SectionThemeConfigurationData` control accesses properties from the current section's configuration (such as the current blog).

For more information on single value controls, please see the discussion of "Single Value Controls" and "Formatting API-Related Single Value Controls" in Chapter 5.

SiteThemeConfigurationDataImage and SectionThemeConfigurationDataImage

The `SiteThemeConfigurationDataImage` and `SectionThemeConfigurationDataImage` controls render images whose URLs are identified by theme configuration data. For example,

```
<CSControl:SiteThemeConfigurationDataImage ImageUrlProperty="logoUrl" runat="server" />
```

would render the image referenced by the `logoUrl` property from the current site theme's configuration.

Both controls expose the `ImageUrlProperty` property, which identifies the `id` of the property whose value identifies the URL of the image to render.

The `SiteThemeConfigurationDataImage` control accesses properties from the site theme's configuration, whereas the `SectionThemeConfigurationDataImage` control accesses properties from the current section's configuration (such as the current blog).

SiteThemeConfigurationDataPropertyComparison and SectionThemeConfigurationDataPropertyComparison

The `SiteThemeConfigurationDataPropertyComparison` and `SectionThemeConfigurationDataPropertyComparison` controls are condition controls that compare two property values within the current theme configuration data.

The `ComparisonProperty1` and `ComparisonProperty2` properties of these controls identify the `id`s of the properties that should be compared.

Both of these controls can be used anywhere that Chameleon condition controls can be used, such as within the `DisplayConditions` property of other Chameleon controls.

The `SiteThemeConfigurationDataPropertyComparison` control compares properties from the site theme's configuration, whereas the `SectionThemeConfigurationDataPropertyComparison` control compares properties from the current section's configuration (such as the current blog).

For more information about these controls, see the "Property Comparison Condition" controls discussion in Chapter 5.

SiteThemeConfigurationPropertyValueComparision and SectionThemeConfigurationPropertyValueComparision

The `SiteThemeConfigurationDataPropertyValueComparison` and `SectionThemeConfigurationDataPropertyValueComparison` controls are condition controls that compare a property value within the current theme configuration data to a static value.

The `ComparisonProperty` property of these controls identifies the `id` of the property that should be compared to the static value.

Both of these controls can be used anywhere that Chameleon condition controls can be used, for example, within the `DisplayConditions` property of other Chameleon controls.

The `SiteThemeConfigurationDataPropertyValueComparison` control compares a property from the site theme's configuration, whereas the `SectionThemeConfigurationDataPropertyValueComparison` control compares a property from the current section's configuration (such as the current blog).

For more information about these controls, see the "Property and Value Comparison Condition" controls discussion in Chapter 5.

SiteThemeConfigurationDataScript and SectionThemeConfigurationDataScript

The `SiteThemeConfigurationDataScript` and `SectionThemeConfigurationDataScript` controls can be used to include a script file identified by a property value within the current theme configuration data.

The `ScriptUrlProperty` of these controls identifies the `id` of the property whose value represents the URL of the script file that should be included in the current page.

The `SiteThemeConfigurationDataScript` control accesses a property from the site theme's configuration whereas the `SectionThemeConfigurationDataScript` control accesses a property from the current section's configuration (such as the current blog).

SiteThemeConfigurationDataStyle and SectionThemeConfigurationDataStyle

The `SiteThemeConfigurationDataStyle` and `SectionThemeConfigurationDataStyle` controls can be used to include a stylesheet file identified by a property value within the current theme configuration data.

The `StyleUrlProperty` of these controls identifies the `id` of the property whose value represents the URL of the stylesheet file that should be included in the current page.

These controls render as a `<link />` tag and should be placed within the `<head></head>` tag of the page.

The `SiteThemeConfigurationDataStyle` control accesses a property from the site theme's configuration, whereas the `SectionThemeConfigurationDataStyle` control accesses a property from the current section's configuration (such as the current blog).

Using Theme Configuration Data in Code

Community Server also provides access to theme configuration data for use in custom code. The site theme's configuration data can be accessed through the `CommunityServer.Components.UserContext.Current.SiteThemeConfigurationData` property and the current section's (for example, the current blog) configuration data can be accessed through the `CommunityServer.Components.UserContext.Current.SectionThemeConfigurationData` property.

Both of these properties are of the type `CommunityServer.Components.ThemeConfigurationData` and expose a set of methods for accessing theme configuration property values.

For example,

```
<%@ Page Language="C#" AutoEventWireup="true" %>
<%@ Import Namespace="CommunityServer.Components" %>
<%@ Import Namespace="System.Drawing" %>

<script language="C#" runat="server">

    protected ThemeConfigurationData ThemeData = CSContext.Current.SiteThemeData;

    protected override void OnInit(EventArgs e)
    {
        base.OnInit(e);
        Page.Response.ContentType = "text/css";
    }

</script>

body
{
    font-family: <%= ThemeData.GetStringValue("textFont", "Arial, Helvetica") %>;
    color: <%= ColorTranslator.ToHtml(ThemeData.GetColorValue("textColor",
ColorTranslator.FromHtml("#333"))) %>;
}
```

would render a stylesheet retrieving body styles from the current site theme's configuration.

The `ThemeConfigurationData` class supports the following methods for retrieving data from the theme's configuration: `GetBoolValue`, `GetIntValue`, `GetDoubleValue`, `GetDateTimeValue`, `GetGuidValue`, `GetColorValue`, `GetUrlValue`, `GetUnitValue`, and `GetStringValue`.

GetBoolValue

The `GetBoolValue(string propertyId, bool defaultValue)` method retrieves a `System.Boolean` value from the theme's configuration data. This method should be used with properties of type `Bool`.

If the property identified by the `propertyId` parameter is not found, the value of the `defaultValue` parameter will be returned by the method. If the property identified by the `propertyId` parameter is found but a value has not yet been selected, the property's default value will be returned (instead of the value of the `defaultValue` parameter).

GetIntValue

The `GetIntValue(string propertyId, int defaultValue)` method retrieves a `System.Int32` value from the theme's configuration data. This method should be used with properties of type `Int`.

If the property identified by the `propertyId` parameter is not found, the value of the `defaultValue` parameter will be returned by the method. If the property identified by the `propertyId` parameter is found but a value has not yet been selected, the property's default value will be returned (instead of the value of the `defaultValue` parameter).

GetDoubleValue

The `GetDoubleValue(string propertyId, double defaultValue)` method retrieves a `System` `.Double` value from the theme's configuration data. This method should be used with properties of type `Double`.

If the property identified by the `propertyId` parameter is not found, the value of the `defaultValue` parameter will be returned by the method. If the property identified by the `propertyId` parameter is found but a value has not yet been selected, the property's default value will be returned (instead of the value of the `defaultValue` parameter).

GetDateTimeValue

The `GetDateTimeValue(string propertyId, DateTime defaultValue)` method retrieves a `System.DateTime` value from the theme's configuration data. This method should be used with properties of type `Date`, `Time`, or `DateTime`.

If the property identified by the `propertyId` parameter is not found, the value of the `defaultValue` parameter will be returned by the method. If the property identified by the `propertyId` parameter is found but a value has not yet been selected, the property's default value will be returned (instead of the value of the `defaultValue` parameter).

GetGuidValue

The `GetGuidValue(string propertyId, Guid defaultValue)` method retrieves a `System.Guid` value from the theme's configuration data. This method should be used with properties of type `Guid`.

If the property identified by the `propertyId` parameter is not found, the value of the `defaultValue` parameter will be returned by the method. If the property identified by the `propertyId` parameter is found but a value has not yet been selected, the property's default value will be returned (instead of the value of the `defaultValue` parameter).

GetColorValue

The `GetColorValue(string propertyId, Color defaultValue)` method retrieves a `System.Drawing.Color` value from the theme's configuration data. This method should be used with properties of type `Color`.

To render a `System.Drawing.Color` value as a color formatted in the #rrggbb format, the `ColorConverter` class can be used, for example:

```
color: <%=
System.Drawing.ColorTranslator.ToHtml(CSContext.Current.SiteThemeData.GetColorValue
("textColor", System.Drawing.ColorTranslator.FromHtml("#333"))) %>;
```

If the property identified by the `propertyId` parameter is not found, the value of the `defaultValue` parameter will be returned by the method. If the property identified by the `propertyId` parameter is found but a value has not yet been selected, the property's default value will be returned (instead of the value of the `defaultValue` parameter).

GetUrlValue

The `GetUrlValue(string propertyId, Uri defaultValue)` method retrieves a `System.Uri` value from the theme's configuration data. This method should be used with properties of type `Url`.

If the property identified by the `propertyId` parameter is not found, the value of the `defaultValue` parameter will be returned by the method. If the property identified by the `propertyId` parameter is found but a value has not yet been selected, the property's default value will be returned (instead of the value of the `defaultValue` parameter).

GetUnitValue

The `GetUnitValue(string propertyId, Unit defaultValue)` method retrieves a `System.Web .UI.WebControls.Unit` value from the theme's configuration data. This method should be used with properties of type `Unit`.

If the property identified by the `propertyId` parameter is not found, the value of the `defaultValue` parameter will be returned by the method. If the property identified by the `propertyId` parameter is found but a value has not yet been selected, the property's default value will be returned (instead of the value of the `defaultValue` parameter).

GetStringValue

The `GetStringValue(string propertyId, string defaultValue)` method retrieves a `System .String` value from the theme's configuration data. This method can be used with properties of any data type; however, it should be used with properties of type `String` and `Custom`.

If the property identified by the `propertyId` parameter is not found, the value of the `defaultValue` parameter will be returned by the method. If the property identified by the `propertyId` parameter is found but a value has not yet been selected, the property's default value will be returned (instead of the value of the `defaultValue` parameter).

Summary

Support for dynamic configuration options in Community Server provides an easy mechanism with which theme developers can expose options to end users, allowing end users to customize themes without knowledge of HTML, Cascading Stylesheets, or other web technologies. Theme developers can customize the options exposed by a theme using custom property controls and rules to enhance the end user's customization experience.

The next chapter will provide specific examples of adding dynamic configuration options to an existing theme.

10

Adding Dynamic Configuration Options to a Theme

You have already learned about some of the many options that are available to you whenever you are creating a theme configuration file. Now that you are familiar with these options on a basic level, this chapter teaches you how to actually apply them. After reading this chapter, you will be familiar with several examples on how dynamic configuration options can be used. In addition, you will also be knowledgeable in the following areas:

q   Adding a simple configuration option

q   Previewing configuration changes

q   Adding a CSS previewable configuration option

q   Adding a conditional rendering option

q   Defining a custom rule

Adding a Simple Configuration Option

By now you should be familiar with some of the different components that make up the `theme.config` file. To review, remember that there is the master Theme node, which contains the name and description of your theme. Inside this node, you can have a `propertyGroup` that contains either a `propertySubGroup` or a property. Also notice that the `propertySubGroup` should only contain child property nodes. At this point, you should have a good understanding of property values and some of the various data types you can use to describe each property.

There are many options that you can enable to be changed through dynamic configuration. Many of the options that you will be enabling are going to be straightforward and actually simple. For example, a simple configuration option might be to change the color of the links on a site. A more advanced option might be to decide between different font options to use on your site. What is important to understand is that even the more advanced configuration options will still be presented in such a manner to the person using it in the Control Panel that it will appear simple.

Site Background Color Configuration

One of the common configuration options that most themes offer administrators is the ability to change the background color of their site. This same option that will be shown for site wide backgrounds can also be used for blog-specific background options. In the following example, you will be using a site `theme.config` to control the color configuration options.

To begin, you need to open the `theme.config` file that you will be using for your theme. If you do not have a `theme.config` created or do not have a theme folder created that is fine. Simply create a new folder in either the `Themes\Blogs` or `Themes` folder with the name of the theme. For the purposes of this demonstration, the theme will be called "Infusion," after all, the name "example" is not very original. Once you have the folder created, you should create a file named `theme.config` and put it in the Infusion folder. You can create this file using Notepad or any other text editor, when you save it, just save it with quotation marks around the name, as in Figure 10-1. The quotation marks are necessary to add a different file extension to the file than the default `.txt` extension.

File name: "theme.config"

Figure 10-1: Notepad Save As Dialog

Once you have your file created, you can now add the following to the file and save it again:

```
<?xml version="1.0" encoding="utf-8" ?>
<Theme title="Infusion">
  <DynamicConfiguration>
    <propertyGroup id="themeVariation" text="General">
        <property id="siteBackgroundColor" text="Background Color"
            dataType="color" defaultValue="#ffffff"
            descriptionText="Select the background color" />
    </propertyGroup>
  </DynamicConfiguration>
</Theme>
```

Now that you have `Themes\Infusion\theme.config` created, you can navigate to the Control Panel of your site. In the Theme Configuration page, you will find a new option in the Site Theme dropdown list for the theme Infusion. When you select this theme, you are presented with a tab that says "General" and a single configuration option for the "Background Color" that should look similar to Figure 10-2.

In Figure 10-2, you can also see how each of the different attributes in the `theme.config` maps to the presentation in the Control Panel. For example, the title of the theme is shown both as the name in the Site Theme dropdown and also the header for the configuration option panel above the configuration option tabs. Additionally, you should note that the `propertyGroup` maps to a tab in the theme configuration option page.

Another handy thing to notice is that the background color is using the default value of #ffffff. This is the hexadecimal representation for the color white. In order to help pick colors for your theme and to understand how they are represented in hexadecimal, you may want to consider using a tool such as Iconico's ColorPic. This tool allows you to grab any color on the screen and see its hexadecimal representation.

Figure 10-2: Theme Configuration Background Color Option

Once you click on the background color and select a different color, then save it, your property value is saved for later use and updated on your live site. Currently, there is no dynamic stylesheet that is in place for this new theme. Therefore, in order to see the theme in action, as well as to understand how the background color property is used in your site, you should create a DynamicStyle.aspx page. You can do this in Notepad if you like; however, it is recommended that you use Visual Studio to accomplish this task.

Create a new folder called Style in which to place your DynamicStyle.aspx page. Remember that the DynamicStyle.aspx actually responds with stylesheet data, so you will actually be including it as you would any normal stylesheet file that has the extension css. Once you have created your Style folder, you can create a new file called DynamicStyle.aspx in this folder and place the following contents in the file:

```
<%@ Page Language="C#" AutoEventWireup="true" %>
<%@ Import Namespace="CommunityServer.Components" %>
<%@ Import Namespace="System.Drawing" %>

<script language="C#" runat="server">
    protected ThemeConfigurationData ThemeData =
        CSContext.Current.ThemePreviewCookie.IsPreviewing() ?
        ThemeConfigurationDatas.GetThemeConfigurationData("Infusion",
        CSContext.Current.ThemePreviewCookie.PreviewID, true) :
        ThemeConfigurationDatas.GetThemeConfigurationData("Infusion", true);

    protected override void OnInit(EventArgs e)
    {
        base.OnInit(e);
        Page.Response.ContentType = "text/css";
        Page.Response.Expires = 30;
    }
</script>
body, html
{
    background-color: <%= ColorTranslator.ToHtml(
```

```
                ThemeData.GetColorValue("siteBackgroundColor",
                ColorTranslator.FromHtml("#ffffff")))%>;
    }
```

The next, and final, step before viewing the final theme is to create a page that you can use that will include the stylesheet. To do this, you can simply create a page called `home.aspx` and place it in a folder called `Common` under your `Infusion` directory. The `home.aspx` page should have the following contents in order to include the stylesheet:

```
<%@ Page EnableViewState="false" Language="C#" AutoEventWireup="true"
Inherits="CommunityServer.Controls.CSThemePage" %>

<html>
<head runat="server">
    <CSControl:Head runat="Server" >
        <meta http-equiv="Content-Type" content="text/html; charset=UTF-8" />
        <CSControl:Style runat="server"
            Href="~/themes/Infusion/Style/DynamicStyle.aspx"
            EnsureNotCachedOnPreview="true" />
    </CSControl:Head>
</head>
<body>
        Hello Dynamic Themes
</body>
</html>
```

Keep in mind that the above pages are just examples and that the `home.aspx` page is not an especially well-formed page. When you actually create a site theme, you should try to use master pages to help keep your theme consistent. If you would like to see an example of the master pages being used, you should look through the files that make up the default theme that ships with Community Server 2007.

Whenever you browse to the homepage on the Community Server site that is running the following pages, with the Infusion theme selected you will see the text "Hello Dynamic Themes" with the background color that you selected inside of the Control Panel. An example of this is shown in Figure 10-3.

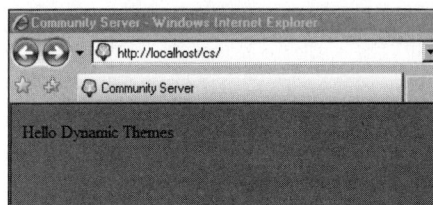

Figure 10-3: Dynamic Configuration Background Color in Action

Site Font Configuration Example

Now that you have added all of the basic files that are required to create a dynamic theme configuration option, it should be easier to add more options. One of the common options that is desirable to offer your theme users is the ability to change the font for your site. This is a slightly more advanced configuration option because you will be providing a dropdown list that a user can select from. The selection will then be used in the dynamic stylesheet file.

Begin by opening your `theme.config` file that you created in the previous subsection. You will be adding a new property inside the same `propertyGroup` that you used for your site background option. You should add a new property that looks like the following, with the various font options:

```
<property id="textFont" text="Font" dataType="string"
        defaultValue="Arial, Helvetica" controlType=
        "Telligent.DynamicConfiguration.Controls.CssValueSelectionControl,
        Telligent.DynamicConfiguration" cssPropertyName="font-family">
    <propertyValue value="Andale Mono" text="Andale Mono" />
    <propertyValue value="Arial, Helvetica" text="Arial" />
    <propertyValue value="Arial Black, Arial, Helvetica" text="Arial Black" />
    <propertyValue value="Book Antiqua" text="Book Antiqua" />
    <propertyValue value="Comic Sans MS" text="Comic Sans MS" />
    <propertyValue value="Courier New" text="Courier New" />
    <propertyValue value="Georgia" text="Georgia" />
    <propertyValue value="Helvetica, Arial" text="Helvetica" />
    <propertyValue value="Impact" text="Impact" />
    <propertyValue value="Tahoma, Arial, Helvetica" text="Tahoma" />
    <propertyValue value="Terminal" text="Terminal" />
    <propertyValue value="Times New Roman" text="Times New Roman" />
    <propertyValue value="Trebuchet MS" text="Trebuchet MS" />
    <propertyValue value="Verdana" text="Verdana" />
</property>
```

After you add the property information above, you will see a new option in the Control Panel theme configuration page. You will also notice that there is no description icon because the property entry above is missing the `descriptionText` attribute. The new dropdown list should look like Figure 10-4 below, and you will notice that it shows a preview of each of the fonts.

Figure 10-4: Site Font Dropdown

Currently, you can save different site fonts, and they will be stored. However, until you update the `DynamicStyle.aspx` page and link up the property to a style, it will not be visible. Therefore, you should open up `DynamicStyle.aspx` and then change the style that you created in the previous example so that it looks like this:

```
body, html
{
    background-color: <%=
        ColorTranslator.ToHtml(ThemeData.GetColorValue("siteBackgroundColor",
        ColorTranslator.FromHtml("#ffffff")))%>;
    font-family: <%= ThemeData.GetStringValue("textFont", "Arial, Helvetica") %>;
}
```

Once you save the changes to the `DynamicStyle.aspx` above, you will be able to see the text on the homepage of your site being updated. Now all you need to do if you want to add or remove font options is to add or remove the `propertyValue` entries from your `theme.config`.

Image Background Configuration Example

Often you will want to enable users of your theme to be able to change what images are used on a site, even background images. This ability is actually quite straightforward to implement using a lot of the knowledge you gained in the previous two subsections. Remember that there is a specific type for URL, which is what will be used to link to the image file.

Begin by opening the `theme.config` file that was used in the previous two subsections. Once you have the file open, you should add the following property entry, which will be used to display a site background image field on the theme configuration Control Panel page:

```
<property id="siteBackgroundImage" text="Background Image URL" dataType="url"
    controlType="CommunityServer.Controls.SiteFileUrlControl,
    CommunityServer.Controls" />
```

If you do not add the `controlType`, and instead have only the `dataType`, to rely on, you will see an empty textbox that can be used to input the URL to the image file you want to use. But because you are including the specific `controlType` with the above value, users are able to upload image files and select the one that they want to use for the background image. An example of what the above property entry adds to the Control Panel is shown below in Figure 10-5.

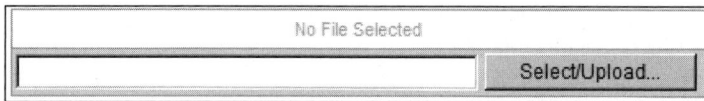

Figure 10-5: File Upload Configuration Option

The image that is selected by the above configuration option is not yet linked to the `DynamicStyle.aspx` page that is used for setting a stylesheet. Therefore, you should open this file for editing and update the HTML body entry so that it now has the following style:

```
background-image: <%= UrlOrNone(ThemeData.GetUrlValue("siteBackgroundImage",
    null))%>;
```

You should notice that this is calling a method called `UrlOrNone`. This method is used in the default theme `DynamicStyle.aspx`, which ships with Community Server 2007. You should use this or a similar method, as it helps format the URL that is used for the background image entry. Therefore, add the following inside the script block:

```
protected string UrlOrNone(Uri url)
{
    if (url == null)
        return "none";
    else
        return "url(" + ResolveUrl(url.ToString()) + ")";
}
```

Once you save these changes, you will be able to load an image from the theme configuration page and view it as the background image on the new theme. This allows administrators to change the background image of their site to anything they want. Additionally, with the combined site background color configuration option that is already available, this empowers these same individuals so that they have full control over how the background of their site looks.

Previewing Configuration Changes

Now that you have added a couple of configuration options to the Infusion theme, you can use the new live preview option. This will allow you to preview any configuration changes before committing them to the live site. One of the nice points about the live preview is that you can actually browse through your site, viewing the theme changes, and yet these changes do not impact what other users are viewing until you actually press the Save button to commit them.

In the configuration options page, you will notice the Preview tab. This is where you control the previewing of your configuration theme changes. Here, you will find the options displayed in Figure 10-6.

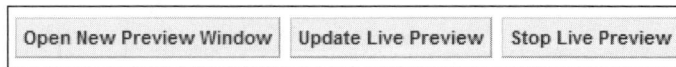

Open New Preview Window	Update Live Preview	Stop Live Preview

Figure 10-6: Theme Preview Options

When you click the Open New Preview Window, a new window will open that you can use to preview your theme changes. Additionally, you can use Update Live Preview to see any recently made configuration changes in your preview window. Remember, though that you will need to refresh the browser window with which you are previewing the site to see these changes.

Adding a CSS Previewable Configuration Option

One of the very nice things that you can do in your `theme.config` file is to specify a preview image for a property. This ability allows you to present an image to the user showing what they can expect to see by enabling a specific option. The main catch to this control is that it is for selection boxes, so it should only be used for dropdown list properties. This would be a property that has different `propertyValue` nodes inside it in the `theme.config`.

In order to add a preview image for a selection option, you first need to have an image that represents the effect of the change. You should try to make this image relatively small and straightforward when demonstrating what will happen if a user selects it. You can see a working example of this feature by looking at the site default theme and then using the Columns option in the Layout section of the configuration page. Next to each of the options is an image that demonstrates how that option will look if selected.

The preview image can be added easily to each `propertyValue` in the following manner. Add the following as a new property entry in the `theme.config`:

```
<property id="previewExample" text="Preview Example" dataType="String"
        selectListWidth="440" selectListHeight="170"
```

```
            controlType=
            "Telligent.DynamicConfiguration.Controls.ImageSelectionControl,
            Telligent.DynamicConfiguration">
      <propertyValue value="Commercial" text="Commercial"
              imageUrl="~/Utility/PoweredByCS_commercial.gif" imageWidth="171px"
              imageHeight="60px" />
      <propertyValue value="Personal" text="Personal"
              imageUrl="~/Utility/PoweredByCS_personal.gif" imageWidth="171px"
              imageHeight="60px" />
   </property>
```

The above example doesn't really connect to any useful stylesheet information; instead, it is useful for demonstrating how you can create a configuration option that provides preview images. Whenever the above is rendered in the theme configuration page and it is expanded, it looks like Figure 10-7.

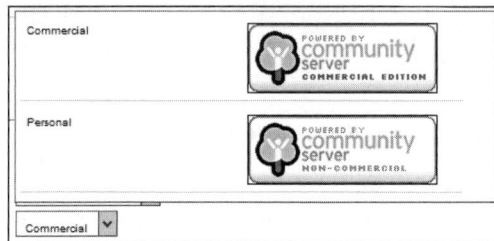

Figure 10-7: Sample Theme Option Preview Selection Box

In order to achieve the above selection box you need to declare that your property uses the `controlType` at `ImageSelectionControl`. This property is set using the fully qualified name of the type so that it can be loaded from the proper assembly. Once you have declared the proper `controlType`, you will want to adjust `selectListWidth` and `selectListHeight` so that the box will properly show the image next to the text used for each selection option. Also, you should note that even if the text for a `propertyValue` is not specified, the image will begin around 200 pixels from the left. This means that your `selectListWidth` should be over 200 pixels in size. Other than that, the select list works like any other in the theme configuration page. If you would like to see another example of this preview option in action, you should refer to the default `theme.config` file, as it has the layout options specified this way.

Adding a Conditional Rendering Option

Many of the controls in Community Server that you will use offer the ability to show or hide themselves based on specific display conditions. There are a set of controls that are used inside the `DisplayConditions` that help determine if a control should be visible or not. One of these conditional controls is used in conjunction with theme configuration files and the values that an administrator has set in the theme configuration page. The control may have the longest name of any control, as it is called `SiteThemeConfigurationDataPropertyValueComparison`. When you combine this property value comparison control with theme configuration settings, the results can be extremely powerful.

For example, consider the homepage that you have set up inside the Infusion theme. Currently, this page simply displays the text "Hello Dynamic Themes." If you want to show or hide this text based on a value set on the configuration theme page, you can use the control above. Here are the steps that you can use to set up this example and hide the text on the homepage based on whether or not a checkbox is selected.

1.   Open the Infusion `theme.config` file for editing.

2.   Add the following property inside the `theme.config` in a `propertyGroup` or `propertySubGroup`:

```
<property id="showText" text="Show Homepage Text" dataType="Bool" />
```

3.   Save the `theme.config` changes, and open the theme configuration page in the Control Panel for the Infusion theme. You should now see a new checkbox for showing the homepage text; it should look like Figure 10-8.

Show Homepage Text ☑

Figure 10-8: Show Homepage Checkbox

4.   Open the `home.aspx` page in your `Infusion\Common` folder for editing, and change the "Hello Dynamic Themes" text to the following:

```
<CSControl:PlaceHolder runat="server">
    <DisplayConditions>
        <CSControl:SiteThemeConfigurationDataPropertyValueComparison
                runat="server"
                ComparisonProperty="showText" Operator="IsSetOrTrue" />
    </DisplayConditions>
    <ContentTemplate>
        Hello Dynamic Themes
    </ContentTemplate>
</CSControl:PlaceHolder>
```

When you view the homepage after making the above changes, you should no longer see the text "Hello Dynamic Themes." This is the case because the new checkbox in the theme configuration page is not set and the `PlaceHolder` controls `DisplayConditions` evaluate to `false`. To see how this works, you should try setting the checkbox, then save your changes and reload the homepage. You will notice when the checkbox is set that the text is displayed, and when the checkbox is unchecked the text is not displayed.

The nice thing about this comparison control is that it inherits from the same base controls that other comparison controls used. As a result of this inheritance, you are able to compare properties using various conditionals for specific values. Another point to remember is that you can combine multiple comparison controls inside the `DisplayConditions` to hide or show content.

Defining a Custom Property Rule

Community Server allows you to create custom rules that can be used to perform a custom action whenever a property is changed. These rules are defined by the `IPropertyRule` interface, which looks like the code below and is defined in the `Telligent.DynamicConfiguration.Components` namespace. This means that a rule occurs whenever a property is changed and that a rule can also read the `theme.config` node that defines the rule. This allows a developer not only to create custom functionality but also to enforce rules that must be followed by properties. For example, if you want to require that any color other than black can be selected, you could create a rule that enforces this behavior by placing a custom rule inside a color property. This example will be demonstrated further at the end of this chapter.

```
ValueChanged(Property property, ConfigurationDataBase data);
LoadConfiguration(PropertyRule rule, XmlNode node);
```

Currently in Community Server, there is only one object that is a property rule; this is the `ValueAutomationRule`. This rule is used in the situation where a theme has predefined theme setting variations. In Community Server, this is used in blog themes in general and in the Paperclip blog theme in particular. The theme variation selector is shown in Figure 10-9. Whenever a theme variation is selected in the Paperclip theme, the `ValueAutomationRule` is executed and custom theme configuration changes are made, depending on the selected variation.

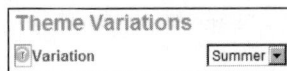

Figure 10-9: Theme Variation Select Field in Paperclip

A `propertyRule` can be defined at a sublevel inside a property. This allows you to easily make a certain property follow certain rules, as you can place multiple rules inside of a property node. The `propertyRule` node takes a couple of attributes, which are `type` and `processImmediately`. You can add more attributes to the node if your rule requires additional information, but these two attributes are the only ones that are needed to declare your rule. Below is an example of the `ValueAutomationRule` declaration in a `theme.config` file. As you will notice, the type is the name of the type that will be used to create an instance of the object using the Activator class. Therefore, you should make sure that the type is properly declared; you may even want to use the fully qualified name of the type to make sure that the correct rule is used.

```
<propertyRule type="Telligent.DynamicConfiguration.Rules.ValueAutomationRule,
    Telligent.DynamicConfiguration" processImmediately="true">
```

This particular rule has two main subnodes that can be used to set configuration values, depending on what value was selected in the theme variation dropdown. For example, if you select the "Summer" variation the following `theme.config` settings will be used to set specific theme configuration values. Note, though, that the following is an abbreviated version of the actual entry. If you would like to see the full entries, look in the `theme.config` file that exists for the Paperclip blog theme.

```
<checkValue value="~/themes/blogs/paperclip/style/summer.css">
    <setValue id="textColor" value="#000000" />
    <setValue id="textFont" value="Tahoma, Arial, Helvetica" />
    <setValue id="linkColor" value="#006ff7" />
    <setValue id="visitedLinkColor" value="#006ff7" />
</checkValue>
```

This means that whenever you select the summer theme variation, the text color entry will be set to #000000 and the link color theme option will be set to #006ff7. As you can see, this is a useful feature, as it allows changes to a particular theme property to impact the values of other properties.

For an example of another rule, go back to the idea at the beginning of this section. The idea is to create a rule that prevents a color property from becoming a specific color. Perhaps a theme has a background color of black, and you would like to prevent the text color from ever becoming black. You can create a rule to accomplish this. The rule itself will take on two extra properties, which are the color you want to replace and the color to substitute. Below is code that you can use to create this custom rule. For the purposes of this example, it is being placed in the `Telligent.DynamicConfiguration` assembly and in the `Telligent.DynamicConfiguration.Rules` namespace.

```
public class ColorReplaceRule : IPropertyRule
{
    private string _originalColor;
    private string _replaceColor;

    public void ValueChanged(Property property, ConfigurationDataBase data)
    {
        if (string.IsNullOrEmpty(_originalColor) ||
                string.IsNullOrEmpty(_replaceColor))
            return;

        object value = data.GetObjectValue(property);
        Color originalColor = (Color)data.ParseObjectValue(_originalColor,
            PropertyType.Color);
        Color replaceColor = (Color)data.ParseObjectValue(_replaceColor,
            PropertyType.Color);

        if (data.ObjectValuesAreEqual(property.DataType, value,
                originalColor))
            data.SetObjectValue(property, replaceColor);
    }

    public void LoadConfiguration(PropertyRule rule, System.Xml.XmlNode node)
    {
        if (rule.Attributes["originalColor"] != null)
            _originalColor = rule.Attributes["originalColor"];

        if (rule.Attributes["replaceColor"] != null)
            _replaceColor = rule.Attributes["replaceColor"];
    }
}
```

To use the above code, you should place it in a class library project, then place the resulting assembly in your website's `bin` directory. As you can see, the class implements the `IPropertyRule` interface, which includes the two methods that were used above. The `LoadConfiguration` method is used primarily to read in any rule-specific data that could be set in the `theme.config` file. The `ValueChanged` method is called whenever the property that the rule is used for is changed. Remember, that a rule is defined for a particular property; this prevents the rule from firing whenever a different property is changed. In other words if you have a rule defined for a property called `FireMe` and then you change the value in the configuration page for a property called `DontFireMe`, the rule will not be executed. It will only be executed when you change the `FireMe` property. Here is an example of how the `ColorReplaceRule` is declared inside a property in the `theme.config`:

```
<property id="siteBackgroundColor" text="Background Color" dataType="color"
    defaultValue="#ffffff" descriptionText="Select the background color">
  <propertyRule type="Telligent.DynamicConfiguration.Rules.ColorReplaceRule,
```

```
                Telligent.DynamicConfiguration" processImmediately="true"
                originalColor="#000000" replaceColor="#444444" />
    </property>
```

Whenever you set the site background color property in the theme configuration page to black, it will automatically be set to #444444. You can even add multiple entries of this rule to prevent a property from ever becoming a specific color. As you can see from the declaration above, the propertyRule is located inside a property, and then the type and processImmediately attributes are both set on it. You can use this example as a template to create other rules in the future. Remember that you only need to implement the IPropertyRule interface to have created a type that is valid for use as a propertyRule node.

Summary

In this chapter, you saw an advanced overview of the theme.config. You were presented with several common examples of properties that are used in this file and also saw how these properties are then used in the theme configuration page inside of the site Control Panel. Also, you were able to see how these configuration settings can be linked to presentation code inside of a stylesheet. Moreover, you also saw how the conditional rendering control could be used to hide or show content on your site based on theme configuration settings. Finally, you were presented with an example of a property rule and learned how you can create your own custom property rule for use in your theme configuration options.

In the next chapter you will learn about content scrubbing and how it will help you create well-formed markup. Additionally, you will see how this powerful feature is already being used inside Community Server.

11

Content Scrubbing

User-entered HTML can adversely affect the rendering of custom themes within Community Server. To ensure that user-entered HTML is formatted properly and does not contain undesirable markup, Community Server includes two components: the `HtmlScrubber` and the `HtmlNestingCorrectionModule`.

Use of these components in a Community Server installation prevents markup-related issues such as use of undesirable tags, cross-site scripting, and breaks in formatting. This chapter includes a discussion of each of these components and provides documentation for their configuration.

Markup Safety and the HtmlScrubber

While themes can define much of the rendered markup of a Community Server-based website, the user-entered HTML content is not controlled by theme developers. This user-defined markup can include malicious scripts, undesired tags, and improperly formatted XHTML.

Malicious scripts can cause a site to be unsafe to browse, potentially compromising the security of both Community Server and the user's computer. Similarly, some tags may compromise the layout or intended use of a custom theme when rendered as part of a post in Community Server. And while theme markup may validate against a version of XHTML, the quality of the user-entered HTML depends largely on the user's editor. Most browser-based editors do not produce XHTML-compliant markup.

The `HtmlScrubber`, included in Community Server, addresses both security and validation issues by processing user-entered HTML and removing unallowed tags and attributes and reformatting badly formed markup.

The tag- and attribute-blocking features can be customized via the `MarkUp` node within the `communityserver.config` file. The configuration options allowed within the `MarkUp` node are defined in the next section in this chapter. The reformatting features of the `HtmlScrubber`, however, cannot be configured. The HtmlScrubber will always perform the following reformatting when enabled:

1. Converts all tag names to lowercase — All tag names are converted to lowercase as required by the XHTML standard.

2. Converts all attribute names to lowercase — Similarly to tag names, all attribute names are converted to lowercase per the XHTML standard.

3. Wraps all attribute values in double quotation marks — All attribute values are wrapped in double quotation marks as required by the XHTML standard.

4. Ensures all attribute values and free text are properly encoded — It ensures that all attribute values and text that are not part of a tag do not contain unencoded quotation marks, double quotations marks, less-than symbols, or greater-than symbols.

Configuring the HtmlScrubber

The HtmlScrubber is enabled by default in Community Server. For each application in Community Server, a CSModule exists that uses the HtmlScrubber to process incoming content for the application.

A sample HtmlScrubber configuration is shown here:

```
<MarkUp>
  <globalAttributes>
    <class enable = "true" />
    <style enable = "true" />
    <align enable = "true" />
    <id enable = "true" />
  </globalAttributes>
  <selfContained>
    <br />
    <img />
    <input />
    <link />
    <meta />
    <base />
    <hr />
  </selfContained>
  <html>
    <h1 />
    <h2 />
    <h3 />
    <h4 />
    <h5 />
    <h6 />
    <strong />
    <em />
    <u />
    <b />
    <i />
    <strike />
    <sub />
    <sup />
    <font size = "true" color = "true" face = "true" />
    <blockquote dir = "true" />
```

```
       <ul />
       <ol start="true" />
       <li />
       <p dir = "true" />
       <address />
       <div />
       <hr />
       <br />
       <a href = "true" title = "true" name = "true" target= "true" rel = "true" />
       <span />
       <img src = "true" alt = "true" title = "true" border = "true" width = "true"
  height = "true" hspace = "true" />
       <table cellpadding = "true" cellspacing = "true" bgcolor = "true" />
       <th />
       <td rowspan = "true" colspan = "true" />
       <tr />
       <pre />
       <code />
     </html>
   </MarkUp>
```

The Markup node supports three subnodes: globalAttributes, selfContained, and html.

globalAttributes

The globalAttributes node, within the MarkUp node, identifies the list of tag attributes that are supported by all tags supported by the HtmlScrubber. Each node within the globalAttributes node identifies an attribute. Each attribute-named node that defines enabled="true" is enabled for all tags enabled by the HtmlScrubber.

For example, the following code:

```
<globalAttributes>
  <class enable = "true" />
  <style enable = "true" />
  <align enable = "true" />
  <id enable = "true" />
</globalAttributes>
```

would enable the class, style, align, and id attributes for all tags enabled by the html node.

selfContained

The selfContained node, within the MarkUp node, identifies the tags that are always self-closed. When reformatting markup, the HtmlScrubber will force all tags identified as self-contained to be self-closed and will remove any associated closing tags.

For example,

```
<selfContained>
  <br />
  <img />
  <input />
  <link />
  <meta />
```

```
  <base />
  <hr />
</selfContained>
```

would ensure that all br, img, input, link, meta, base, and hr tags are self-closed and would reformat the following markup:

```
<hr>
<input type="text" name="input1"></input><br>
```

by self-closing the hr, input, and br tags and removing the unnecessary closing input tag as shown here:

```
<hr />
<input type="text" name="input1" /><br />
```

html

The html node, within the MarkUp node, contains the tags and associated attributes that should be allowed by the HtmlScrubber. All tags not listed within the html node will be removed by the HtmlScrubber. Additionally, any attributes on supported tags that are not defined on the tag-named node within the html node or within the selfContained node will be removed.

For example,

```
<html>
  <strong />
  <em />
  <font size = "true" color = "true" face = "true" />
  <p />
  <br />
  <a href = "true" title = "true" name = "true" target= "true" rel = "true" />
</html>
```

would configure the HtmlScrubber to only allow strong, em, font, p, br, and a tags. Furthermore, only the size, color, and face attributes will be allowed on the font tag and only the href, title, name, target, and rel attributes will be allowed on the a tag.

With this configuration, the following markup:

```
<p>
<i>This</i> markup is <strong>not</strong> <font color="#f00"
style="background-color: #ccc;">good</font>.
</p>
```

would be reformatted as:

```
<p>
This markup is <strong>not</strong> <font color="#f00">good</font>.
</p>
```

This removes the unsupported i tag and the style attribute from the font tag.

Additionally, the `html` node exposes the `protocols` attribute, which can be used to define the colon-separated list of supported URL protocols supported by the `HtmlScrubber`. Any protocol used in `href` or `src` attributes on allowed tags that is not listed in the supported protocols list, will cause the `href` or `src` attribute to be removed.

For example,

```
<html protocols="http;https;mailto">
  <p />
  <font />
  <br />
  <a href = "true" title = "true" name = "true" target= "true" rel = "true" />
</html>
```

would only support the `http`, `https`, and `mailto` protocols in absolute URLs. This would cause the following markup:

```
<a href="http://getben.com/">Visit Ben's Site</a> or
<a href="ftp://getben.com/">visit his FTP site</a>
```

to be reformatted as:

```
<a href="http://getben.com/">Visit Ben's Site</a> or
<a>visit his FTP site</a>
```

This is because the `ftp` protocol is not allowed.

Well-formed Markup and the HtmlNestingCorrectionModule

User-defined HTML and HTML generated from some office and development applications may not be well formed. This markup can often contain improperly nested and unnecessary tags, such as this tag:

```
<b><i>Text</b></i></div>
```

When improperly nested HTML is saved in a post and rendered within Community Server, the errors in the post's content can affect the markup of a custom theme, which can cause the rendered page to be unviewable. To correct HTML nesting issues, the `HtmlNestingCorrectionModule` can be used.

When the `HtmlNestingCorrectionModule` processes the sample invalid markup above, the result is this:

```
<b><i>Text</i></b>
```

which corrects the reversed closing tags for the `i` and `b` tag and removes the unnecessary `div` tag.

Configuring the HtmlNestingCorrectionModule

The `HtmlNestingCorrectionModule` is included in Community Server but is disabled by default. To enable the `HtmlNestingCorrectionModule`, the `communityserver.config` file can be updated to set the `enabled` attribute to `true` on the `add` node for the `HtmlNestingCorrectionModule` within the `CSModules` region. Alternatively, if a `communityserver_override.config` file is used, the following can be added within the `Overrides` node to enable the `HtmlNestingCorrectionModule`:

```
<Override xpath="/CommunityServer/CSModules/add[@name='HtmlNestingCorrectionModule']"
mode="change" name="enabled" value="true" />
```

The `HtmlNestingCorrectionModule` is configured using subnodes within the `add` node for the `HtmlNestingCorrectionModule` within the `CSModules` region of the `communityserver.config` file. The module is preconfigured and should not require modifications, but supports two configuration node types: `CloseBeforeNext` and `SelfContained`.

CloseBeforeNext

`CloseBeforeNext` nodes can be added within the `add` node for the `HtmlNestingCorrectionModule` within the `CSModules` node. Each `CloseBeforeNext` node identifies a tag name, identified using the `Tag` attribute that cannot contain a tag with the same name.

Additionally, each `CloseBeforeNext` node can identify a comma-separated list of valid parent tags via the `Parents` attribute. Tags can be nested within similarly named tags as long as the nested tag is within a valid parent tag. For example,

```
<li>Item<li>Item</li></li>
```

is not valid because a `li` tag cannot be directly nested within another `li` tag, however,

```
<li>Item<ul><li>Item</li></ul></li>
```

is valid because the `ul` tag defines a sublist and is therefore a valid parent of the nested `li` tag.

The default configuration of the `HtmlNestingCorrectionModule` includes the following `CloseBeforeNext` nodes:

```
<CloseBeforeNext Tag="li" Parents="ul,ol" />
<CloseBeforeNext Tag="option" />
<CloseBeforeNext Tag="td" Parents="tr" />
<CloseBeforeNext Tag="tr" Parents="table" />
<CloseBeforeNext Tag="th" Parents="table" />
<CloseBeforeNext Tag="dt" Parents="dl" />
<CloseBeforeNext Tag="dd" Parents="dl" />
```

This prevents similarly named tags from being nested within `li`, `option`, `td`, `tr`, `th`, `dt`, and `dd` tags unless the nested tag is within a valid parent tag.

SelfContained

SelfContained nodes can be added within the add node for the HtmlNestingCorrectionModule within the CSModules node. Each SelfContained node identifies a tag name, identified using the Tag attribute, that is always self-closed.

Note that the SelfContained nodes used to configure the HtmlNestingCorrectionModule do not affect the HtmlScrubber. The configuration of each module is completely independent.

When processing markup, the HtmlNestingCorrectionModule will force all tags identified as self-contained to be self-closed and will remove any associated closing tags.

The default configuration of the HtmlNestingCorrectionModule includes the following SelfContained nodes:

```
<SelfContained Tag="br" />
<SelfContained Tag="img" />
<SelfContained Tag="input" />
<SelfContained Tag="link" />
<SelfContained Tag="meta" />
<SelfContained Tag="base" />
<SelfContained Tag="hr" />
```

This causes all br, img, input, link, meta, base, and hr tags to be self-closed.

Summary

The HtmlScrubber and HtmlNestingCorrectionModule can be used to ensure that HTML-based content entered by end users into custom themes does not break the formatting of the theme or enable security vulnerabilities. The HtmlScrubber removes disallowed tags and attributes and reformats each tag to be XHTML compliant, whereas the HtmlNestingCorrectionModule corrects inter-tag nesting issues.

The next chapter discusses how to create custom Chameleon controls and provides code samples for custom controls of each Chameleon control type.

12

Creating Custom Chameleon Controls

Chameleon supports external, custom controls. These custom controls take advantage of Chameleon's well-defined base class structure to implement new features with a minimum amount of code, and participate in and extend implicit data binding.

This chapter takes you a step beyond Chapter 5 and provides the necessary information and instructions to create custom Chameleon controls. This chapter identifies the base classes for each of the Chameleon control types, defines the abstract and protected members of each base class, and provides a sample implementation of each control type.

Using Implicit Data Binding

All Chameleon base controls, from which all Chameleon controls inherit, implement support for implicit data binding by ensuring that each control will be data bound. To complete the requirements for implicit data binding, each control only needs to define its own, default value for its DataSource property.

In general, each existing Chameleon control implements logic that allows the control to determine its own data source based on the context in which the control is placed. For example, the DataSource property of a control that renders Post-related data could be implemented as follows:

```
private Post _post = null;
public override object DataSource
{
    get
    {
```

```
            if (_post == null)
                _post = CSControlUtility.Instance().GetCurrentPost(this);

            return _post;
        }
        set
        {
            if (value is Post)
                _post = value as Post;
            else
                throw new InvalidCastException("DataSource must be a valid Post object");
        }
    }
```

Notice that when the value of the DataSource property is retrieved, if the value has not been set manually, the control calls the CSControlUtility.Instance().GetCurrentPost method. This method uses the control's context to determine the current post relative to this control. The GetCurrentPost method of the CSControlUtility class implements logic based on Community Server API object relationships to retrieve the current Post object according to the objects being bound on parent controls.

The CSControlUtility class provides methods for retrieving implicit, contextual data sources. For example, the generic GetCurrentBoundObject method of the CSControlUtility class, whose method signature is:

```
public virtual T GetCurrentBoundObject<T>(Control currentControl) where T : class
```

supports retrieving any object (of type T) based on the context of a control. For example, to retrieve the current User object, the following code could be executed within a control:

```
User currentUser = CSControlUtility.Instance().GetCurrentBoundObject<User>(this);
```

The GetCurrentBoundObject method, however, does not implement object relationship logic. If no User is in the context of the control, but a Post is, the GetCurrentBoundObject method will not be able to retrieve the author User of the Post. For each Community Server API object, the CSControlUtility class defines a method that implements data relationship logic. To retrieve the current User, including the author User of the current Post, the following code could be used within a control:

```
User currentUser = CSControlUtility.Instance().GetCurrentUser(this);
```

The Community Server API object-specific methods exposed by the CSControlUtility class provide easy access to contextual data.

Additionally, each application in Community Server implements an override of the CSControlUtility class, which provides access to application-specific object types. For example, the WeblogControlUtility class defined in the CommunityServer.Blogs assembly exposes methods for blog-related objects, such as the GetCurrentWeblogPost method, which retrieves the current WeblogPost object relative to the current control.

The methods exposed by the CSControlUtility class and its child classes are described in the documentation for Chameleon.

Custom Single-value Controls

Single-value controls render a single user interface widget or data from a single object.

All Chameleon single-value controls inherit from the `CommunityServer.Controls.WrappedContentBase` class. This class provides the base support for Chameleon behavior such as ensured data binding, leader and trailer template rendering, conditional rendering via the `DisplayConditions` property, and wrapper tag rendering.

Community Server also includes other single-value control base classes that inherit from the `WrappedContentBase` class. You can find these child classes by browsing the Community Server SDK or reviewing documentation for Chameleon.

Abstract Members of WrappedContentBase

`WrappedContentBase` defines abstract members that must be implemented by child controls to define the basic behavior of the custom control.

The following method must be implemented by controls inheriting from `WrappedContentBase`: `BindDefaultContent`.

BindDefaultContent

The abstract `BindDefaultContent` method is defined as:

```
protected abstract void BindDefaultContent(Control control, IDataItemContainer
dataItemContainer)
```

This allows single-value controls to create and bind their rendered content. All content must be added to the `control.Controls` collection in the form of a `System.Web.UI.Control`. To render HTML markup directly, use `System.Web.UI.LiteralControls`.

Utility Members of WrappedContentBase

`WrappedContentBase` also provides a set of utility and overridable members to help implement single-value controls, such as `GetContentTemplate`, `DataSource`, `DefaultLeaderTemplate`, `DefaultTrailerTemplate`, `CreateDefaultContentControls`, `AutomatedVisible`, `RenderControl`, `EnsureDataBound`, `RecreateChidlControlsOnDataBind`, `AddPropertyControls`, `AddLeaderControls`, `AddContentControls`, `GetContentTemplateWrapper`, and `AddTrailerControls`.

GetContentTemplate

The `GetContentTemplate` method is defined as:

```
protected virtual ITemplate GetContentTemplate()
```

This returns an `ITemplated` that causes the `BindDefaultContent` and `CreateDefaultContentControls` methods to be called to add and bind the content controls. You can override this method to identify any programmatic or user-defined `ITemplate` to be used as the content of the control.

DataSource

The DataSource property is defined as:

```
public virtual DataSource { get; set; }
```

This identifies the data source for the control. Most Chameleon controls override the DataSource property to check for a compatible type in the set and to implicitly load the expected data source using the CSControlUtility class (or one of its application-specific overrides) in the get when the value of the DataSource property is not explicitly set.

DefaultLeaderTemplate

The DefaultLeaderTemplate property is defined as:

```
protected virtual ITemplate DefaultLeaderTemplate { get; }
```

This identifies the default leader template. By default, the value of the DefaultLeaderTemplate property is null. You can override this property to identify the ITemplate that defines the default leader template.

DefaultTrailerTemplate

The DefaultTrailerTemplate property is defined as:

```
protected virtual ITemplate DefaultTrailerTemplate { get; }
```

This identifies the default trailer template. By default, the value of the DefaultTrailerTemplate property is null. You can override this property to identify the ITemplate, which defines the default trailer template.

CreateDefaultContentControls

The CreateDefaultContentControls property is defined as:

```
protected virtual void CreateDefaultContentControls(Control control)
```

This is called by the default content template, then returned by the default implementation of the GetContentTemplate method when child controls are being created (due to a call to the EnsureChildControls or CreateChildControls methods).

By default, this method performs no actions and creates no content controls. You can override this method, however, to create controls that must exist before data binding occurs.

When overriding the CreateDefaultContentControls method, it is often also necessary to set the RecreateChildControlsOnDataBind property to false. The RecreateChildControlsOnDataBind property is discussed later in this section.

AutomatedVisible

The AutomatedVisible property is defined as:

```
protected virtual bool AutomatedVisible { get; set; }
```

This property is used to identify the control-defined visibility for the control. By default, the `DataBind` method of `WrappedContentBase` resets the `AutomatedVisible` property's value to `false` and allows the value to be set based on automated control logic, for example when processing the `DisplayConditions` property of Chameleon controls.

The `AutomatedVisible` property should be used whenever control logic identifies the visibility of the control. Setting `AutomatedVisible` to `false`, for example, will cause the standard `Visible` property to also return `false`. However, whenever the `DataBind` method is called, the value of the `AutomatedVisible` property is reset to `true` and the value of the `Visible` property is restored to the user-defined value.

RenderControl

The `RenderControl` method is defined as:

```
public virtual void RenderControl(HtmlTextWriter writer, bool renderWrapper)
```

This allows the control to be rendered without rendering the wrapper tag. When the `renderWrapper` parameter is set to `false`, the control will be rendered without its defined wrapper tag (defined by the standard `Tag`, `ContainerId`, `CssClass` properties and unrecognized attributes on the control).

Rendering a control without its wrapper tag is useful when updating the content of a control using AJAX as the wrapper tag can be used as the placeholder for the control. The wrapperless rendering of the control can then be used to replace the contents of the placeholding wrapper tag as the result of an AJAX request.

EnsureDataBound

The `EnsureDataBound` method is defined as:

```
public virtual void EnsureDataBound()
```

This can be called to ensure that the control is bound. If the control has already been data bound, calling the `EnsureDataBound` method will not cause data binding to reoccur.

RecreateChildControlsOnDataBind

The `RecreateChildControlsOnDataBind` property is defined as:

```
protected virtual bool RecreateChildControlsOnDataBind { get; set; }
```

This allows controls to identify whether their child controls should be recreated when the control is data bound. When the `RecreateChildControlsOnDataBind` property is set to `true`, all of the control's child controls will be removed and recreated whenever the `DataBind` method is called. When the property is set to `false`, child controls are only created once.

The default value for the `RecreateChildControlsOnDataBind` property is `true`.

AddPropertyControls

The `AddPropertyControls` method is defined as:

```
protected virtual void AddPropertyControls()
```

. This method provides a mechanism for re-adding property child controls, such as `DisplayConditions`, `SuccessActions`, and `QueryOverrides`, to the control when child controls are recreated. All control-based inner-properties should have their values readded to the control's `Controls` collection via overriding the `AddPropertyControls` method.

AddLeaderControls

The `AddLeaderControls` method is defined as:

```
protected virtual void AddLeaderControls()
```

This is called when the content of the leader template should be added to the control. By default, this method adds the content defined by value of the `LeaderTemplate` property to the control's `Controls` collection. You can override this method to modify leader-rendering behavior.

AddContentControls

The `AddContentControls` method is defined as:

```
protected virtual void AddContentControls()
```

This is called when the child controls defining the content of the control should be added to the control's `Controls` collection. By default, this method adds the controls defined by the `ITemplate` returned by the `GetContentTemplate` method, optionally wrapping it in the result of the `GetContentTemplateWrapper` method (if non-null), to the control.

You can override this method to modify content rendering behavior.

GetContentTemplateWrapper

The `GetContentTemplateWrapper` method is defined as:

```
protected virtual Control GetContentTemplateWrapper()
```

This method returns a wrapper control into which the current content of the control should be added. By default, this method returns `null`.

You can override this method to add support for wrapping the content of the control in a wrapper control. For example, the `LinkTo` property on API-related single-value Chameleon controls identifies a link to wrap the content of the control. The `LinkTo` property, if set to a valid value, causes a configured `HyperLink` control to be returned by the `GetContentTemplateWrapper` method. The content of the control is then added to this `Hyperlink` control.

AddTrailerControls

The `AddTrailerControls` method is defined as:

```
protected virtual void AddTrailerControls()
```

This is called when the content of the trailer template should be added to the control. By default, this method adds the content defined by value of the `TrailerTemplate` property to the control's `Controls` collection. This method can be overridden to modify trailer-rendering behavior.

Implementing the *PostExtendedAttributeLink* Control

The API-related single-value controls in Community Server that relate to Post objects expose the LinkTo property which provides theme developers with a list of selectable links associated to posts. The LinkTo property, however, does not support linking to a URL stored within an extended attribute on the current Post object. The following is a sample implementation of a single-value Chameleon control that provides support for linking to a URL stored in an extended attribute on the current Post object, the PostExtendedAttributeLink control.

Because the PostExtendedAttributeLink control is a single-value control, it inherits from the WrappedContentBase class via the PreTemplatedWrappedContentBase class. The PreTemplatedWrappedContentBase class extends the WrappedContentBase class, adding support for the ContentTemplate property, allowing theme developers to override the default content of the control (defined by the BindDefaultContent method).

The PostExtendedAttributeLink control implements the BindDefaultContent method and overrides the DataSource and GetContentTemplateWrapper members of the WrappedContentBase class. The PostExtendedAttributeLink control also adds a property, UrlExtendedAttribute, that allows the theme developer to identify the name of the extended attribute on the current Post object from which to load the link URL.

The full source of the PostExtendedAttributeLink control is:

```
using System;
using System.Collections.Generic;
using System.Text;
using CommunityServer.Controls;
using CommunityServer.Components;
using System.Web.UI.WebControls;
using System.Web.UI;

namespace ProfessionalThemes
{
    public class PostExtendedAttributeLink : PreTemplatedWrappedContentBase
    {
        #region Public Properties

        public string UrlExtendedAttribute
        {
            get { return ((string)ViewState["UrlExtendedAttribute"]) ?? string.Empty; }
            set { ViewState["UrlExtendedAttribute"] = value; }
        }

        #endregion

        #region WrappedContentBase Overrides

        private Post _post = null;
        public override object DataSource
        {
            get
            {
```

```
                    if (_post == null)
                        _post = CSControlUtility.Instance().GetCurrentPost(this);

                    return _post;
                }
            set
            {
                if (value is Post)
                    _post = (Post) value;
                else
                    throw new InvalidCastException("The DataSource property must be
set to a valid Post object");
            }
        }

        protected override Control GetContentTemplateWrapper()
        {
            HyperLink link = null;

            Post post = this.DataSource as Post;
            if (!string.IsNullOrEmpty(this.UrlExtendedAttribute)
                && post != null
                &&
!string.IsNullOrEmpty(post.GetExtendedAttribute(this.UrlExtendedAttribute)))
            {
                link = new HyperLink();
                link.NavigateUrl =
post.GetExtendedAttribute(this.UrlExtendedAttribute);
            }
            else
                this.AutomatedVisible = false;

            return link;
        }

        protected override void BindDefaultContent(Control control,
IDataItemContainer dataItemContainer)
        {
            Post post = this.DataSource as Post;
            if (!string.IsNullOrEmpty(this.UrlExtendedAttribute)
                && post != null
                &&
!string.IsNullOrEmpty(post.GetExtendedAttribute(this.UrlExtendedAttribute)))
            {
                control.Controls.Add(new
LiteralControl(post.GetExtendedAttribute(this.UrlExtendedAttribute)));
            }
        }

        #endregion
    }
}
```

First, the `UrlExtendedAttribute` property, which is used to identify the name of the extended attribute on the current `Post` from which the link URL should be retrieved, is implemented as a standard control property using `ViewState`. This property should be familiar to ASP.Net server control developers.

Next, the `DataSource` property of `WrappedContentBase` is overridden as:

```
private Post _post = null;
      public override object DataSource
      {
          get
          {
              if (_post == null)
                  _post = CSControlUtility.Instance().GetCurrentPost(this);

              return _post;
          }
          set
          {
              if (value is Post)
                  _post = (Post) value;
              else
                  throw new InvalidCastException("The DataSource property must be
set to a valid Post object");
          }
      }
```

This implements the default implicit data-binding behavior by retrieving the current `Post` object via the `CSControlUtility.GetCurrentPost` method when the `DataSource` is not otherwise manually set. When set, the `DataSource` property ensures that the value is a valid `Post` object and, if it is not, throws a meaningful exception.

The `GetContentTemplateWrapper` method of `WrappedContentBase` is overridden to add support for wrapping the content of the control in a link, which navigates to a URL stored in the extended attribute identified by the `UrlExtendedAttribute` property. The `GetContentTempalteWrapper` override is defined as:

```
protected override Control GetContentTemplateWrapper()
      {
          HyperLink link = null;

          Post post = this.DataSource as Post;
          if (!string.IsNullOrEmpty(this.UrlExtendedAttribute)
              && post != null
              &&
!string.IsNullOrEmpty(post.GetExtendedAttribute(this.UrlExtendedAttribute)))
          {
              link = new HyperLink();
              link.NavigateUrl =
post.GetExtendedAttribute(this.UrlExtendedAttribute);
          }
          else
```

```
                    this.AutomatedVisible = false;

        return link;
    }
```

This retrieves the `Post` object from the `DataSource` property and ensures that the `UrlExtendedAttribute` property's value is set, the `Post` object is not null, and the post has a value for the identified extended attribute name. If all of these checks are successful, the method returns a `HyperLink` control configured to link to the value of the extended attribute. If any of the checks fail, the `AutomatedVisible` property will be set to `false`, causing the control to not render.

The `BindDefaultContent` method of `WrappedContentBase` must also be implemented (it is abstract on the `WrappedContentBase` class). While this method could define no content and depend on the theme developer to specify content using the `ContentTemplate` property exposed by the `PreTemplatedWrappedContentBase` class from which the `PostExtendedAttributeLink` control inherits, in this example the control will render the URL as text by default. For example,

```
protected override void BindDefaultContent(Control control, IDataItemContainer
dataItemContainer)
        {
            Post post = this.DataSource as Post;
            if (!string.IsNullOrEmpty(this.UrlExtendedAttribute)
                && post != null
                &&
!string.IsNullOrEmpty(post.GetExtendedAttribute(this.UrlExtendedAttribute)))
            {
                control.Controls.Add(new
LiteralControl(post.GetExtendedAttribute(this.UrlExtendedAttribute)));
            }
        }
```

This uses similar logic to the `GetContentTemplateWrapper` method to ensure that the `Post` object is not `null`, the extended attribute name is set, and the `Post` object contains a value for the identified extended attribute. If these checks are successful, a new `LiteralControl` is added to the content of the control, which will render the URL stored in the identified extended attribute as text.

After compiling the assembly in which this control is defined and deploying it into Community Server's `web/bin` folder, the control can be used in themed pages. For example,

```
<CSThemes:PostExtendedAttributeLink runat="server" UrlExtendedAttribute="RelatedPostUrl" />
```

The above code would render a link to the URL stored in the `RelatedPostUrl` extended attribute on the current `Post`.

Note that this usage example assumes that the namespace of the control is associated to the `CSThemes` tag prefix.

Custom List Controls

List controls render lists of data and can support theme-defined queries.

All Chameleon list controls inherit from the `CommunityServer.Controls.WrappedRepeater` class. This class provides the base support for Chameleon behavior such as leader, trailer, ad, and row separator template rendering, conditional rendering via the `DisplayConditions` property, and wrapper tag rendering.

Most Chameleon list controls, however, inherit from `CommunityServer.Controls.PreTemplatedListBase` which extends `WrappedRepeater` to add support for predefined template contents and ensured data binding. This section outlines the `PreTemplatedListBase` class.

Abstract Members of PreTemplatedListBase

`PreTemplatedListBase` defines abstract members that must be implemented by child controls to define the basic behavior of the custom control.

The following method must be implemented by controls inheriting from `PreTemplatedListBase`: `BindDefaultItemContent`.

BindDefaultItemContent

The `BindDefaultItemContent` method is defined as:

```
protected abstract void BindDefaultItemContent(ListItemTemplateListItem listItem,
    IDataItemContainer dataItemContainer)
```

This must be implemented to create and bind each rendered item's content. All content must be added to the `listItem.Controls` collection in the form of a `System.Web.UI.Control`. To render HTML markup directly, `System.Web.UI.LiteralControls` can be used.

Utility Members of PreTemplatedListBase

`PreTemplatedListBase` also provides a set of utility members to help implement list controls, such as `DefaultItemTemplate`, `DefaultAlternatingTemplate`, `DefaultHeaderTemplate`, `DefaultTrailerTemplate`, `DefaultSeparatorTemplate`, `DefaultAdTemplate`, `DefaultLeaderTemplate`, `DefaultFooterTemplate`, `DefaultNoneTemplate`, `FlagForDataBinding`, `AddPropertyControls`, `AddLeaderControls`, `AddTrailerControls`, `AutomatedVisible`, and `RenderControl`.

DefaultItemTemplate

The `DefaultItemTemplate` property, defined as:

```
protected override ITemplate DefaultItemTemplate { get; }
```

identifies the default `ITemplate` used to render each item in the list. By default, the `DefaultItemTemplate` property returns an `ITemplate` that causes each item to be bound using the `BindDefaultItemContent` method wrapped in an `<li>` tag with its `class` attribute set to the value of the `ListItemCssClass` property.

DefaultAlternatingTemplate

The `DefaultAlternatingTemplate` property, defined as:

```
protected override ITemplate DefaultAlternatingTemplate { get; }
```

identifies the default `ITemplate` used to render each alternating item in the list. By default, the `DefaultAlternatingTemplate` property returns an `ITemplate` that causes each item to be bound using the `BindDefaultItemContent` method wrapped in an `<li>` tag with its `class` attribute set to the value of the `AlternateListItemCssClass` property.

DefaultHeaderTemplate

The `DefaultHeaderTemplate` property, defined as:

```
protected override ITemplate DefaultHeaderTemplate { get; }
```

identifies the default `ITemplate` used to render the header of the list. By default, the `DefaultHeaderTemplate` property returns an `ITemplate` that renders the header followed by a `<ul>` tag defined by the `ListCssClass`, `HeaderCssClass`, `HeaderText`, `HeaderSourceName`, `HeaderResourceFile`, and `HeaderTag` properties.

DefaultTrailerTemplate

The `DefaultTrailerTemplate` property is defined as:

```
protected virtual ITemplate DefaultTrailerTemplate { get; }
```

This identifies the default trailer template. By default, the value of the `DefaultTrailerTemplate` property is `null`. This property can be overridden to identify the `ITemplate` that defines the default trailer template.

DefaultSeparatorTemplate

The `DefaultSeparatorTemplate` property is defined as:

```
protected virtual ITemplate DefaultSeparatorTemplate { get; }
```

This identifies the default `ITemplate` used to render the separator between each item in the list. By default, the `DefaultSeparatorTemplate` is `null`, causing no separator to be rendered.

DefaultAdTemplate

The `DefaultAdTemplate` property is defined as:

```
protected virtual ITemplate DefaultAdTemplate  { get; }
```

This identifies the default `ITemplate` used to render advertisements between list items in the list. By default, the `DefaultAdTemplate` is `null`, causing no advertisements to be rendered.

DefaultLeaderTemplate

The `DefaultLeaderTemplate` property is defined as:

```
protected virtual ITemplate DefaultLeaderTemplate { get; }
```

This identifies the default leader template. By default, the value of the `DefaultLeaderTemplate` property is `null`. This property can be overridden to identify the `ITemplate` that defines the default leader template.

DefaultFooterTemplate

The `DefaultFooterTemplate` property is defined as:

```
protected override ITemplate DefaultFooterTemplate { get; }
```

This identifies the default `ITemplate` used to render the footer of the list. By default, the `DefaultFooterTemplate` property returns an `ITemplate` that renders a `</ul>` tag.

DefaultNoneTemplate

The `DefaultNoneTemplate` property is defined as:

```
protected override ITempalte DefaultNoneTemplate { get; }
```

This identifies the default `ITemplate` used to render content when no items are bound to the list. By default, the `DefaultNoneTemplate` is `null`, causing no content to be rendered when no items are bound to the list.

FlagForDataBinding

The `FlagForDataBinding` method is defined as:

```
public virtual void FlagForDataBinding()
```

This notifies the control that its items should be data bound (or data bound again). This method can be called when a paging event occurs that requires that the list be updated, for example.

AddPropertyControls

The `AddPropertyControls` method is defined as:

```
protected virtual void AddPropertyControls(bool dataBinding)
```

This provides a mechanism for re-adding property child controls, such as `DisplayConditions`, `SuccessActions`, and `QueryOverrides`, to the control when child controls are recreated. All control-based inner-properties should have their values re-added to the control's `Controls` collection by overriding the `AddPropertyControls` method.

AddLeaderControls

The `AddLeaderControls` method is defined as:

```
protected virtual void AddLeaderControls(bool dataBinding)
```

This is called when the content of the leader template should be added to the control. By default, this method adds the content defined by value of the `LeaderTemplate` property to the control's `Controls` collection. This method can be overridden to modify leader-rendering behavior.

AddTrailerControls

The `AddTrailerControls` method is defined as:

```
protected virtual void AddTrailerControls(bool dataBinding)
```

This is called when the content of the trailer template should be added to the control. By default, this method adds the content defined by value of the `TrailerTemplate` property to the control's `Controls` collection. This method can be overridden to modify trailer-rendering behavior.

AutomatedVisible

The `AutomatedVisible` property is defined as:

```
protected virtual bool AutomatedVisible
```

This is used to identify the control-defined visibility for the control. By default, the `DataBind` method of `PreTemplatedListBase` resets the `AutomatedVisible` property's value to `false` and allows the value to be set based on automated control logic, such as when processing the `DisplayConditions` property of Chameleon controls.

The `AutomatedVisible` property should be used whenever control logic identifies the visibility of the control. Setting `AutomatedVisible` to `false`, for example, will cause the standard `Visible` property to also return `false`. However, whenever the `DataBind` method is called, the value of the `AutomatedVisible` property is reset to `true` and the value of the `Visible` property is restored to the user-defined value.

RenderControl

The `RenderControl` method is defined as:

```
public virtual void RenderControl(HtmlTextWriter writer, bool renderWrapper)
```

This allows the control to be rendered without rendering the wrapper tag. When the `renderWrapper` parameter is set to `false`, the control will render without its defined wrapper tag (defined by the standard `Tag`, `ContainerId`, `CssClass` properties and unrecognized attributes on the control).

Rendering a control without its wrapper tag is useful when updating the content of a control using AJAX, as the wrapper tag can be used as the placeholder for the control. The wrapperless rendering of the control can then be used to replace the contents of the placeholding wrapper tag as the result of an AJAX request.

Implementing the GroupList Control

The following example of a list control uses the source of the GroupList control included in Community Server, which is used to list Group objects.

Because the GroupList control is a list control, it inherits from PreTemplatedListBase. The PreTemplatedListBase control extends PreTemplatedWrappedRepeaterBase, which inherits from WrappedRepeaterBase.

The GroupList control implements the BindDefaultItemContent method of PreTemplatedListBase and also overrides the DataSource property and FlagForDataBinding methods. Additionally, the GroupList control provides support for overriding the default implicit query by exposing the QueryOverrides property.

The full source of the GroupList control is:

```
using System;
using System.Collections.Generic;
using System.Text;
using CommunityServer.Components;
using System.Web.UI;
using System.ComponentModel;

namespace CommunityServer.Controls
{
    public class GroupList : PreTemplatedListBase
    {
        [PersistenceMode(PersistenceMode.InnerProperty)]
        public virtual CommunityServer.Controls.GroupQuery QueryOverrides
        {
            get { return _queryOverrides; }
            set
            {
                if (_queryOverrides != null)
                    this.Controls.Remove(_queryOverrides);

                _queryOverrides = value;
                if (_queryOverrides != null)
                    this.Controls.Add(_queryOverrides);
            }
        }
        private CommunityServer.Controls.GroupQuery _queryOverrides;

        protected override void AddPropertyControls(bool dataBinding)
        {
            if (this.QueryOverrides != null)
                this.Controls.Add(this.QueryOverrides);

            base.AddPropertyControls(dataBinding);
        }

        private bool _isImplicitDataSource = true;
        private List<Group> _groups = null;
```

```csharp
            public override object DataSource
        {
            get
            {
                if (_groups == null)
                {
                    CSContext csContext =
CSControlUtility.Instance().GetCurrentCSContext(this.Page);

                    CommunityServer.Components.GroupQuery query = new
CommunityServer.Components.GroupQuery();
                    query.ApplicationType = csContext.ApplicationType;

                    Group group =
CSControlUtility.Instance().GetCurrentGroup(this);
                    if (group != null)
                    {
                        query.GroupID = group.GroupID;
                        query.ApplicationType = group.ApplicationType;
                    }

                    if (this.QueryOverrides != null)
                        this.QueryOverrides.ApplyQueryOverrides(query);

                    List<Group> groups = null;
                    if (query.ApplicationType != ApplicationType.Unknown)
                        groups =
ApplicationSet.Applications[query.ApplicationType].Groups();
                    else
                    {
                        groups = new List<Group>();
                        foreach (CSApplicationData appData in
ApplicationSet.Applications)
                        {
                            List<Group> appGroups = appData.Groups();
                            if (appGroups != null)
                            {
                                foreach (Group s in appGroups)
                                    groups.Add(s);
                            }
                        }
                    }

                    int totalCount = 0;
                    _groups = Groups.Filter(groups, query, ref totalCount);

                    if (this.QueryOverrides != null && this.QueryOverrides.Pager != null)
                    {
                        this.QueryOverrides.Pager.PageIndex = query.PageIndex;
                        this.QueryOverrides.Pager.PageSize = query.PageSize;
                        this.QueryOverrides.Pager.TotalRecords = totalCount;
                        this.QueryOverrides.Pager.OnPageIndexChanged += new
PagerEventHandler(this.PageIndexChanged);
                        this.QueryOverrides.Pager.DataBind();
```

```
                }
            }

            return _groups;
        }
        set
        {
            if (value is List<Group>)
            {
                _groups = value as List<Group>;
                _isImplicitDataSource = false;
                RequiresDataBinding = true;
                OnDataPropertyChanged();
            }
            else if (value == null)
            {
                _groups = null;
                _isImplicitDataSource = true;
                RequiresDataBinding = true;
                OnDataPropertyChanged();
            }
            else
                throw new InvalidCastException("DataSource must be a valid
List<Group> object");
        }
    }

    public override void FlagForDataBinding()
    {
        this.DataSource = null;
        base.FlagForDataBinding();
    }

    protected void PageIndexChanged(IPager sender, PagerEventArgs e)
    {
        if (_isImplicitDataSource)
            FlagForDataBinding();
    }

    protected override void
BindDefaultItemContent(PreTemplatedListBase.ListItemTemplateListItem listItem,
System.Web.UI.IDataItemContainer dataItemContainer)
    {
        Group item = dataItemContainer.DataItem as Group;
        if (item != null)
        {
            GroupData gd = new GroupData();
            gd.DataSource = item;
            gd.Text = item.Name;
            listItem.Controls.Add(gd);
        }
    }
  }
 }
}
```

First, the QueryOverrides property is defined; it provides support for theme developers to customize the default implicit query used to retrieve Group objects. The QueryOverrides property is implemented as:

```
[PersistenceMode(PersistenceMode.InnerProperty)]
public virtual CommunityServer.Controls.GroupQuery QueryOverrides
{
    get { return _queryOverrides; }
    set
    {
        if (_queryOverrides != null)
            this.Controls.Remove(_queryOverrides);

        _queryOverrides = value;
        if (_queryOverrides != null)
            this.Controls.Add(_queryOverrides);
    }
}
private CommunityServer.Controls.GroupQuery _queryOverrides;
```

Note that the property has the PersistenceMode(PersistenceMode.InnerProperty) attribute. This attribute identifies the fact that the property will be defined within a subnode when configured declaratively.

The data type of the QueryOverrides property is the GroupQuery control. The GroupQuery control exists in Community Server and provides access to properties that affect the way that Group objects will be loaded implicitly within the DataSource property.

Because the GroupList control defines a control inner-property (QueryOverrides), the AddPropertyControls method must be used to ensure that the control representing the QueryOverrides property is added to the GroupList's Controls collection when its child controls are recreated. The AddPropertyControls method is overridden as:

```
protected override void AddPropertyControls(bool dataBinding)
{
    if (this.QueryOverrides != null)
        this.Controls.Add(this.QueryOverrides);

    base.AddPropertyControls(dataBinding);
}
```

This simply adds the value of the QueryOverrides property to the GroupList's Controls collection when it is not null. It is important to call the base.AddPropertyControls method when overriding the AddPropertyControls method to ensure that control inner-properties defined on the parent control (PreTemplatedListBase) are also properly added to the Controls collection.

The DataSource property is overridden next. The DataSource property provides support for loading the implicit data source and also ensures that manually assigned data sources are of the proper data type. The DataSource property is implemented as:

```
private bool _isImplicitDataSource = true;
private List<Group> _groups = null;
public override object DataSource
{
```

```
            get
            {
                if (_groups == null)
                {
                    CSContext csContext =
CSControlUtility.Instance().GetCurrentCSContext(this.Page);

                    CommunityServer.Components.GroupQuery query = new
CommunityServer.Components.GroupQuery();
                    query.ApplicationType = csContext.ApplicationType;

                    Group group =
CSControlUtility.Instance().GetCurrentGroup(this);
                    if (group != null)
                    {
                        query.GroupID = group.GroupID;
                        query.ApplicationType = group.ApplicationType;
                    }

                    if (this.QueryOverrides != null)
                        this.QueryOverrides.ApplyQueryOverrides(query);

                    List<Group> groups = null;
                    if (query.ApplicationType != ApplicationType.Unknown)
                        groups =
ApplicationSet.Applications[query.ApplicationType].Groups();
                    else
                    {
                        groups = new List<Group>();
                        foreach (CSApplicationData appData in
ApplicationSet.Applications)
                        {
                            List<Group> appGroups = appData.Groups();
                            if (appGroups != null)
                            {
                                foreach (Group s in appGroups)
                                    groups.Add(s);
                            }
                        }
                    }

                    int totalCount = 0;
                    _groups = Groups.Filter(groups, query, ref totalCount);

                    if (this.QueryOverrides != null && this.QueryOverrides.Pager !=
null)
                    {
                        this.QueryOverrides.Pager.PageIndex = query.PageIndex;
                        this.QueryOverrides.Pager.PageSize = query.PageSize;
                        this.QueryOverrides.Pager.TotalRecords = totalCount;
                        this.QueryOverrides.Pager.OnPageIndexChanged += new
PagerEventHandler(this.PageIndexChanged);
                        this.QueryOverrides.Pager.DataBind();
                    }
                }
```

```
                    return _groups;
            }
            set
            {
                if (value is List<Group>)
                {
                    _groups = value as List<Group>;
                    _isImplicitDataSource = false;
                    RequiresDataBinding = true;
                    OnDataPropertyChanged();
                }
                else if (value == null)
                {
                    _groups = null;
                    _isImplicitDataSource = true;
                    RequiresDataBinding = true;
                    OnDataPropertyChanged();
                }
                else
                    throw new InvalidCastException("DataSource must be a valid
    List<Group> object");
            }
        }
```

When the value of the DataSource is null (the _groups field is null), the GroupList control loads the data source implicitly using a CommunityServer.Components.GroupQuery object.

Note how the GroupList control first assigns contextual information loaded from the CSControlUtility class to the query object and then applies the theme-defined configuration stored in the QueryOverrides property. When the query object is properly configured contextually and manually, the query is processed using the ApplicationSet class, which provides application-generic access to common data such as Groups.

When the groups list is populated, it is filtered using the Groups.Filter method, which processes the query object, filtering the groups list and returning only the current page of groups.

If the QueryOverrides property identifies a pager control, the pager control is populated and the PageIndexChanged event handler is attached to ensure that the GroupList control is properly updated if the associated pager control causes the current page index to change.

Next, the FlagForDataBinding method is overridden as:

```
public override void FlagForDataBinding()
{
    this.DataSource = null;
    base.FlagForDataBinding();
}
```

This ensures that the DataSource is set to null when the control is set to be data bound. This ensures that the implicit data source will be reloaded.

The `FlagForDataBinding` method is called by the method that handles the `OnPageIndexChanged` event of the pager associated to the `GroupList` via the `QueryOverrides` property. The `PageIndexChanged` method is implemented as:

```
protected void PageIndexChanged(IPager sender, PagerEventArgs e)
{
    if (_isImplicitDataSource)
        FlagForDataBinding();
}
```

This causes the `FlagForDataBinding` method to be called when the `GroupList` is using an implicit data source and the associated pager control changes the current page index to render.

All Chameleon list controls supporting paging implement the same basic paging/event/data-binding process. In general, this code can be copied and adapted to other Chameleon list controls.

Finally, the implementation of the `BindDefaultItemContent` method is defined as:

```
protected override void
BindDefaultItemContent(PreTemplatedListBase.ListItemTemplateListItem listItem,
System.Web.UI.IDataItemContainer dataItemContainer)
{
    Group item = dataItemContainer.DataItem as Group;
    if (item != null)
    {
        GroupData gd = new GroupData();
        gd.DataSource = item;
        gd.Text = item.Name;
        listItem.Controls.Add(gd);
    }
}
```

The `BindDefaultItemContent` method is rendered for each item in the rendered list if the `ItemTemplate` is not defined by the theme.

In this example, the `GroupList` control will add a `GroupData` control configured to show the `Group` object's name to each list item.

Custom Form Controls

Form controls implement behaviors that initiate a process or modify data by automating child form element controls.

All Chameleon form controls inherit from the `CommunityServer.Controls.WrappedFormBase` class. This class provides the base support for Chameleon behavior such as leader and trailer template rendering, conditional rendering via the `DisplayConditions` property, and wrapper tag rendering. This base class also implements the base structure for rendering forms and provides utility methods related to form processing.

Abstract Members of WrappedFormBase

The following method must be implemented by controls inheriting from `WrappedFormBase`: `AttachChildControls`.

AttachChildControls

The `AttachedChildControls` method is defined as:

```
protected abstract void AttachChildControls()
```

These should be used by form controls to find and store references to child form elements. In this method, the form control should use the `CSControlUtility` class (or one of its application-specific overrides) to locate child form element controls by their IDs.

Utility Members of WrappedFormBase

`WrappedFormBase` also provides a set of utility members to help implement form controls, such as `DefaultLeaderTemplate`, `DefaultTrailerTemplate`, `AutomatedVisible`, `RenderControl`, `DataBind`, `IsValid`, `AddPropertyControls`, `AddLeaderControls`, `AddFormControls`, `GetFormTemplateWrapper`, and `AddTrailerControls`.

DefaultLeaderTemplate

The `DefaultLeaderTemplate` property is defined as:

```
protected virtual ITemplate DefaultLeaderTemplate { get; }
```

This identifies the default leader template. By default, the value of the `DefaultLeaderTemplate` property is `null`. This property can be overridden to identify the `ITemplate` that defines the default leader template.

DefaultTrailerTemplate

The `DefaultTrailerTemplate` property is defined as:

```
protected virtual ITemplate DefaultTrailerTemplate { get; }
```

This identifies the default trailer template. By default, the value of the `DefaultTrailerTemplate` property is `null`. This property can be overridden to identify the `ITemplate` that defines the default trailer template.

AutomatedVisible

The `AutomatedVisible` property is defined as:

```
protected virtual bool AutomatedVisible
```

This is used to identify the control-defined visibility for the control. By default, the `DataBind` method of `WrappedFormBase` resets the `AutomatedVisible` property's value to `false` and allows the value to be set based on automated control logic, such as when processing the `DisplayConditions` property of Chameleon controls.

The `AutomatedVisible` property should be used whenever control logic identifies the visibility of the control. Setting `AutomatedVisible` to `false`, for example, will cause the standard `Visible` property to also return `false`. However, whenever the `DataBind` method is called, the value of the `AutomatedVisible` property is reset to `true` and the value of the `Visible` property is restored to the user-defined value.

RenderControl

The `RenderControl` method is defined as:

```
public virtual void RenderControl(HtmlTextWriter writer, bool renderWrapper)
```

This allows the control to be rendered without rendering the wrapper tag. When the `renderWrapper` parameter is set to `false`, the control will render without its defined wrapper tag (defined by the standard `Tag`, `ContainerId`, `CssClass` properties and unrecognized attributes on the control).

Rendering a control without its wrapper tag is useful when updating the content of a control using AJAX, as the wrapper tag can be used as the placeholder for the control. The wrapperless rendering of the control can then be used to replace the contents of the placeholding wrapper tag as the result of an AJAX request.

DataBind

The `DataBind` method is defined as:

```
public virtual void DataBind()
```

This should be overridden and used to directly assign values to and otherwise data bind child form element controls.

Note that, when overridden, `base.DataBind()` should be called to ensure that `DisplayConditions` are process properly.

IsValid

The `IsValid` method is defind as:

```
public virtual bool IsValid()
```

This returns the result of processing the validation rules associated to the form's assigned `ValidationGroup`. If the `ValidationGroup` property is not set, the `IsValid` method will always return `true`.

AddPropertyControls

The `AddPropertyControls` method is defined as:

```
protected virtual void AddPropertyControls()
```

This provides a mechanism for re-adding property child controls, such as `DisplayConditions`, `SuccessActions`, and `QueryOverrides`, to the control when child controls are recreated. All control-based inner-properties should have their values re-added to the control's `Controls` collection via overriding the `AddPropertyControls` method.

AddLeaderControls

The `AddLeaderControls` method is defined as:

```
protected virtual void AddLeaderControls()
```

This is called when the content of the leader template should be added to the control. By default, this method adds the content defined by the value of the `LeaderTemplate` property to the control's `Controls` collection. This method can be overridden to modify leader-rendering behavior.

AddFormControls

The AddFormControls method is defined as:

```
protected virtual void AddFormControls()
```

This is called when the child controls defining the content of the control should be added to the control's `Controls` collection. By default, this method adds the controls defined by the `ITemplate` returned by the `GetFormTemplate` method, optionally wrapping it in the result of the `GetFormTemplateWrapper` method (if non-`null`), to the control.

This method can be overridden to modify content-rendering behavior or provide a default implementation of the form.

GetFormTemplate

The `GetFormTemplate` method is defined as:

```
protected virtual ITemplate GetFormTemplate()
```

This returns the value of the `FormTemplate` property as the `ITemplate` containing the implementation of the form. This method can be overridden to provide a default or alternate rendering of the form.

GetFormTemplateWrapper

The `GetFormTemplateWrapper` is defined as:

```
protected virtual Control GetFormTemplateWrapper()
```

This returns a child control in which the content of the form should be added. By default, this method returns `null`.

AddTrailerControls

The `AddTrailerControls` method is defined as:

```
protected virtual void AddTrailerControls()
```

This is called when the content of the trailer template should be added to the control. By default, this method adds the content defined by value of the `TrailerTemplate` property to the control's `Controls` collection. This method can be overridden to modify trailer-rendering behavior.

Implementing the SendEmailForm Control

Community Server includes a `ContactForm` control, which supports emailing blog owners, but it does not include a general-purpose email form. The generic contact form, `SendEmailForm`, will be implemented as an example of a Chameleon form control.

Because the `SendEmailForm` control is a form control, it inherits from the `WrappedFormBase` class. It implements the `AttachChildControls` method and overrides the `DataBind` and `AddPropertyControls` methods of `WrappedFormBase`. The `SendEmailForm` control also defines properties to support identifying child form element control IDs and success actions and defines a custom event handler for the form's Submit button.

The full source of the `SendEmailForm` control is:

```
using System;
using System.Collections.Generic;
using System.Text;
using CommunityServer.Controls;
using CommunityServer.Components;
using System.Web.UI.WebControls;
using System.Web.UI;
using CommunityServer.MailRoom.Components;
using System.Net.Mail;

namespace ProfessionalThemes
{
    public class SendEmailForm : WrappedFormBase
    {
        private TextBox SubjectTextBox, MessageTextBox, FromTextBox;
        private IButton SubmitButton;

        protected List<WrappedSubFormBase> SubForms;

        #region Public Properties

        [PersistenceMode(PersistenceMode.InnerProperty)]
        public virtual Actions SuccessActions
        {
            get { return _successActions; }
            set
            {
                if (_successActions != null)
                    this.Controls.Remove(_successActions);

                _successActions = value;
                if (_successActions != null)
                    this.Controls.Add(_successActions);
            }
        }
    }
```

```
        private Actions _successActions;

        public string SubFormIds
        {
            get { return (string)(ViewState["SubFormIds"] ?? string.Empty); }
            set { ViewState["SubFormIds"] = value; }
        }

        public string SubjectTextBoxId
        {
            get { return (string)(ViewState["SubjectTextBoxId"] ?? string.Empty); }
            set { ViewState["SubjectTextBoxId"] = value; }
        }

        public string MessageTextBoxId
        {
            get { return (string)(ViewState["MessageTextBoxId"] ?? string.Empty); }
            set { ViewState["MessageTextBoxId"] = value; }
        }

        public string FromTextBoxId
        {
            get { return (string)(ViewState["FromTextBoxId"] ?? string.Empty); }
            set { ViewState["FromTextBoxId"] = value; }
        }

        public string SubmitButtonId
        {
            get { return (string)(ViewState["SubmitButtonId"] ?? string.Empty); }
            set { ViewState["SubmitButtonId"] = value; }
        }

        public string ToEmailAddress
        {
            get { return (string)(ViewState["ToEmailAddress"] ?? string.Empty); }
            set { ViewState["ToEmailAddress"] = value; }
        }

        #endregion

        #region WrappedFormBase Overrides

        protected override void AddPropertyControls()
        {
            if (this.SuccessActions != null)
                this.Controls.Add(this.SuccessActions);

            base.AddPropertyControls();
        }

        protected override void AttachChildControls()
        {
            SubjectTextBox = CSControlUtility.Instance().FindControl(this,
this.SubjectTextBoxId) as TextBox;
            MessageTextBox = CSControlUtility.Instance().FindControl(this,
this.MessageTextBoxId) as TextBox;
```

```
            FromTextBox = CSControlUtility.Instance().FindControl(this,
this.FromTextBoxId) as TextBox;
            SubmitButton = CSControlUtility.Instance().FindButtonControl(this,
this.SubmitButtonId);

            if (SubjectTextBox == null || MessageTextBox == null || FromTextBox ==
null || SubmitButton == null)
                throw new InvalidOperationException("The SubjectTextBoxId,
MessageTextBoxId, FromTextBoxId, and SubmitButtonId properties must reference valid
controls.");

            this.SubForms = new List<WrappedSubFormBase>();
            if (!string.IsNullOrEmpty(this.SubFormIds))
            {
                foreach (string id in this.SubFormIds.Split(','))
                {
                    WrappedSubFormBase subForm =
CSControlUtility.Instance().FindControl(this, id) as WrappedSubFormBase;
                    if (subForm != null)
                    {
                        subForm.HostForm = this;
                        this.SubForms.Add(subForm);
                    }
                }
            }

            SubmitButton.Click += new EventHandler(SubmitButton_Click);
        }

        public override void DataBind()
        {
            base.DataBind();

            foreach (WrappedSubFormBase subForm in this.SubForms)
            {
                subForm.DataSource = this.DataSource;
                subForm.DataBind();
            }
        }

        #endregion

        #region Event Handlers

        void SubmitButton_Click(object sender, EventArgs e)
        {
            if ((SubmitButton.CausesValidation && !Page.IsValid) || !this.IsValid())
                return;

            foreach (WrappedSubFormBase subForm in this.SubForms)
            {
                if (!subForm.IsValid())
                    return;
            }
```

```
                MailMessage message = new MailMessage(FromTextBox.Text, ToEmailAddress,
        SubjectTextBox.Text, MessageTextBox.Text);

            foreach (WrappedSubFormBase subForm in this.SubForms)
            {
                subForm.ApplyChangesBeforeCommit(message);
            }

            Emails.QueueMessage(message);

            foreach (WrappedSubFormBase subForm in this.SubForms)
            {
                subForm.ApplyChangesAfterCommit(message);
            }

            if (this.SuccessActions != null)
                this.SuccessActions.Execute(this, message);
        }

        #endregion
    }
}
```

First, the private fields are defined for storing references to the child form element controls and subforms. The following code identifies TextBox controls that will be used to store the subject, message, and "from" email address for the email being sent, the IButton control used to submit the form, and the list of sub-forms that will interact with this form:

```
        private TextBox SubjectTextBox, MessageTextBox, FromTextBox;
        private IButton SubmitButton;

        protected List<WrappedSubFormBase> SubForms;
```

These fields will be populated by the AttachChildControls method.

When the SendEmailForm is successfully submitted, the control supports allowing the theme developer to identify the actions to execute. To add this support, the SuccessActions property is defined as:

```
        [PersistenceMode(PersistenceMode.InnerProperty)]
        public virtual Actions SuccessActions
        {
            get { return _successActions; }
            set
            {
                if (_successActions != null)
                    this.Controls.Remove(_successActions);

                _successActions = value;
                if (_successActions != null)
                    this.Controls.Add(_successActions);
            }
        }
        private Actions _successActions;
```

This allows Chameleon action controls to be used to interact with this control. Note that the property has the `PersistenceMode(PersistenceMode.InnerProperty)` attribute. This attribute identifies that the property will be defined as a subnode within the control when defined declaratively.

The child control properties are defined next. The properties for `SubFormIds`, `SubjectTextBoxId`, `MessageTextBoxId`, `FromTextBoxId`, and `SubmitButtonId` all identify IDs for form element controls with which the `SendEmailForm` control will interact. All of these properties are simple `string` properties whose values are stored in `ViewState`.

The `ToEmailAddress` property, which is also a `string` property stored in `ViewState`, is used to identify the email address to which the email will be sent when the submit button is clicked.

Because the `SendEmailForm` control defines a control inner-property (`SuccessActions`), the `AddPropertyControls` method must be used to ensure that the control representing the `SuccessActions` property is added to the `SendEmailForm`'s `Controls` collection when its child controls are recreated. The `AddPropertyControls` method is overridden as:

```
protected override void AddPropertyControls()
{
    if (this.SuccessActions != null)
        this.Controls.Add(this.SuccessActions);

    base.AddPropertyControls();
}
```

This simply adds the value of the `SuccessActions` property to the `SendEmailForm`'s `Controls` collection when it is not `null`. It is important to call the `base.AddPropertyControls` method when overriding the `AddPropertyControls` method to ensure that control inner-properties defined on the parent control (`WrappedFormBase`) are also properly added to the `Controls` collection.

Next, the `AttachChildControls` method is implemented. The `AttachChildControls` method is defined below and uses `CSControlUtility` to find controls and buttons for each of the properties identifying child form element controls, assigning the results to the appropriate fields:

```
protected override void AttachChildControls()
{
    SubjectTextBox = CSControlUtility.Instance().FindControl(this,
this.SubjectTextBoxId) as TextBox;
    MessageTextBox = CSControlUtility.Instance().FindControl(this,
this.MessageTextBoxId) as TextBox;
    FromTextBox = CSControlUtility.Instance().FindControl(this,
this.FromTextBoxId) as TextBox;
    SubmitButton = CSControlUtility.Instance().FindButtonControl(this,
this.SubmitButtonId);

    if (SubjectTextBox == null || MessageTextBox == null || FromTextBox ==
null || SubmitButton == null)
        throw new InvalidOperationException("The SubjectTextBoxId,
MessageTextBoxId, FromTextBoxId, and SubmitButtonId properties must reference valid
controls.");

    this.SubForms = new List<WrappedSubFormBase>();
```

```
                    if (!string.IsNullOrEmpty(this.SubFormIds))
                    {
                        foreach (string id in this.SubFormIds.Split(','))
                        {
                            WrappedSubFormBase subForm =
        CSControlUtility.Instance().FindControl(this, id) as WrappedSubFormBase;
                            if (subForm != null)
                            {
                                subForm.HostForm = this;
                                this.SubForms.Add(subForm);
                            }
                        }
                    }

                    SubmitButton.Click += new EventHandler(SubmitButton_Click);
                }
```

If the required child form element controls are not defined or could not be found, an
InvalidOperationException is thrown with a meaningful message.

If all of the required child form element controls are available, the SubForms field is populated using the
comma-separated list of subform IDs identified by the value of the SubFormIds property. As subforms
are found, their HostForm property is set to the SendEmailForm control (this) and they're added to the
SubForms field for later use.

Finally, an event handler, the SubmitButton_Click method, is added for the SubmitButton.Click
event. The SubmitButton_Click method will be defined later in the SendFormControl class.

The SendEmailForm control does not edit an existing object, so it has no data to bind within the
DataBind method. However, because the control supports subforms, the DataBind method is overridden to support binding subforms. The DataBind method is overridden as:

```
            public override void DataBind()
            {
                base.DataBind();

                foreach (WrappedSubFormBase subForm in this.SubForms)
                {
                    subForm.DataSource = this.DataSource;
                    subForm.DataBind();
                }
            }
```

This loops through each of the registered subforms, passing on the value of the DataSource property
and calling each subform's DataBind method.

Next, the SubmitButton_Click method, which handles the SubmitButton.Click event, is
defined. This method will be executed when the SendEmailForm is submitted and implements validation checks, email sending, subform handling, and processing of the SuccessActions property.
The SubmitButton_Click method is defined as:

```
            void SubmitButton_Click(object sender, EventArgs e)
            {
```

```
            if ((SubmitButton.CausesValidation && !Page.IsValid) || !this.IsValid())
                return;

            foreach (WrappedSubFormBase subForm in this.SubForms)
            {
                if (!subForm.IsValid())
                    return;
            }

            MailMessage message = new MailMessage(FromTextBox.Text, ToEmailAddress,
    SubjectTextBox.Text, MessageTextBox.Text);

            foreach (WrappedSubFormBase subForm in this.SubForms)
            {
                subForm.ApplyChangesBeforeCommit(message);
            }

            Emails.QueueMessage(message);

            foreach (WrappedSubFormBase subForm in this.SubForms)
            {
                subForm.ApplyChangesAfterCommit(message);
            }

            if (this.SuccessActions != null)
                this.SuccessActions.Execute(this, message);
        }
```

This first ensures that the `SendEmailForm` and all of its subforms are valid. If the form and subforms are valid, the `MailMessage` object is created using the values of the child form element controls. Any registered subforms are then allowed to modify the `MailMessage` object before it is sent by use of their `ApplyChangesBeforeCommit` method. After processing subforms, the `MailMessage` object is queued for processing by the Community Server email task by calling the `Emails.QueueMessage` method. The `ApplyChangesAfterCommit` method of all registered subforms is then called, allowing them to log or otherwise process the completed `MailMessage` object.

When all processing has been completed, the `SuccessActions` are processed by calling their `Execute` method.

After compiling the assembly in which this control is defined and deploying it into Community Server's `web/bin` folder, the control can be used in theme pages. For example,

```
<CSThemes:SendEmailForm runat="server"
  FromTextBoxId="From"
  SubjectTextBoxId="Subject"
  MessageTextBoxId="Message"
  SubmitButtonId="Send"
  ToEmailAddress="test@getben.com"
  >
  <SuccessActions>
    <CSControl:GoToModifiedUrlAction runat="server" />
  </SuccessActions>
```

```
    <FormTemplate>
      From: <asp:TextBox runat="server" id="From" /><br />
      Subject: <asp:TextBox runat="server" id="Subject" /><br />
      Message: <asp:TextBox runat="server" id="Message" /><br />
      <asp:Button runat="server" id="Send" Text="Send Email" />
    </FormTemplate>
  </CSThemes:SendEmailForm>
```

This would render a SendEmailForm that sends an email to test@getben.com and, after being sent, redirects the user to the current page (which clears the form).

Note that this assumes that the namespace of the control is associated with the CSThemes tag prefix.

Custom SubForm Controls

Subform controls interact with form controls to add new behaviors to existing forms.

All Chameleon subform controls inherit from the CommunityServer.Controls.WrappedSubFormBase class. This class provides the base support for Chameleon behavior such as leader and trailer template rendering, conditional rendering via the DisplayConditions property, and wrapper tag rendering. This class also implements the basic structure of subform controls and provides utility methods for interacting with host form controls.

Abstract Members of WrappedSubFormBase

All WrappedSubFormBase controls must implement the abstract members defined by WrappedFormBase in addition to the following method: IsEnabled.

IsEnabled

The IsEnabled method is defined as:

```
public abstract bool IsEnabled()
```

This should be implemented to return true if the subform control is enabled to be used in the current context.

Utility Members of WrappedSubFormBase

WrappedSubFormBase also provides a set of utility members (in addition to those exposed by WrappedFormBase) to help implement single-value controls, such as HostForm, GetPropertyFromHostForm, ApplyChangesBeforeCommit, ApplyChangesAfterCommit, and IsValid.

HostForm

The HostForm property is defined as:

```
public virtual Control HostForm { get; set; }
```

This provides access to the form control hosting this subform control.

GetPropertyFromHostForm

The GetPropertyFromHostForm method is defined as:

```
public T GetPropertyFromHostForm<T>() where T: class
```

This provides a mechanism for this subform control to retrieve properties of a specific type, T, from the hosting form control.

ApplyChangesBeforeCommit

The ApplyChangesBeforeCommit method, defined as:

```
public virtual void ApplyChangesBeforeCommit(object activeObject)
```

This can be overridden to implement the behavior of the subform control before the host form commits the object being manipulated.

ApplyChangesAfterCommit

The ApplyChangesAfterCommit method is defined as:

```
public virtual void ApplyChangesAfterCommit(object activeObject)
```

This can be overridden to implement the behavior of the subform control after the host form commits the object being manipulated.

IsValid

The IsValid method is defined as:

```
public virtual bool IsValid()
```

This returns the result of processing the validation rules associated to the subform's assigned ValidationGroup. If the ValidationGroup property is not set or the subform's IsEnabled method returns false, the IsValid method will always return true.

Implementing the ExtendedAttributeSubForm Control

The single-value control example, PostExtendedAttributeLink control renders links to URLs stored in an extended attribute on a Post object. The following subform example, ExtendedAttributeSubForm, adds support for specifying values on objects supporting extended attributes and is suitable for use with the PostExtendedAttributeLink control example.

Because the ExtendedAttributeSubForm control is a subform control, it inherits from the WrappedSubFormBase class. It implements AttachChildControls, DataBind, ApplyChangesBeforeCommit, and IsEnabled methods of WrappedSubFormBase. Additionally, the ExtendedAttributeSubForm control defines properties for a list of extended attributes to edit and their associated TextBox controls.

The full source of the `ExtendedAttributeSubForm` control is:

```csharp
using System;
using System.Collections.Generic;
using System.Text;
using CommunityServer.Controls;
using CommunityServer.Components;
using System.Web.UI.WebControls;
using System.Web.UI;

namespace ProfessionalThemes
{
    public class ExtendedAttributeSubForm : WrappedSubFormBase
    {
        #region Public Properties

        public string ExtendedAttributeNames
        {
            get { return (string)(ViewState["ExtendedAttributeNames"] ?? string.Empty); }
            set { ViewState["ExtendedAttributeNames"] = value; }
        }

        public string ExtendedAttributeTextBoxIds
        {
            get { return (string)(ViewState["ExtendedAttributeTextBoxIds"] ??
string.Empty); }
            set { ViewState["ExtendedAttributeTextBoxIds"] = value; }
        }

        #endregion

        #region WrappedSubFormBase Overrides

        protected override void AttachChildControls()
        {
            // Attach child controls in DataBind()
        }

        public override void DataBind()
        {
            base.DataBind();

            ExtendedAttributes extendedAttributes =
GetPropertyFromHostForm<ExtendedAttributes>();
            if (extendedAttributes != null)
            {
                string[] names = this.ExtendedAttributeNames.Split(',');
                string[] textBoxIds = this.ExtendedAttributeTextBoxIds.Split(',');

                for (int i = 0; i < names.Length && i < textBoxIds.Length; i++)
                {
                    TextBox textBox = CSControlUtility.Instance().FindControl(this,
textBoxIds[i].Trim()) as TextBox;
                    if (textBox != null)
```

```
                                   textBox.Text =
        Globals.HtmlDecode(extendedAttributes.GetExtendedAttribute(names[i].Trim()));
                    }
                }
            }

            public override void ApplyChangesBeforeCommit(object activeObject)
            {
                ExtendedAttributes extendedAttributes = activeObject as ExtendedAttributes;
                if (extendedAttributes != null)
                {
                    string[] names = this.ExtendedAttributeNames.Split(',');
                    string[] textBoxIds = this.ExtendedAttributeTextBoxIds.Split(',');

                    for (int i = 0; i < names.Length && i < textBoxIds.Length; i++)
                    {
                        TextBox textBox = CSControlUtility.Instance().FindControl(this,
        textBoxIds[i].Trim()) as TextBox;
                        if (textBox != null)
                            extendedAttributes.SetExtendedAttribute(names[i].Trim(),
        Globals.HtmlEncode(textBox.Text));
                    }
                }
            }

            public override bool IsEnabled()
            {
                return true;
            }

            #endregion
        }
    }
```

First, the two properties, ExtendedAttributeNames and ExtendedAttributeTextBoxIds, are defined as simple string properties with values stored in ViewState. The ExtendedAttributeNames property allows for one or more comma-separated extended attribute names to be specified to be edited by the ExtendedAttributeSubForm control. Each extended attribute identified in the value of the ExtendedAttributeNames property should have an associated control ID referencing a TextBox control in the comma-separated TextBox ID list property, ExtendedAttributeTextBoxIds.

Next, the AttachChildControls method is implemented as:

```
        protected override void AttachChildControls()
        {
            // Attach child controls in DataBind()
        }
```

This method would normally contain code to find controls referenced by properties; however, because the ExtendedAttributeSubForm control loads a dynamic list of TextBox controls, the child controls are found in the DataBind and ApplyChangesBeforeCommit methods instead of in the AttachChildControls method.

The `DataBind` method is used to bind the existing values of each of the extended attributes to their associated `TextBox` controls. The method is implemented as:

```
public override void DataBind()
{
    base.DataBind();

    ExtendedAttributes extendedAttributes =
GetPropertyFromHostForm<ExtendedAttributes>();
    if (extendedAttributes != null)
    {
        string[] names = this.ExtendedAttributeNames.Split(',');
        string[] textBoxIds = this.ExtendedAttributeTextBoxIds.Split(',');

        for (int i = 0; i < names.Length && i < textBoxIds.Length; i++)
        {
            TextBox textBox = CSControlUtility.Instance().FindControl(this,
textBoxIds[i].Trim()) as TextBox;
            if (textBox != null)
                textBox.Text =
Globals.HtmlDecode(extendedAttributes.GetExtendedAttribute(names[i].Trim()));
        }
    }
}
```

This first loads the `ExtendedAttributes` object from the control's host form. All Community Server API objects supporting extended attributes inherit from the `ExtendedAttributes` class, allowing this form to interact with any form control editing an object supporting extended attributes.

If an `ExtendedAttributes` object is found, the control loops through the list of extended attributes and their associated `TextBox` control IDs, finding each `TextBox` and assigning its value to the current value of the associated extended attribute.

The `ApplyChangesBeforeCommit` method saves the values of the `TextBox` controls related to extended attribute values back to the `ExtendedAttributes` object before it is committed. The method is implemented as:

```
public override void ApplyChangesBeforeCommit(object activeObject)
{
    ExtendedAttributes extendedAttributes = activeObject as ExtendedAttributes;
    if (extendedAttributes != null)
    {
        string[] names = this.ExtendedAttributeNames.Split(',');
        string[] textBoxIds = this.ExtendedAttributeTextBoxIds.Split(',');

        for (int i = 0; i < names.Length && i < textBoxIds.Length; i++)
        {
            TextBox textBox = CSControlUtility.Instance().FindControl(this,
textBoxIds[i].Trim()) as TextBox;
            if (textBox != null)
                extendedAttributes.SetExtendedAttribute(names[i].Trim(),
Globals.HtmlEncode(textBox.Text));
        }
    }
}
```

This works similar to the `DataBind` method, but instead of assigning each `TextBox` control's value to the current value of the associated extended attribute, this method assigns each extended attribute the current value of its associated `TextBox` control. After these changes have been applied, the control's host form should commit the changes.

Finally, the `IsEnabled` method is implemented. Because the `ExtendedAttributeSubForm` control does not implement any permission checks, the `IsEnabled` method is implemented as:

```
public override bool IsEnabled()
{
    return true;
}
```

This always reports that the subform is enabled. If the control depended on the current user having a specific permission, the permission could be checked in this method and the result of the permission check would be returned.

After compiling the assembly in which this control is defined and deploying it to Community Server's `web/bin` folder, the control can be used in theme pages. For example,

```
<CSForum:CreateEditForumPostForm runat="server"
  PostBodyEditorId="Body"
  PostSubjectTextBoxId="Subject"
  SubmitButtonId="Submit"
  SubFormIds="RelatedUrlForm"
  >
  <SuccessActions>
    <CSControl:GoToModifiedUrlAction runat="server" />
  </SuccessActions>
  <FormTemplate>
    Subject: <asp:TextBox id="Subject" runat="server" /><br />
    Body: <CSControl:Editor id="Body" runat="server" /><br />

    <CSThemes:ExtendedAttributeSubForm runat="server"
      id="RelatedUrlForm"
      ExtendedAttributeNames="RelatedUrl"
      ExtendedAttributeTextBoxIds="RelatedUrl"
      >
      <FormTemplate>
        Related URL: <asp:TextBox id="RelatedUrl" runat="server" /><br />
      </FormTemplate>
    </CSThemes:ExtendedAttributeSubForm>

    <asp:Button runat="server" id="Submit" Text="Submit" runat="server" />
  </FormTemplate>
</CSForum:CreateEditForumPostForm>
```

This would render an `ExtendedAttributeSubForm` attached to a `CreateEditForumPostForm` that adds support for specifying the value of the `RelatedUrl` extended attribute on the `ForumPost` being created or edited.

Note that this assumes that the namespace of the control is associated with the `CSThemes` tag prefix.

Custom Condition Controls

Condition controls are the building blocks for defining custom conditional behavior.

All Chameleon condition controls inherit from the `CommunityServer.Controls.ConditionBase` class. This class provides the basic structure for implementing condition controls and defines the interface with which other Chameleon controls can interact with conditions.

Abstract Members of ConditionBase

The following property must be implemented by controls inheriting from `ConditionBase`: `Result`.

Result

The `Result` property is defined as:

```
protected abstract bool Result { get; }
```

This should be implemented to return the result of the condition implemented by the control.

Utility Members of ConditionBase

`ConditionBase` also provides a single utility property: `ProcessDuring`.

ProcessDuring

The `ProcessDuring` property is defined as:

```
public virtual ConditionProcessEvent ProcessDuring { get; }
```

This identifies the control event during which this condition can be executed. By default, the `ProcessDuring` property returns `ConditionProcessingEvent.DataBind`, but it can be overridden to return `ConditionProcessingEvent.PreRender`.

Implementing the CurrentTimeCondition Control

As an example of implementing a Chameleon condition control, the `CurrentTimeCondition` control will be implemented. The `CurrentTimeCondition` control ensures that the current time (adjusted for the accessing user's time zone) is within a theme-developer-defined window.

Because the `CurrentTimeCondition` control is a condition control, it inherits from the `ConditionBase` class and implements the `Result` property. Additionally, to allow the theme developer to specify the time window, the `CurrentTimeCondition` control exposes two properties: `BeforeTime` and `AfterTime`.

The full source of the `CurrentTimeCondition` control is:

```
using System;
using System.Collections.Generic;
using System.Text;
```

```csharp
using CommunityServer.Controls;

namespace ProfessionalThemes
{
    public class CurrentTimeCondition : ConditionBase
    {
        #region Public Properties

        public TimeSpan BeforeTime
        {
            get { return (TimeSpan)(ViewState["BeforeTime"] ?? TimeSpan.MaxValue); }
            set { ViewState["BeforeTime"] = value; }
        }

        public TimeSpan AfterTime
        {
            get { return (TimeSpan)(ViewState["AfterTime"] ?? TimeSpan.MinValue); }
            set { ViewState["AfterTime"] = value; }
        }

        #endregion

        #region ConditionBase Overrides

        public override bool Result
        {
            get
            {
                TimeSpan now =
CSControlUtility.Instance().GetCurrentCSContext(this.Page).User.GetTimezone().TimeOfDay;
                return now >= AfterTime && now <= BeforeTime;
            }
        }

        #endregion
    }
}
```

First, the configuration properties, BeforeTime and AfterTime, are implemented. Both properties are of type TimeSpan. The BeforeTime property defaults to TimeSpan.MinValue, and the AfterTime property defaults to TimeSpan.MaxValue to ensure that, by default, the condition will always evaluate to true (the user's time will, by default, always be between the values of the BeforeTime and AfterTime properties).

Next, the Result property is implemented. The Result property implements the condition and is defined as:

```csharp
        public override bool Result
        {
            get
            {
                TimeSpan now =
CSControlUtility.Instance().GetCurrentCSContext(this.Page).User.GetTimezone().TimeOfDay;
```

```
                    return now >= AfterTime && now <= BeforeTime;
            }
        }
```

This first determines the current `TimeSpan` relative to the accessing user's current time. Then, the user's current time is compared against the values of the `BeforeTime` and `AfterTime` properties. If the user's time is within the specified time window, the condition will evaluate to `true`. If the user's time is outside of the window, the condition will evaluate to `false`.

After compiling the assembly in which this control is defined and deploying it to Community Server's `web/bin` folder, the control can be used in theme pages. For example,

```
<CSControl:PlaceHolder runat="server">
  <DisplayConditions>
    <CSThemes:CurrentTimeCondition runat="server" BeforeTime="8:00" AfterTime="2:00" />
  </DisplayConditions>
  <ContentTemplate>
    Good Morning!
  </ContentTemplate>
</CSControl:PlaceHolder>
```

This would render the text "Good Morning!" only when the accessing user's current time is between 2:00 AM and 8:00 AM.

Note that this assumes that the namespace of the control is associated with the `CSThemes` tag prefix.

Custom Action Controls

Action controls are used to define custom actions related to events initiated by other Chameleon controls.

All Chameleon condition controls inherit from the `CommunityServer.Controls.ConditionBase` class. This class defines the interface with which other Chameleon controls can interact with actions.

Abstract Members of ActionBase

The following method must be implemented by controls inheriting from `ActionBase`: `Execute`.

Execute

The `Execute` method is defined as:

```
public abstract void Execute(Control sender, object parameter)
```

This should be implemented to execute the action defined by the action control. The action control is passed a reference to the control initiating the execution as well as an appropriate, contextual parameter.

Implementing the IncludeStyleAction Control

As an example of implementing a Chameleon action control, the `IncludeStyleAction` control will be implemented. The `IncludeStyleAction` control implements support for including a Cascading Style Sheets file when executed.

Because the `IncludeStyleAction` control is an action control, it inherits from `ConditionBase` and implements the `Execute` method. Additionally, the control defines configuration properties for `Href` and `Media`.

The full source of the `IncludeStyleAction` control is:

```
using System;
using System.Collections.Generic;
using System.Text;
using CommunityServer.Controls;
using System.Web.UI;

namespace ProfessionalThemes
{
    public class IncludeStyleAction : ActionBase
    {
        #region Public Properties

        public string Href
        {
            get { return (string)(ViewState["Href"] ?? string.Empty); }
            set { ViewState["href"] = value; }
        }

        public string Media
        {
            get { return (string)(ViewState["Media"] ?? "screen"); }
            set { ViewState["Media"] = value; }
        }

        #endregion

        #region ActionBase Overrides

        public override void Execute(Control sender, object parameter)
        {
            if (!string.IsNullOrEmpty(this.Href))
            {
                if (this.Page.Header != null)
                    this.Page.Header.Controls.Add(new
LiteralControl(string.Format("<link href=\"{0}\" media=\"{1}\" type=\"text/css\"
rel=\"stylesheet\" />", this.Href, this.Media)));
                else
                    Head.AddStyle(this.Href, this.Media, this.Context,
CommunityServer.Components.StyleRelativePosition.Last);
            }
        }
```

```
            #endregion
        }
    }
```

First, the `Href` and `Media` properties are defined. Both are string properties stored in `ViewState`. The `Href` property stores the URL of the stylesheet to include on the page when this action is executed. The `Media` property identifies the stylesheet media type and defaults to "screen."

Next, the `Execute` method is implemented. The `Execute` method is defined as:

```
public override void Execute(Control sender, object parameter)
{
    if (!string.IsNullOrEmpty(this.Href))
    {
        if (this.Page.Header != null)
            this.Page.Header.Controls.Add(new
LiteralControl(string.Format("<link href=\"{0}\" media=\"{1}\" type=\"text/css\"
rel=\"stylesheet\" />", this.Href, this.Media)));
        else
            Head.AddStyle(this.Href, this.Media, this.Context,
CommunityServer.Components.StyleRelativePosition.Last);
    }
}
```

This implements the action of the control. The method first ensures that the `Href` property contains a value. If it does, it attempts to add the `<link />` tag for the specified URL and media type to the `Page.Header.Controls` collection (if the `Page.Header` property is not `null`); otherwise, it enqueues the stylesheet using the Community Server `Head` class, which will render the stylesheet after all other queued stylesheets.

After compiling the assembly in which this control is defined and deploying it into Community Server's web/bin folder, the control can be used in theme pages. For example,

```
<CSControl:ConditionalAction runat="server">
  <Conditions>
    <CSThemes:CurrentTimeCondition BeforeTime="8:00" AfterTime="2:00" runat="server" />
  </Conditions>
  <Actions>
    <CSThemes:IncludeStyleAction Href="/style/morning.css" runat="server" />
  </Actions>
</CSControl:ConditionalAction>
```

This would include the `/style/morning.css` stylesheet file whenever the accessing user's current time is between 2:00 AM and 8:00 AM.

Note that this assumes that the namespace of the control is associated with the `CSThemes` tag prefix.

Distributing Custom Controls

Custom controls can be easily distributed by sharing the assembly containing the controls.

When distributing custom control assemblies, other theme developers will need to do the following:

1. Copy the assembly into Community Server's `bin/` folder.

2. Update Community Server's root `web.config` file to include a tag prefix for the assembly.

3. Add the markup for the new controls to the desired theme pages, master files, and user controls.

The tag prefix in step two can be added after the other tag prefix registrations in the root `web.config` file for Community Server. These registrations exist within the `controls` node located within the `pages` node of the `web.config` file.

When distributing controls that use script files or images, consider including the scripts or images as embedded resources in the control assembly. Embedding resources into an assembly causes the contents of the embedded files to be literally embedded into the compiled assembly. This simplifies the distribution process, as no external files need to be installed. For more information on embedding resources, see the Microsoft KB article number 910445.

Summary

Community Server provides extendable base classes for each of the Chameleon base control types to help custom control developers extend the Chameleon theming engine. Much of the behavior of Chameleon controls is built into these base classes, facilitating the creation of new controls.

The next chapter will discuss creating custom property controls and rules to enhance the dynamic configuration options exposed by custom themes.

13

Creating Custom Dynamic Configuration Controls and Rules

As discussed in Chapter 9, Community Server supports extending the dynamically generated theme configuration form using custom property controls and property rules.

Custom controls can be used to customize the user interface of a single configuration property, whereas custom rules can be used to automate configuration data when it is changed. This chapter outlines the support for these extensions, identifies and explains the code requirements, and provides a sample implementation of both a property control and a property rule.

Custom Property Controls

Community Server supports creating custom property controls to allow theme developers to customize the configuration form user interface as needed. All custom property controls must implement the `Telligent.DynamicConfiguration.Components.IPropertyControl` interface, located within the `Telligent.DynamicConfiguration.dll` assembly.

Additionally, property controls that support rendering selectable property values should also implement the `Telligent.DynamicConfiguration.Components.IPropertyValuesControl` interface, also located within the `Telligent.DynamicConfiguration.dll` assembly.

IPropertyControl

The `Telligent.DynamicConfiguration.Components.IPropertyControl` interface is used by Community Server to interact with property controls within the theme configuration pages. All custom property controls must implement this interface.

The `IPropertyControl` interface is defined as:

```
using System;

namespace Telligent.DynamicConfiguration.Components
{
    public interface IPropertyControl
    {
        Property ConfigurationProperty
        {
            get;
            set;
        }

        ConfigurationDataBase ConfigurationData
        {
            get;
            set;
        }

        System.Web.UI.Control Control
        {
            get;
        }

        void SetConfigurationPropertyValue(object value);

        object GetConfigurationPropertyValue();

        event ConfigurationPropertyChanged ConfigurationValueChanged;
    }
}
```

The defining the members are: `ConfigurationProperty`, `ConfigurationData`, `Control`, `SetConfigurationPropertyValue`, `GetConfigurationPropertyValue`, and `ConfigurationValueChanged`.

ConfigurationProperty

The `ConfigurationProperty` property is used by Community Server to assign the `Telligent .DynamicConfiguration.Components.Property` object that the property control will be rendering.

The property control can use the `ConfigurationProperty` property to access attribute values of the property as defined in the theme's `theme.config` file.

ConfigurationData

The `ConfigurationData` property is used by Community Server to assign the `Telligent .DynamicConfiguration.Components.ConfigurationDataBase` object containing the configuration data set currently being edited.

The property control can use the `ConfigurationData` property to get configuration property values, load language resources, and retrieve default error messages.

Control

The `Control` property identifies the `System.Web.UI.Control` that implements the user interface of the property control. Community Server will render this control on the theme configuration form when the associated configuration property is editable.

SetConfigurationPropertyValue

The `SetConfigurationPropertyValue(object value)` method is called by Community Server to set the value displayed on the control property. This method is called when initially binding the control and is also called after property rules are executed to update the visible property value when changed by a rule.

GetConfigurationPropertyValue

The `GetConfigurationPropertyValue()` method is called by Community Server to retrieve the value of the associated configuration property from the property control. This value will be saved to the current configuration data store by Community Server.

ConfigurationValueChanged

The `ConfigurationValueChanged` event should be executed when the value of the property control is changed by the user.

When an event handler is registered to the `ConfigurationValueChanged` event, the property control should automatically post back and execute the `ConfigurationValueChanged` event when the property value is changed on the client side.

IPropertyValuesControl

The `Telligent.DynamicConfiguration.Components.IPropertyValuesControl` interface is used by Community Server to interact with property controls that support rendering selectable property values.

The `IPropertyValuesControl` interface is defined as:

```
using System;

namespace Telligent.DynamicConfiguration.Components
{
    public interface IPropertyValuesControl
    {
        void SetPropertyValues(PropertyValue[] values);
    }
}
```

This defines a single method: `SetPropertyValues`.

SetPropertyValues

The `SetPropertyValues(PropertyValue[] values)` method is called by Community Server to assign the selectable values that are configured in the theme's `theme.config` file for the property rendered by the control.

Implementing the RadioButtonListPropertyControl

The default control rendered for configuration properties that define selectable values is a dropdown list. For short lists of selectable values, however, a radio button list is sometimes desirable. A custom property control can easily be defined to render selectable options in a radio button list.

To begin, a new class can be added to a class library assembly. For the purposes of this example, the control will be named `ProfessionalThemes.RadioButtonListPropertyControl` in the `ProfessionalThemes.dll` class library assembly.

Because the `RadioButtonListPropertyControl` will be rendered as a `RadioButtonList`, the class inherits from `RadioButtonList`. Additionally, it implements the `IPropertyControl` and `IPropertyValuesControl` interfaces from the `Telligent.DynamicConfiguration.dll` assembly to identify that this class supports rendering configuration properties and supports rendering selectable values. Allowing Visual Studio to automatically implement the interfaces results in the following:

```
using System;
using System.Collections.Generic;
using System.Text;
using Telligent.DynamicConfiguration.Components;
using System.Web.UI.WebControls;

namespace ProfessionalThemes
{
    public class RadioButtonListPropertyControl : RadioButtonList,
IPropertyControl, IPropertyValuesControl
    {
        #region IPropertyControl Members

        ConfigurationDataBase IPropertyControl.ConfigurationData
        {
            get
            {
                throw new Exception("The method or operation is not
implemented.");
            }
            set
            {
                throw new Exception("The method or operation is not
implemented.");
            }
        }

        Property IPropertyControl.ConfigurationProperty
        {
```

```csharp
            get
            {
                throw new Exception("The method or operation is not
implemented.");
            }
            set
            {
                throw new Exception("The method or operation is not
implemented.");
            }
        }

        event ConfigurationPropertyChanged
IPropertyControl.ConfigurationValueChanged
        {
            add { throw new Exception("The method or operation is not
implemented."); }
            remove { throw new Exception("The method or operation is not
implemented."); }
        }

        System.Web.UI.Control IPropertyControl.Control
        {
            get { throw new Exception("The method or operation is not
implemented."); }
        }

        object IPropertyControl.GetConfigurationPropertyValue()
        {
            throw new Exception("The method or operation is not
implemented.");
        }

        void IPropertyControl.SetConfigurationPropertyValue(object value)
        {
            throw new Exception("The method or operation is not
implemented.");
        }

        #endregion

        #region IPropertyValuesControl Members

        void IPropertyValuesControl.SetPropertyValues(PropertyValue[] values)
        {
            throw new Exception("The method or operation is not
implemented.");
        }

        #endregion
    }
}
```

The `ConfigurationData` and `ConfigurationProperty` properties are simple get and set members that can be implemented as:

```
ConfigurationDataBase _configurationDataBase = null;
public ConfigurationDataBase ConfigurationData
{
    get { return _configurationDataBase; }
    set { _configurationDataBase = value; }
}

Property _configurationProperty = null;
public Property ConfigurationProperty
{
    get { return _configurationProperty; }
    set { _configurationProperty = value; }
}
```

This allows the control to use these properties elsewhere.

The next `IPropertyControl` member, the `ConfigurationValueChanged` event, is implemented to support registering event handlers, automatically setting the `RadioButtonList`'s `AutoPostBack` property to `true` when an event handler is added. For example,

```
public event ConfigurationPropertyChanged ConfigurationValueChanged
{
    add
    {
        base.Events.AddHandler(EventConfigurationValueChanged, value);
        this.AutoPostBack = true;
    }
    remove { base.Events.RemoveHandler(EventConfigurationValueChanged, value); }
}
private static readonly object EventConfigurationValueChanged = new object();

protected virtual void OnConfigurationValueChanged(object value)
{
    ConfigurationPropertyChanged handler =
(ConfigurationPropertyChanged)base.Events[EventConfigurationValueChanged];
    if (handler != null)
        handler(this, value);
}
```

This is a standard event implementation and should be familiar to ASP.NET control developers. The `OnConfigurationValueChanged` method will be wired into the `RadioButtonList` later.

The remaining `IPropertyControl` members can simply interact with the `RadioButtonList` control. For example,

```
public System.Web.UI.Control Control
{
    get { return this; }
}
```

```
public object GetConfigurationPropertyValue()
{
    return this.SelectedValue;
}


public void SetConfigurationPropertyValue(object value)
{
    if (value != null && this.Items.FindByValue(value.ToString()) != null)
        this.SelectedValue = value.ToString();
}
```

The Control property simply returns a reference to the current instance, since it is based on RadioButtonList and RadioButtonList is the Control that should be rendered on the configuration form. The GetConfigurationPropertyValue() and SetConfigurationPropertyValue(object value) methods get and set the existing SelectedValue property exposed by the RadioButtonList class.

The RadioButtonListPropertyControl also implements the IPropertyValuesControl interface, which allows it to render selectable property values. The SetPropertyValues(PropertyValue[] values) method populates the RadioButtonList.Items collection. For example,

```
public void SetPropertyValues(PropertyValue[] values)
{
    string currentValue = this.SelectedValue;

    this.Items.Clear();
    foreach (PropertyValue pv in values)
    {
        this.Items.Add(new
ListItem(this.ConfigurationData.GetResourceOrText(pv.ResourceName, pv.ResourceFile,
pv.Text), pv.Value));
    }

    if (this.Items.FindByValue(currentValue) != null)
        this.SelectedValue = currentValue;
}
```

This ensures that the rendered RadioButtonList displays all of the selectable options for the current property.

The OnConfigurationValueChanged(object value) method still needs to be wired into the RadioButtonList control using the following code:

```
protected override void OnInit(EventArgs e)
{
    base.OnInit(e);
    this.SelectedIndexChanged += new
EventHandler(RadioButtonListPropertyControl_SelectedIndexChanged);
}


void RadioButtonListPropertyControl_SelectedIndexChanged(object sender, EventArgs e)
{
    OnConfigurationValueChanged(this.SelectedValue);
}
```

This causes the `OnConfigurationValueChanged` method to be executed whenever the `RadioButtonList`
`.SelectedIndexChanged` event occurs.

To provide additional control over how the `RadioButtonList` is rendered within the configuration
form, support for the extended attribute `"columns"` is added to define the number of columns in which
to render selectable options. The value for the `"columns"` extended attribute can be retrieved from the
`ConfigurationProperty` property of the control, which is set to an instance of the property being
rendered. For example,

```
protected override void OnPreRender(EventArgs e)
{
    if (this.ConfigurationProperty != null &&
!string.IsNullOrEmpty(this.ConfigurationProperty.Attributes["columns"]))
    {
        this.RepeatColumns = int.Parse(this.ConfigurationProperty.Attributes["columns"]);
        this.RepeatLayout = RepeatLayout.Table;
        this.RepeatDirection = RepeatDirection.Horizontal;
    }

    base.OnPreRender(e);
}
```

If the `"columns"` attribute is defined on the property for which this property control is rendered, the
`RadioButtonList` will be rendered across the defined number of columns. If the `"columns"` attribute is
not defined, the `RadioButtonList` will render in its default format, a single vertical column.

After compiling the assembly in which this control is defined and deploying it into Community Server's
web/bin folder, the control can be referenced in a theme's `theme.config` file by specifying the
`controlType` attribute on a `property` node, such as:

```
<property id="layout" text="Layout" dataType="Int"
controlType="ProfessionalThemes.RadioButtonListPropertyControl,
ProfessionalThemes" columns="2">
  <propertyValue value="-1" text="Two columns, sidebar on left" />
  <propertyValue value="0" text="Three columns" />
  <propertyValue value="1" text="Two columns, sidebar on right" />
</property>
```

This will render the defined selectable values in two horizontal columns as shown in Figure 13-1.

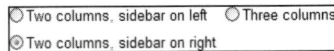

**Figure 13-1: Rendering a Property Using the
RadioButtonListPropertyControl**

Custom Property Rules

Community Server supports creating custom property rules implementing custom theme configuration logic. All custom property rules must implement the `Telligent.DynamicConfiguration.Components.IPropertyRule` interface, located within the `Telligent.DynamicConfiguration.dll` assembly.

IPropertyRule

The `Telligent.DynamicConfiguration.Components.IPropertyRule` interface is used by Community Server to interact with property rules.

The `IPropertyRule` interface is defined as:

```
using System;
using System.Xml;

namespace Telligent.DynamicConfiguration.Components
{
    public interface IPropertyRule
    {
        void ValueChanged(Property property, ConfigurationDataBase data);
        void LoadConfiguration(PropertyRule rule, XmlNode node);
    }
}
```

This defines two methods: `ValueChanged` and `LoadConfiguration`.

ValueChanged

The `ValueChanged(Property property, ConfigurationDataBase data)` method is called by Community Server when the value of the property in which the property rule is defined in the theme's `theme.config` file is changed. The changed property and the configuration data set containing the updated value are passed as parameters.

The rule's behavior should be initiated from this method call. The rule can get and set property values by interacting with the `ConfigurationDataBase` parameter. The rule should not call the `ConfigurationDataBase.Commit()` method, however, as Community Server will call it automatically after all rules have been processed.

LoadConfiguration

The `LoadConfiguration(PropertyRule rule, XmlNode node)` method is called when the rule is first instantiated as Community Server parses the theme's `theme.config` file. The rule is passed the `PropertyRule` object representing the `<propertyRule />` node in the `theme.config` file for which this property rule object was instantiated, allowing the rule to access configuration attributes specified on the `<propertyRule />` node. Additionally, the method is passed the `XmlNode` representing the `<propertyRule />` node, allowing the custom rule to parse any subnodes containing additional configuration data for the rule.

Implementing the AcceptableIntRangeRule

By default, the dynamic configuration support in Community Server does not implement configuration value range checking. A rule, however, can ensure that values are saved within acceptable ranges.

To begin, a new class can be added to a class library assembly. For the purposes of this example, the rule will be named `ProfessionalThemes.AcceptableIntRangeRule` in the `ProfessionalThemes.dll` class library assembly.

Because the `AcceptableIntRangeRule` is a rule, it implements the `IPropertyRule` interface from the `Telligent.DynamicConfiguration.dll` assembly. Allowing Visual Studio to automatically implement the interface results in the following code:

```
using System;
using System.Collections.Generic;
using System.Text;223
using Telligent.DynamicConfiguration.Components;

namespace ProfessionalThemes
{
    public class AcceptableIntRangeRule : IPropertyRule
    {
        #region IPropertyRule Members

        public void LoadConfiguration(PropertyRule rule, System.Xml.XmlNode node)
        {
            throw new Exception("The method or operation is not implemented.");
        }

        public void ValueChanged(Property property, ConfigurationDataBase data)
        {
            throw new Exception("The method or operation is not implemented.");
        }

        #endregion
    }
}
```

To support defining the acceptable range for the property's value, support for the extended attributes `"upperBound"` and `"lowerBound"` is added to the rule. These attribute values can be loaded within the `LoadConfiguration(PropertyRule rule, System.Xml.XmlNode node)` method as in:

```
private int _lowerBound = int.MinValue;
private int _upperBound = int.MaxValue;
public void LoadConfiguration(PropertyRule rule, System.Xml.XmlNode node)
{
    if (!string.IsNullOrEmpty(rule.Attributes["upperBound"]))
        _upperBound = int.Parse(rule.Attributes["upperBound"]);

    if (!string.IsNullOrEmpty(rule.Attributes["lowerBound"]))
        _lowerBound = int.Parse(rule.Attributes["lowerBound"]);
}
```

This loads the `"upperBound"` and `"lowerBound"` attributes from the `propertyRule` node in the theme's `theme.config` file. The values of these extended attributes are stored on the private instance fields `_lowerBound` and `_upperBound`, which default to supporting the full range of integer values.

The logic of the rule is implemented within the `ValueChanged(Property property, ConfigurationDataBase data)` method. In this method, the current value of the property is retrieved from the configuration data store and compared against the upper- and lower-bound values loaded from the `theme.config` file. For example,

```
public void ValueChanged(Property property, ConfigurationDataBase data)
{
    if (property.DataType != PropertyType.Int)
        return;

    int value = data.GetIntValue(property);
    if (value < _lowerBound)
        data.SetIntValue(property, _lowerBound);
    else if (value > _upperBound)
        data.SetIntValue(property, _upperBound);
}
```

This implements the range validation rule, automatically adjusting out-of-bounds values to the nearest in-range value. Note too, that this code also ensures that the property is of type `Int`, ensuring that the rule can be applied to the value of the property.

When this class is complied and the class library assembly is deployed to Community Server's `web/bin` folder, a theme's `theme.config` file can use the rule by adding a `propertyRule` node within a property node, such as:

```
<property id="numberOfColumns" text="Number of Columns (3 - 10)" dataType="Int"
defaultValue="5">
  <propertyRule type="ProfessionalThemes.AcceptableIntRangeRule,
ProfessionalThemes" lowerBound="3" upperBound="10" />
</property>
```

which would ensure that the `numberOfColumns` property's value is always within the range of 3 to 10.

Summary

Custom property controls and rules can be created and used to enhance the default dynamic configuration form that renders theme configuration options. Custom property controls can implement any user interface and must simply implement the `IPropertyControl interface`. Custom property rules implement automated behaviors when configuration data changes and must implement the `IPropertyRule` interface.

14

Creating a Custom Editor

In the previous chapter, you learned how to customize a theme using the theme configuration file. You will expand your knowledge of customizing a theme in this chapter by learning how to create a custom editor. The editor is a central component in a Community Server site, as it is what enables a user to create a post. After reading this chapter, you will be familiar with the following areas:

- ❏ Editor overview
- ❏ Existing editors
- ❏ Installing an editor
- ❏ Custom editor example

Editor Overview

The editor component of a Community Server site is nothing more than a "what you see is what you get" (WYSIWYG) editor. This type of an editor allows a user to see how a post is going to look before actually saving the post to the site. At the most basic level a Community Server editor must allow a user to type out the actual content of a post. For example, if a user types out the words "hello editor" inside of an editor and clicks the post button to save it to the server, then the text "hello editor" will be displayed when the user views the post.

A Community Server editor is not limited to only providing the basic input of text; it can also be used to insert more complex HTML elements. Even more, it also allows for complex objects to be inserted inside of a post. Basically, any text or items that you can insert into an HTML file can be created, using an editor. For example, you could even embed an MP3 player into a post with the click of an editor button.

All of the editors that are installed on a site are selectable in the Edit Profile page for a user. As a result, each user is able to select the editor that they would like to use throughout the site. Once they save their selection then whenever they make a blog post or forum post or any other main application post they are presented with the editor that they selected. This allows a site to target the different types of users who are posting to a site. For example, a site may have many members who are developers and others who are nontechnical users. The site could offer a custom editor just for the developers that allows them to post highlighted code samples. Meanwhile, the same site is capable of providing an editor for the nontechnical users without the advanced code choices.

Existing Editors

Out of the box Community Server ships with three levels of WYSIWYG editors. They are all selectable from the edit profile page under the Site Options tab. The available editors are listed below; however, it is important to realize that you can change the available editors.

❑ Plain Text

❑ Standard

❑ Enhanced

The Plain Text editor provides a very simple editor that will output any text you input into the editor to the screen. It is essentially an HTML editor without any buttons or code highlighting. For example if you want to insert bold text into your post using the Plain Text editor you would be forced to write `<b>Hello Bold Text</b>`.

The Standard editor actually offers several buttons that help control the presentation of a post. It includes a dropdown list for selecting a font family and font size. In addition, it is able to change any selected text using these buttons. The Standard editor is the default editor that is selected for all new users.

The Enhanced editor has all of the features that the Standard editor has along with a few more. One of the main additions is the ability to select the color for the text as well as the background. Furthermore, the Enhanced editor allows you to select the font family and size of your text.

The Standard and Enhanced editors both are a form of the tinyMCE editor. If you would like to change the buttons that are available in each of these editors, you can do so by altering the editor options in the `communityserver.config` file. For example, if you look at the editor's section in the `communityserver .config` file, you will find several `editorOption` entries that are used to alter the parent editor. The Standard editor has some of the following `editorOptions` defined.

```
<editorOption name="theme_advanced_statusbar_location" value="'bottom'" />
<editorOption name="theme_advanced_resize_horizontal" value="false" />
<editorOption name="plugins" value="'contentselector,smilies,iespell'" />
<editorOption name="theme_advanced_buttons1_add" value="'iespell'" />
```

If you change the `theme_advanced_resize_horizontal` value to be true, you would be able to resize the editor horizontally. The advanced resizing is enabled, and this allows the editor to be able to be resized. Many more options are available for the tinyMCE editor. If you are interested in learning about more of these options, you should consult the tinyMCE website at `http://tinymce.moxiecode.com`.

Custom Editor Example

In order to create an editor, you will need to implement the ITextEditor interface. This is found in the CommunityServer.Components namespace and project. This type is activated whenever your editor is loaded from the communityserver.config file. The following code shows what the ITextEditor interface looks like. In fact, the only difference between the code below and that found in Community Server is that the code below is missing comments.

```
public interface ITextEditor : System.Web.UI.ITextControl
{
    Unit Height { get; set;}

    Unit Width { get; set;}

    int Rows { get; set;}

    int Columns { get; set;}

    bool EnableHtmlModeEditing
    {
        get;
        set;
    }

    bool IsRichTextCapable
    {
        get;
    }

    bool IsSupported(System.Web.HttpBrowserCapabilities browser);

    string GetContentScript();

    string GetBookmarkScript();

    string GetContentInsertScript(string contentVariableName);

    string GetContentUpdateScript(string contentVariableName);

    string GetFocusScript();

    void ApplyConfigurationOption(string name, string value);
}
```

The ITextEditor expects several methods that are used to return JavaScript code that do such things as return the content inside of the editor or focus the editor. In the Plain Text editor, the scripts are returned from an included JavaScript file. You do not need to do this; as you will see in the example below, you can write the script inline.

One thing to note is that the IsSupported method determines if the editor will work correctly in the current browser. The browser is passed in from the Request object and is the browser of the accessing user. If you would like to explicitly make certain browsers not be able to load your editor, you can do so inside this method by returning `false`. In the next example, all browsers are supported except for the AOL browser.

In the following example, you will create an editor that allows a user to recover any text that was lost from closing the browser or accidentally hitting the Back button. This is useful because it means that users don't have to worry about saving their posts before they are complete. Instead, if something should happen to the browser while a user is writing a post, he or she can simply return to the same create post page and recover the contents of the post, using the editor.

For this recovery feature to work, the example will store the value of the editor inside of a cookie each time the user presses a key while the editor has focus. This means that every letter will be remembered inside of a cookie. As a result, the value of the editor is able to stay on the clients machine for a specific amount of time or until the user decides to clear the cookies. You will notice that, by default, the cookie is set to expire after 24 hours, which should be more than adequate for returning to a post and recovering its contents.

To begin creating this editor, you should create a new class library project in Visual Studio and call it `CS.Custom.Editors`. Once you have the project created you can create a new class and name it `ForgetItNotEditor`, which is the name of the custom editor. After you have the class created, you can add the following code to it. You should notice that the class implements `ITextEditor` as well as inherits from `TextBox`. The `TextBox` was added so that it is easier to access some of the page-level events.

```
using System;
using System.Text;
using System.Web.UI.WebControls;
using CommunityServer.Controls;

namespace CS.Custom.Editors
{
    public class ForgetItNotEditor : System.Web.UI.WebControls.TextBox,
        ITextEditor
    {

        const string OnKeyDownAttribute = "return KeyDownHandler{0}();";

        public ForgetItNotEditor() : base() {  }

        public void Configure()
        {
            if (this.Height == Unit.Empty)
                this.Style["height"] = "250px;";

            if (this.Width == Unit.Empty)
                this.Style["width"] = "95%";

            this.TextMode = TextBoxMode.MultiLine;
        }

        protected override void OnLoad(EventArgs e)
        {
            base.OnLoad(e);
            this.Configure();
        }
```

```
protected override void Render(System.Web.UI.HtmlTextWriter writer)
{
    base.Render(writer);
    System.Web.UI.LiteralControl lit = new
            System.Web.UI.LiteralControl("<input type=\"button\"
            name=\"recoverContentButton\" onClick=\"RecoverContent()\"
            value=\"Recover\" />");
    lit.RenderControl(writer);
}

protected override void OnPreRender(EventArgs e)
{
    base.OnPreRender(e);
    RegisterContentScripts();
    this.Attributes.Add("onkeydown", string.Format(OnKeyDownAttribute,
            this.ClientID));
}

protected void RegisterContentScripts()
{
    StringBuilder sb = new StringBuilder();
    sb.Append("<script type=\"text/javascript\">\n");
    sb.Append("<!--\n");

    sb.Append("function RecoverContent()\n");
    sb.Append("{\n");
    sb.Append(string.Format("var editor =
            document.getElementById('{0}');\n", this.ClientID));
    sb.Append("var start =
            document.cookie.indexOf(\"editPost=\");\n");
    sb.Append("if (start == -1) return; \n");
    sb.Append("start = start+9;\n");
    sb.Append("var end = document.cookie.indexOf(\";\", start);\n");
    sb.Append("editor.value =
            decodeURIComponent(document.cookie.substring(start,
            end));\n");
    sb.Append("}\n");
    sb.Append("\n");

    sb.Append("function KeyDownHandler");
    sb.Append(this.ClientID);
    sb.Append("()\n");
    sb.Append("{\n");
    sb.Append("var day = new Date();\n");
    sb.Append("day.setDate(day.getDate()+1);\n");
    sb.Append(string.Format("var editor =
            document.getElementById('{0}');\n", this.ClientID));
    sb.Append("document.cookie = \"editPost=\" +
            encodeURIComponent(editor.value) + \" ; max-age=\" +
            (60*60*24) + \"; expires=\" + day.toGMTString();\n");
    sb.Append("}\n");
    sb.Append("\n");

    sb.Append("//-->\n");
    sb.Append("</script>\n");
```

```csharp
        CSControlUtility.Instance().RegisterClientScriptBlock(this,
                typeof(ForgetItNotEditor), this.ClientID, sb.ToString(),
                false);
}

#region ITextEditor Members

public void ApplyConfigurationOption(string name, string value)
{

}

private bool _enableHtmlModeEditing = true;
public bool EnableHtmlModeEditing
{
    get
    {
        return _enableHtmlModeEditing;
    }
    set
    {
        _enableHtmlModeEditing = value;
    }
}

public string GetBookmarkScript()
{
    return "";
}

public string GetContentInsertScript(string contentVariableName)
{
    return string.Format("document.getElementById({0}).value += {1};",
            this.ClientID, contentVariableName);
}

public string GetContentScript()
{
    return string.Format("return document.getElementById({0}).value;",
            this.ClientID);
}

public string GetContentUpdateScript(string contentVariableName)
{
    return string.Format("document.getElementById({0}).value = {1};",
            this.ClientID, contentVariableName);
}

public string GetFocusScript()
{
    return string.Format("document.getElementById({0}).focus();",
            this.ClientID);
}
```

```
public bool IsRichTextCapable
{
    get { return false; }
}

public bool IsSupported(System.Web.HttpBrowserCapabilities browser)
{
    return !browser.AOL;
}

Unit ITextEditor.Height
{
    get
    {
        return Unit.Parse(this.Style["height"]);
    }
    set
    {
        this.Style["height"] = value.ToString();
    }
}

Unit ITextEditor.Width
{
    get
    {
        return Unit.Parse(this.Style["width"]);
    }
    set
    {
        this.Style["width"] = value.ToString();
    }
}

#endregion

    }
}
```

Notice in the above code that all of the JavaScript is declared inline. One thing that you can do to make this process easier is to simply reference the JavaScript in an included resource file. For an example of this, you can consult the default text editor or Plain Text editor. Another solution is to create the JavaScript externally and then include it line by line, as was done in this example.

After you are done adding the above code, you should try compiling your project to make sure that everything was added correctly. Remember to add the references for the CommunityServer.Components assembly. After you have compiled the assembly, you should copy it to your site's bin directory. Once this is done, the only thing left to do is to install it. Please consult the next section on installing a new editor, as it demonstrates how to install this particular editor.

Once the ForgetItNot editor is installed and running, you should see an option to select it from the Site Options tab of the Edit Profile page. On this tab, there is a new entry for the editor that looks like Figure 14-1. After you select the new editor and save the changes to your profile, you will be able to use it whenever you create or edit a post.

Content Editor		Forget It Not	▼

Figure 14-1: New Editor Option in Edit Profile

The Forget It Not editor works by recording the value of the editor, or the text that the user enters, after every keystroke. It records this value to a cookie that lasts for a day and that is called `editPost`. The `editPost` cookie has the potential to be used by other users on the same machine; therefore, this approach is not a great one for users who are on a shared workstation. Whenever the user would like to recover text that was stored, he or she simply presses the Recover button. This action copies the contents of the cookie into the editor. All of these actions occur on the client side in the JavaScript that was created from the editor component.

After you have installed the editor and selected it, you will see an editor that is very similar to the Plain Text editor. The main difference is the Recover button, which is wired up to copy contents from the `editPost` cookie into the editor whenever it is clicked. The Forget It Not editor looks like the message area of Figure 14-2.

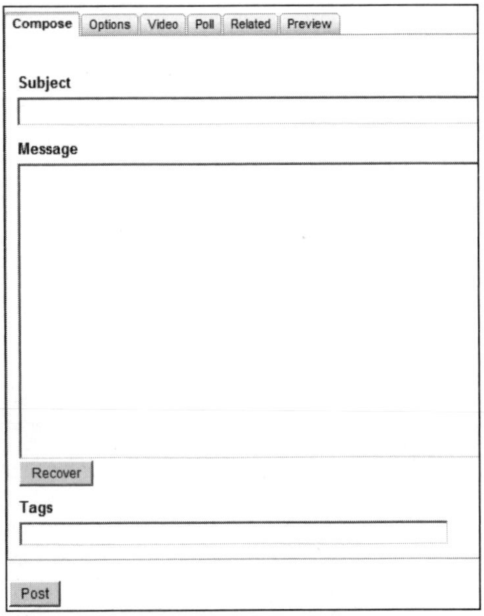

Figure 14-2: Rendered Forget It Not Editor

Whenever the Forget It Not editor is selected and you make a new post, you will see the JavaScript in the source code for the post creation page. The code that is in the `RegisterContentScripts` method will be rendered to the page as the code shown below. As you can see, the `ClientID` is populated along with the code to read the value of the cookie:

```
<SCRIPT type=text/javascript>
<!--
function RecoverContent()
{
var editor =
```

```
document.getElementById('ctl00_ctl00_bcr_bcr_PostForm_ctl04_PostBody_ctl00_Editor');
var start = document.cookie.indexOf("editPost=");
if (start == -1) return;
start = start+9;
var end = document.cookie.indexOf(";", start);
editor.value = decodeURIComponent(document.cookie.substring(start, end));
}


function KeyDownHandlerctl00_ctl00_bcr_bcr_PostForm_ctl04_PostBody_ctl00_Editor()
{
var day = new Date();
day.setDate(day.getDate()+1);
var editor =
document.getElementById('ctl00_ctl00_bcr_bcr_PostForm_ctl04_PostBody_ctl00_Editor');
document.cookie = "editPost=" + encodeURIComponent(editor.value) + " ; max-age=" +
(60*60*24) + "; expires=" + day.toGMTString();
}


//-->
</SCRIPT>
```

To see the editor in action you should enter some text into it. After you do this, you can close the browser window and then open it again. After the browser is open, again browse to a page where you can create a post and click the Recover button. The contents of your original message should now be the value of the editor.

If you have inserted the text that is shown in Figure 14-3, the value of your cookie will be the value of the text.

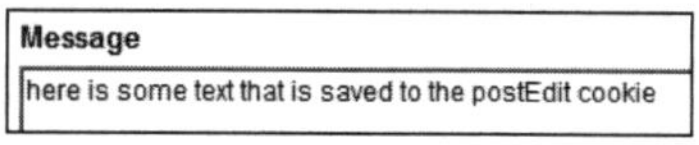

Message
here is some text that is saved to the postEdit cookie

Figure 14-3: Forget It Not Editor with Text

Whenever you look at the value of the `editPost` cookie after entering the above text, you will see something similar to Figure 14-4. You will notice that the JavaScript call to `encodeURIComponent` results in the value of the `editPost` being encoded. As a result, you are able to type HTML code into the editor and have it encoded properly for easy retrieval. You will also notice that the cookie is set to expire in a day from the time that the last letter was entered into the editor. This information can also be useful for reporting, as it gives you an accurate time of when your post was created on the client. You could extend this cookie to also store a timestamp of when a user begins to create a post. Because of this information, you would have a time span of how long it takes to create a post. Even more, you also have the length of the post, or the number of characters, so that you could calculate the time it takes to type each letter.

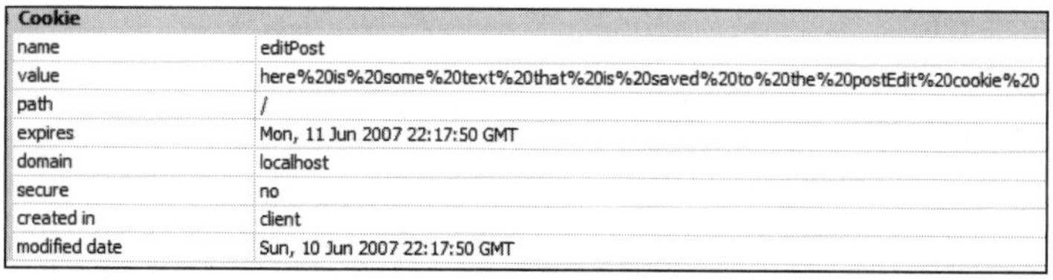

Cookie	
name	editPost
value	here%20is%20some%20text%20that%20is%20saved%20to%20the%20postEdit%20cookie%20
path	/
expires	Mon, 11 Jun 2007 22:17:50 GMT
domain	localhost
secure	no
created in	client
modified date	Sun, 10 Jun 2007 22:17:50 GMT

Figure 14-4: editPost Cookie Value

Installing an Editor

Community Server makes it rather easy to install an editor. You only need to alter a single configuration file and copy the editor assembly into the `bin` folder. Start by copying the editor assembly file into the `bin` folder of your site. After this is done, open the `communityserver.config` file with an editor.

With the `communityserver.config` file open, navigate to the `editors` node. Inside this node, you will find a few child editor nodes. Each of the editor nodes represents a different selectable editor in your site. To install the Forget It Not editor that was created in the previous example, you simply need to add the following line of code:

```
<editor name="Forget It Not" type="CS.Custom.Editors.ForgetItNotEditor,
    CS.Custom.Editors " />
```

The editor node requires a name as well as a type be supplied. The type is made up of the namespace to your editor as well as the assembly that it is contained in. The type will be used to activate your editor object whenever it is in use. The name is the text that will be displayed from the selection dropdown list inside the Edit Profile page. This is the name that users will associate with your editor, in this situation it will be Forget It Not.

After you have added the editor node, you can optionally add any child `editorOption` nodes to your editor. This is useful if your editor has configurable options, such as hiding or showing certain buttons. In this example, there are not any extra options, so you should simply save the `communityserver.config` file. Once the file is saved, you may need to touch the `web.config` file to reload the Community Server configuration settings.

Summary

In this chapter, you learned how you cannot only configure existing editors in a Community Server site but also how you can add your own custom editors. Now you should see that creating a custom editor in Community Server is actually quite forward and only requires that you implement the `ITextEditor` interface.

In the next chapter, you will learn about another component you can customize and create called the browseable list. The browseable list is a button that is visible in the tinyMCE editors that exist in Community Server and allow you to extend the power of your editors.

15

Creating a Custom Browseable List

In the previous chapter, you learned how to create a custom editor that you can use with Community Server. In this chapter, you will learn about another area of Community Server that you can customize called a *browseable list*. This is not a well-known feature, but one that is extremely powerful. By the end of this chapter, you should feel comfortable with the following topics regarding a browseable list:

- ❑ Browseable list overview
- ❑ Existing browseable lists
- ❑ Installing a browseable list
- ❑ Custom browseable list example

Browseable List Overview

Browseable lists allow a user to choose from different types of items and have them added to a post. For example, if you want to add a photo from the photo gallery inside of a blog post, you can do so using a browseable list. Simply select the photo from the browseable list modal whenever you are creating the blog post. Likewise, you can essentially make any type of content that can be rendered on the web into a selectable list that is usable while editing a post.

The browseable list feature of Community Server is found in the default editor whenever you are creating or editing a post. The icon that gives access to the browseable list functionality is shown in Figure 15-1. One thing to notice is that you will want to have the Enhanced editor enabled for your profile in order to see this icon. You can do this by editing your profile and changing the editor selection in the Site Options tab.

Figure 15-1: Browseable List Selector Icon on Default Editor

Existing Browseable Lists

Community Server ships with four different browseable lists. Each one is available for adding application-specific files to a post. In addition to the application-specific file type browseable lists, there is one available for sitewide files. This means that a community can potentially have shared files that members can insert into their posts. Below is the list of these different types of default browseable lists that are available.

❑   WeblogFiles

❑   FileGallery

❑   Gallery

❑   SiteFiles

Each of these browseable lists shows only the content that the user can access. This means that a system administrator will see more files than an anonymous user can with the default settings. This is important as you may need to add view permissions to the role that you want to be able to access certain content. For example, if you want to make a picture accessible in the gallery browseable list so that anyone can use it, then you will need to make sure that everyone can view the picture. This can be done in the permissions grid on a specific gallery.

Installing a Browseable List

Installing a browseable list is just as easy as installing a Community Server module. You only need to edit a single configuration file. Aside from editing the configuration file, you need to have the assembly containing the browseable list you want to install inside of your site's `bin` folder.

Inside the `communityserver.config` file in your web site, you will find the following `BrowseableLists` section. This is the only section that you will need to edit to install or uninstall a browseable list. If you are interested in uninstalling an existing list, you can simply remove it from the `BrowseableLists` section.

```
<BrowseableLists>
    <add type = "CommunityServer.Blogs.Providers.WeblogFilesBrowseableList,
        CommunityServer.Blogs" />
    <add type = "CommunityServer.Files.Providers.FileGalleryBrowseableList,
        CommunityServer.Files" />
    <add type = "CommunityServer.Galleries.Providers.GalleryBrowseableList,
        CommunityServer.Galleries" />
    <add type ="CommunityServer.Components.Providers.SiteFilesBrowseableList,
        CommunityServer.Components" />
</BrowseableLists>
```

In the `BrowseableLists` section, you find that there is a collection of qualified types that point to a class that is of type `IBrowseableList`. To help explain how the type is value is found, consider the following example. Assume that you want to install a browseable list called `BlogTemplatesBrowseableList` that is contained in the assembly `CS.BrowseableLists` under the namespace `CS.BrowseableLists`, then you can use the following `BrowseableList` entry in your `communityserver.config` file:

```
<add type="CS.BrowseableLists.BlogTemplateBrowseableList,
    CS.BrowseableLists" />
```

In order for this to work, the `CS.BrowseableLists` assembly needs to be accessible in the `bin` folder of the website where this entry was added. In addition, you will need to touch (change the modified date stamp) the `web.config` file to force the application to reload the configuration settings found in the `communityserver.config` file. Therefore, if you do not see your browseable list after installing it into the `communityserver.config`, you may want to double-check that you also touched the `web.config`.

Custom Browseable List Example

There are three types that you must create in order for your browseable list to work correctly. The three types are the `IBrowseableList`, `IBrowseableListContainer`, and `IBrowseableListItem`. Each one of these interfaces needs to be implemented in order for your browseable list to work correctly. Below you will see an example of how you could implement each of these interfaces.

The `IBrowseableList` is an interface that you should implement that can contain multiple containers. The class that you implement `IBrowseableList` will be the type that you define in the `communityserver.config` `BrowseableLists` collection. The `IBrowseableList` interface contains the following members that you must implement.

```
string Name { get;}
List<IBrowseableListContainer> Containers { get; }
object GetNode(string listKey);
StringCollection GetPathToNode(string listKey);
bool Enabled { get; }
```

The `Containers` property should contain a collection of `IBrowseableListContainer` types. These containers are the folder-like elements that are displayed on the left side of the browseable list. In the default browseable list weblog files that ship with Community Server, they are actually the folders that contain the different files. You will see an example of how the various members can be implemented below.

The `IBrowseableListContainer` interface must contain the following members:

```
string ID { get; }
string Name { get; }
List<IBrowseableListItem> Items { get; }
List<IBrowseableListContainer> Containers { get; }
void CreateConfigurationControls(System.Web.UI.Control control,
        IBrowseableListItemSelector selector);
void DataBindConfigurationControls();
```

As you can see, the list container can not only contain child browseable list items but also child browseable list containers. This allows a hierarchy of containers to exist, much like a normal folder structure.

The `IBroseableListItem` interface must contain the following members:

```
string ID { get; }
string Name { get; }
string PreviewHTML { get; }
string RenderHTML { get; }
string RenderURL { get; }
```

The `IBrowseableListItem` is the most basic element in the browseable list family. It simply represents an item that when selected will render specific HTML code. The `PreviewHTML` element is nice because it allows you to create an abbreviated version of the completely rendered code. Below you will see a couple of examples of possible `IBrowseableListItem` objects.

Now that you have a basic idea of what the different types are that make up the browseable lists, you should try out the following example to see them in action. The example is simply going to offer a couple of blog templates that set the background color for a post along with a custom table. This can be useful if you want to adhere to a specific presentation in your posts.

You can begin by creating a new class inside of a project. In this example, the class file is called `BlogTemplatesBrowseableList`. If you do not have a project in place to store your browseable lists, you may want to create a class library project to hold your different browseable lists. In the following example, the class library project is called `CS.BrowseableLists`.

In order for the following code example to work, you will need to make sure that you have the appropriate references set up and the following `using` statements at the beginning of your new class file:

```
using System;
using System.Collections.Generic;
using System.Web;
using CommunityServer.Components;
using CommunityServer.Blogs.Components;
```

Once you have the `using` statements in place, you will want to add the following code to the `BlogTemplatesBrowseableList.cs` file in your `BrowseableLists` project:

```
namespace CS.BrowseableLists
{
    public class BlogTemplatesBrowseableList : IBrowseableList
    {
        #region IBrowseableList Members

        public List<IBrowseableListContainer> Containers
        {
            get
            {
                List<IBrowseableListContainer> containers = new
                    List<IBrowseableListContainer>();
                containers.Add(new BlogTemplatesBrowseableListContainer(
                    GetCurrentBlog()));
```

```csharp
            return containers;
        }
    }

    public bool Enabled
    {
        get { return true; }
    }

    public object GetNode(string listKey)
    {
        string[] keyComponents = listKey.Split(new char[] { ':' }, 3);
        if (keyComponents.Length != 3)
            return null;

        Weblog blog = Weblogs.GetWeblog(int.Parse(keyComponents[2]));
        switch (keyComponents[0])
        {
            case "C":
                return new BlogTemplatesBrowseableListContainer(blog);

            case "I":
                if (keyComponents[1].Equals("Grey"))
                    return new BlogGreyTemplateBrowseableListItem(blog);
                else if (keyComponents[1].Equals("Blue"))
                    return new BlogBlueTemplateBrowseableListItem(blog);

                return new BlogGreyTemplateBrowseableListItem(blog);
        }

        return null;
    }

    public System.Collections.Specialized.StringCollection
            GetPathToNode(string listKey)
    {
        return null;
    }

    public string Name
    {
        get { return "Blog Templates"; }
    }

    #endregion

    public static Weblog GetCurrentBlog()
    {
        Weblog blog = null;
        CSContext csContext = CSContext.Current;

        if (csContext.SectionID > 0)
        {
```

```
                try
                {
                    blog = Weblogs.GetWeblog(csContext.SectionID);
                }
                catch { }
            }

            if (blog == null &&
                    !string.IsNullOrEmpty(csContext.ApplicationKey))
            {
                try
                {
                    blog = Weblogs.GetWeblog(csContext.ApplicationKey);
                }
                catch { }
            }

            if (blog == null)
            {
                try
                {
                    string cookieName = string.Format("{0}_{1}_{2}",
                        csContext.SettingsID, csContext.User.Username,
                        "weblog");
                    HttpCookie cookie =
                        csContext.Context.Request.Cookies[cookieName];
                    if (cookie != null)
                    {
                        if (!Globals.IsNullorEmpty(cookie.Values["BlogID"]))
                            blog =
                                Weblogs.GetWeblog(Int32.Parse(
                                cookie.Values["BlogID"]), true, false);
                    }
                }
                catch { }
            }

            return blog;
        }
    }

    public class BlogTemplatesBrowseableListContainer :
            IBrowseableListContainer
    {
        Weblog _blog = null;

        public BlogTemplatesBrowseableListContainer(Weblog blog)
        {
            _blog = blog;
        }

        #region IBrowseableListContainer Members
```

```csharp
        public List<IBrowseableListContainer> Containers
        {
            get { return null; }
        }

        public void CreateConfigurationControls(System.Web.UI.Control control,
                IBrowseableListItemSelector selector)
        {

        }

        public void DataBindConfigurationControls()
        {

        }

        public string ID
        {
            get { return string.Format("C:BlogTemplate:{0}", _blog.SectionID); }
        }

        public List<IBrowseableListItem> Items
        {
            get
            {
                List<IBrowseableListItem> items = new
                        List<IBrowseableListItem>();
                items.Add(new BlogGreyTemplateBrowseableListItem(_blog));
                items.Add(new BlogBlueTemplateBrowseableListItem(_blog));

                return items;
            }
        }

        public string Name
        {
            get { return "Template Container"; }
        }

        #endregion
    }

    public class BlogGreyTemplateBrowseableListItem : IBrowseableListItem
    {
        Weblog _blog = null;

        public BlogGreyTemplateBrowseableListItem(Weblog blog)
        {
            _blog = blog;
        }

        #region IBrowseableListItem Members
```

```csharp
        public string ID
        {
            get { return string.Format("I:Grey:{0}", _blog.SectionID); }
        }

        public string Name
        {
            get { return "Grey"; }
        }

        public string PreviewHTML
        {
            get { return "<table bgcolor='#ECECEC'><tr><td>Grey</td></tr></table>"; }
        }

        public string RenderHTML
        {
            get { return "<table cellpadding='40px'
                    bgcolor='#ECECEC'><tr><td>Grey</td></tr></table>"; }
        }

        public string RenderURL
        {
            get { return null; }
        }

        #endregion
}


public class BlogBlueTemplateBrowseableListItem : IBrowseableListItem
{
    Weblog _blog = null;

    public BlogBlueTemplateBrowseableListItem(Weblog blog)
    {
        _blog = blog;
    }

    #region IBrowseableListItem Members

    public string ID
    {
        get { return string.Format("I:Blue:{0}", _blog.SectionID); }
    }

    public string Name
    {
        get { return "Blue"; }
    }

    public string PreviewHTML
    {
```

```
        get { return "<table
            bgcolor='#6497C4'><tr><td>Blue</td></tr></table>"; }
    }

    public string RenderHTML
    {
        get { return "<table cellpadding='40px'
            bgcolor='#6497C4'><tr><td>Blue</td></tr></table>"; }
    }

    public string RenderURL
    {
        get { return null; }
    }

    #endregion
    }
}
```

As a result of the above code, you will be presented with a couple of options for selecting a blog template. The options are shown in Figure 15-2 and are a result of the `PreviewHTML` property on each of the `BrowseableListItem` objects. In addition to the `PreviewHTML` property, the name of the browseable list item is displayed below the selectable item, which is controlled by the `Name` property. Also, it is important to realize that the `RenderHTML` property is the code that will actually be inserted into the post, which can be different than what is displayed in the preview.

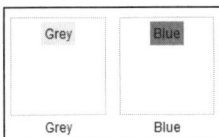

Figure 15-2: Browseable List Item Rendered Preview Example

Whenever the `BlogTemplatesBrowseableList` is rendered in the browseable list selector a new tab is created with the name of the browseable list. Therefore, the name of the tab is Blog Templates, as specified in the `Name` property. This is shown in Figure 15-3.

Figure 15-3: Blog Templates Browseable List Selector Tab

As mentioned previously, the container is displayed in a folder type fashion on the left-hand side of the browseable list modal. This structure allows for child containers to be presented as though they are child folders. As a result, this type of organization is not only common to most users but also very straightforward for finding items. See Figure 15-4.

Figure 15-4: Browseable List Container Display

There are many other possibilities for a browseable list than simply offering a template. For example, Scott Watermasysk has created a custom browseable list that allows you to insert pictures from a flickr account into a post. You can obtain this browseable list from the downloads section of http://communityserver.org. There are many possibilities, as in the flickr example, to allow users to easily access items contained in other applications.

Summary

In this chapter, you learned about some of the power and flexibility that is available with browseable lists. You learned about the existing browseable lists as well as how to access them. In the code example, you learned how it is possible to create a custom post template with a browseable list. Furthermore, you learned how you could go about installing new browseable lists.

SiteUrls.config Reference

Node Structure

The following list shows the nodes and child nodes in a `SiteUrls.config` file. You will notice that the children nodes are spaced further to the right and the parent nodes are aligned to the left.

> **locations**
>> **location**
>>> **url**
>
> **transformers**
>
> **navigation**
>> **link**

Node Attributes

The locations node can contain the following attributes:

❑ **type** — The default type is `CommunityServer.Components.CSLocation`.

The location node can contain the following attributes:

❑ **type** — If no type is specified, the `Location` object will be used by default. The `Location` object can be found in the `CommunityServer.Components` project and namespace. In Community Server 2007, the `CSLocation` is specified as the type to use.

❑ **name** — The unique name that describes the location entry. You should make sure that all of your location elements have a name attribute; otherwise they will not be loaded correctly.

❑ **path** — The path to the folder where the pages to be controlled are located. This path should begin and end with a forward slash. The path element is required just like the name element is; therefore, you should make sure to include this.

❑ **physicalPath** — This is similar to path; you should surround it with a forward slash. This is not a required element, and if you do not include it,then the path will be stored as physicalPath in the Location object.

❑ **exclude** — A Boolean value indicating whether a path should be included in URL rewriting.

❑ **themeDir** — The theme directory where the pages for the location will be rewritten to. This value will be transformed to /themes/default/themeDir/. In this example, default is the name of your theme and themeDir is the value you put into the themeDir attribute of the location node.

The url node can contain the following attributes:

❑ **name** — Unique name to identify the url entry.

❑ **path** — The path to the original page that the request comes in on. This can be used to indicate any special query string values that are used with the incoming request.

❑ **pattern** — The pattern to match to identify that the requested URL maps to the url entry. If the pattern does not begin with a forward slash, then the path will be prepended to the pattern to get the full path. The pattern can be a regular expression, as the eventual pattern will be matched using a regular expression to indicate that the page begins with the provided pattern.

❑ **physicalPath** — The path where the page that will be rewritten to is located. In most situations, this is going to be found in the theme directory; therefore, the transformer ##themeDir## is used.

❑ **vanity** — Specifies any extra query string or page changes that you want to include when the url is rewritten. The vanity can include string.Format placeholders, since this is applied to it. The value for {0} will be the Theme page name, {1} is the theme directory, and {2} is the page name specified in the page attribute.

❑ **page** — The page that should be rewritten to. For example, if you specify Test.aspx, this will be the page that will be loaded when a request is made for a page with the related url pattern.

❑ **redirect** — A Booelan value indicating if the request should be redirected to the new page. If this is true then a 301 status code will be sent to the client.

❑ **navigateUrl** — Used in conjunction with only a name attribute to specify a direct URL. This is intended to be the full URL that is associated with the url name. If you supply this attribute, all other attributes will be ignored and the url name will be mapped to this specific URL.

The link node can contain the following attributes:

❑ **name** — A descriptive name or key for a given link entry.

❑ **resourceUrl** — The name of a url entry in the SiteUrls.config that should be used to create the URL to link to.

❏ **resourceName** — The name of a `resources.xml` entry to use for the text that will be displayed in for the link. This is useful for international sites where you have a different language and local than the default en-US local.

❏ **navigateUrl** — If you want to supply a full URL that is not provided in your `SiteUrls.config`, then you can do so with this attribute.

❏ **text** — The text to display for the link when you choose not to use a resource entry.

❏ **roles** — A comma-delimited list of roles to display the link to. If none is supplied, then the default role becomes Everyone.

❏ **target** — Used like a standard target in an anchor tag. This can be used to open a link in a new window or in a specific window.

❏ **type** — If you would like to use a custom link type other than the CSLink object, you can do so with this attribute.

❏ **applicationType** — The application that your link belongs to so that when the application is currently being accessed the navigation link for that application can show that the application link is selected.

SiteUrls.config Examples

```
<locations type ="CommunityServer.Components.CSLocation,
    CommunityServer.Components">
  <location name="themes" path="/themes/" exclude = "true" />

  <location name="message" path="/msgs/" themeDir="msgs">
    <url name="message"  path="default.aspx?MessageID={0}"
        pattern="default.aspx" physicalPath="##themeDir##" vanity="{2}"
        page="message.aspx" />
    <url name="message_modal" path="modalmessage.aspx?MessageID={0}"
        pattern="modalmessage.aspx" physicalPath="##themeDir##" vanity="{2}"
        page="modalmessage.aspx" />
  </location>
</locations>
```

```
<transformers>
  <add key = "^" value = "&amp;" />
  <add key = "##themeDir##" value = "/themes/{0}/{1}/" />
  <add key = "##blogthemeDir##" value = "/themes/blogs/{0}/" />
  <add key = "##blogdirectory##" value = "{0}/" />
</transformers>
```

```
<navigation>
  <link name="home" resourceUrl="home" resourceName="home" roles="Everyone" />
  <link name="blog" resourceUrl="webloghome" resourceName="weblogs"
      roles="Everyone" applicationType = "Weblog" />
  <link name="forums" resourceUrl="forumshome" resourceName="forums"
      roles="Everyone" applicationType = "Forum" />
</navigation>
```

B

Chameleon Controls — Common

This appendix includes a list of controls that exist in the `CommunityServer.Controls` assembly and also lists the properties of the related Community Server API objects.

Common Controls

The following table lists controls within the `CommunityServer.Controls` assembly. All of the controls use the "CSControl" tag prefix. For more information about the specific properties of each control, see Chapter 5 or consult the Chameleon Control Documentation.

Control Name	Control Type
`<CSControl:AcceptInvitationForm />`	Form
`<CSControl:Actions />`	Action
`<CSControl:AdPart />`	Single Value
`<CSControl:ApplicationData />`	Single Value
`<CSControl:ApplicationPropertyComparison />`	Condition
`<CSControl:ApplicationPropertyValueComparison />`	Condition
`<CSControl:BaseTagCloud />`	Single Value

Continued

Control Name	Control Type
`<CSControl:ButtonActionForm />`	Form
`<CSControl:CallbackPager />`	Pager
`<CSControl:ChangePasswordForm />`	Form
`<CSControl:ClearAndDataBindRepeaterAction />`	Action
`<CSControl:ConditionalAction />`	Utility
`<CSControl:ConditionalContent />`	Single Value
`<CSControl:Conditions />`	Condition
`<CSControl:ContentData />`	Single Value
`<CSControl:ContentPart />`	Single Value
`<CSControl:ControlVisibilityCondition />`	Condition
`<CSControl:CreateEditContentForm />`	Form
`<CSControl:CreateUserForm />`	Form
`<CSControl:CSButton />`	Utility
`<CSControl:CSConfigurationData />`	Single Value
`<CSControl:CSConfigurationPropertyComparison />`	Condition
`<CSControl:CSConfigurationPropertyValueComparison />`	Condition
`<CSControl:CSConfirmationPage />`	Utility
`<CSControl:CSLabel />`	Utility
`<CSControl:CSLinkButton />`	Utility
`<CSControl:CSLinkData />`	Single Value
`<CSControl:CSLinkPropertyComparison />`	Condition
`<CSControl:CSLinkPropertyValueComparison />`	Condition
`<CSControl:CSLiteral />`	Utility

Control Name	Control Type
`<CSControl:CSThemePage />`	Utility
`<CSControl:CurrentSiteUrlCondition />`	Condition
`<CSControl:CurrentUserIsAccessingUserCondition />`	Condition
`<CSControl:CustomAction />`	Action
`<CSControl:CustomCondition />`	Condition
`<CSControl:DefaultButtonTextBox />`	Utility
`<CSControl:DefaultTextEditor />`	Utility
`<CSControl:DelayedContent />`	Single Value
`<CSControl:DeleteFavoritePostsForm />`	Form
`<CSControl:DeleteFavoriteSectionsForm />`	Form
`<CSControl:DeleteFavoriteUsersForm />`	Form
`<CSControl:Editor />`	Single Value
`<CSControl:EditorOption />`	Utility
`<CSControl:EditorOptions />`	Utility
`<CSControl:EditUserForm />`	Form
`<CSControl:ExecuteScriptAction />`	Action
`<CSControl:FavoritePopupMenu />`	Single Value
`<CSControl:FavoriteToggleButton />`	Single Value
`<CSControl:ForgottenPasswordForm />`	Form
`<CSControl:FormLabel />`	Single Value
`<CSControl:GoToCurrentContentAction />`	Action
`<CSControl:GoToCurrentPostAction />`	Action
`<CSControl:GoToModifiedUrlAction />`	Action

Continued

Control Name	Control Type
`<CSControl:GoToReferralUrlAction />`	Action
`<CSControl:GoToSiteUrlAction />`	Action
`<CSControl:GroupCollapsableArea />`	Single Value
`<CSControl:GroupData />`	Single Value
`<CSControl:GroupList />`	List
`<CSControl:GroupPropertyComparison />`	Condition
`<CSControl:GroupPropertyValueComparison />`	Condition
`<CSControl:GroupVisibilityToggleButton />`	Single Value
`<CSControl:Head />`	Utility
`<CSControl:HelpToolTip />`	Single Value
`<CSControl:HtmlEditorStringControl />`	Single Value
`<CSControl:Image />`	Utility
`<CSControl:IndexPostData />`	Single Value
`<CSControl:IndexPostList />`	List
`<CSControl:IndexPostPropertyComparison />`	Condition
`<CSControl:IndexPostPropertyValueComparison />`	Condition
`<CSControl:IndexPostRssLink />`	Single Value
`<CSControl:InlineContentEditor />`	Utility
`<CSControl:InviteUserForm />`	Form
`<CSControl:LinkCategoryData />`	Single Value
`<CSControl:LinkCategoryList />`	List
`<CSControl:LinkCategoryPropertyComparison />`	Condition
`<CSControl:LinkCategoryPropertyValueComparison />`	Condition

Control Name	Control Type
`<CSControl:LinkData />`	Single Value
`<CSControl:LinkList />`	List
`<CSControl:LinkPropertyComparison />`	Condition
`<CSControl:LinkPropertyValueComparison />`	Condition
`<CSControl:LoginForm />`	Form
`<CSControl:LogOutForm />`	Form
`<CSControl:MessageData />`	Single Value
`<CSControl:Modal />`	Utility
`<CSControl:ModalButton />`	Utility
`<CSControl:ModalImage />`	Utility
`<CSControl:ModalLink />`	Utility
`<CSControl:ModifiedUrl />`	Single Value
`<CSControl:NavigationList />`	List
`<CSControl:Pager />`	Pager
`<CSControl:PagerData />`	Single Value
`<CSControl:PagerGroup />`	Utility
`<CSControl:PlaceHolder />`	Single Value
`<CSControl:PlainTextContentPart />`	Single Value
`<CSControl:PostbackPager />`	Pager
`<CSControl:PostCategoryData />`	Single Value
`<CSControl:PostCategoryPropertyComparison />`	Condition
`<CSControl:PostCategoryPropertyValueComparison />`	Condition
`<CSControl:PostCheckBox />`	Single Value

Continued

Control Name	Control Type
`<CSControl:PostData />`	Single Value
`<CSControl:PostEmoticon />`	Single Value
`<CSControl:PostList />`	List
`<CSControl:PostPollSubForm />`	Subform
`<CSControl:PostPropertyComparison />`	Condition
`<CSControl:PostPropertyValueComparison />`	Condition
`<CSControl:PostTagsSubForm />`	Subform
`<CSControl:PostVideoSubForm />`	Subform
`<CSControl:PreTemplatedBreadCrumb />`	List
`<CSControl:QuoteValidator />`	Utility
`<CSControl:RatingControl />`	Single Value
`<CSControl:RatingData />`	Single Value
`<CSControl:RatingList />`	List
`<CSControl:RatingPropertyComparison />`	Condition
`<CSControl:RatingPropertyValueComparison />`	Condition
`<CSControl:RegistrationData />`	Single Value
`<CSControl:RegistrationPropertyComparison />`	Condition
`<CSControl:RegistrationPropertyValueComparison />`	Condition
`<CSControl:RelatedIndexPostList />`	List
`<CSControl:RequiredCheckBoxValidator />`	Utility
`<CSControl:ResourceButton />`	Utility
`<CSControl:ResourceControl />`	Single Value
`<CSControl:ResourceLinkButton />`	Utility

Control Name	Control Type
`<CSControl:Script />`	Utility
`<CSControl:ScrollingPager />`	Pager
`<CSControl:ScrollingPagerData />`	Single Value
`<CSControl:ScrollingPagerItem />`	Utility
`<CSControl:SearchForm />`	Form
`<CSControl:SectionCheckBox />`	Single Value
`<CSControl:SectionData />`	Single Value
`<CSControl:SectionList />`	List
`<CSControl:SectionPermissionCondition />`	Condition
`<CSControl:SectionPropertyComparison />`	Condition
`<CSControl:SectionPropertyValueComparison />`	Condition
`<CSControl:SectionSubscriptionToggleButton />`	Single Value
`<CSControl:SectionThemeConfigurationData />`	Single Value
`<CSControl:SectionThemeConfigurationDataImage />`	Single Value
`<CSControl:SectionThemeConfigurationDataPropertyComparison />`	Condition
`<CSControl:SectionThemeConfigurationDataPropertyValueComparison />`	Condition
`<CSControl:SectionThemeConfigurationDataScript />`	Utility
`<CSControl:SectionThemeConfigurationDataStyle />`	Utility
`<CSControl:SectionVisibilityToggleButton />`	Single Value
`<CSControl:SelectContentForm />`	Form
`<CSControl:SelectedNavigation />`	Utility
`<CSControl:SelectTagsForm />`	Form
`<CSControl:SendEmailForm />`	Form

Continued

257

Control Name	Control Type
`<CSControl:SetVisibilityAction />`	Action
`<CSControl:SinglePager />`	Single Value
`<CSControl:SiteFileUrlControl />`	Utility
`<CSControl:SiteSettingsData />`	Single Value
`<CSControl:SiteSettingsEditableData />`	Single Value
`<CSControl:SiteSettingsPropertyComparison />`	Condition
`<CSControl:SiteSettingsPropertyValueComparison />`	Condition
`<CSControl:SiteStatisticsData />`	Single Value
`<CSControl:SiteStatisticsPropertyComparison />`	Condition
`<CSControl:SiteStatisticsPropertyValueComparison />`	Condition
`<CSControl:SiteThemeConfigurationData />`	Single Value
`<CSControl:SiteThemeConfigurationDataImage />`	Single Value
`<CSControl:SiteThemeConfigurationDataPropertyComparison />`	Condition
`<CSControl:SiteThemeConfigurationDataPropertyValueComparison />`	Condition
`<CSControl:SiteThemeConfigurationDataScript />`	Utility
`<CSControl:SiteThemeConfigurationDataStyle />`	Utility
`<CSControl:SiteUrl />`	Single Value
`<CSControl:Style />`	Utility
`<CSControl:TagBreadCrumb />`	List
`<CSControl:TagCloud />`	Single Value
`<CSControl:TagData />`	Single Value
`<CSControl:TagList />`	List
`<CSControl:TagRssLink />`	Single Value

Control Name	Control Type
`<CSControl:TemporaryRssFeedData />`	Single Value
`<CSControl:TemporaryRssFeedItemData />`	Single Value
`<CSControl:TemporaryRssFeedItemList />`	List
`<CSControl:TemporaryRssFeedItemPropertyComparison />`	Condition
`<CSControl:TemporaryRssFeedItemPropertyValueComparison />`	Condition
`<CSControl:TemporaryRssFeedList />`	List
`<CSControl:TemporaryRssFeedPropertyComparison />`	Condition
`<CSControl:TemporaryRssFeedPropertyValueComparison />`	Condition
`<CSControl:ThemeImage />`	Utility
`<CSControl:ThemeScript />`	Utility
`<CSControl:ThemeStyle />`	Utility
`<CSControl:ThreadSubscriptionToggleButton />`	Single Value
`<CSControl:ToggleButton />`	Single Value
`<CSControl:UserAvatar />`	Single Value
`<CSControl:UserAvatarSubForm />`	Subform
`<CSControl:UserCheckBox />`	Single Value
`<CSControl:UserContactPopupMenu />`	Single Value
`<CSControl:UserData />`	Single Value
`<CSControl:UserInRoleCondition />`	Condition
`<CSControl:UserList />`	List
`<CSControl:UserOnlineData />`	Single Value
`<CSControl:UserOnlineList />`	List
`<CSControl:UserOnlinePropertyComparison />`	Condition

Continued

Control Name	Control Type
`<CSControl:UserOnlinePropertyValueComparison />`	Condition
`<CSControl:UserPostIcons />`	Single Value
`<CSControl:UserProfileData />`	Single Value
`<CSControl:UserProfilePropertyComparison />`	Condition
`<CSControl:UserProfilePropertyValueComparison />`	Condition
`<CSControl:UserPropertyComparison />`	Condition
`<CSControl:UserPropertyValueComparison />`	Condition
`<CSControl:UserRoleIcons />`	Single Value
`<CSControl:UserSearchForm />`	Form
`<CSControl:UsersOnlineData />`	Single Value
`<CSControl:WrappedControlItem />`	Utility
`<CSControl:WrappedLiteral />`	Single Value
`<CSControl:WrappedRepeater />`	Utility
`<CSControl:WrappedRepeaterItem />`	Utility
`<CSControl:YesNoCheckBox />`	Utility

Related API Object Properties

The following tables list the properties of objects from the Community Server API that are exposed through Chameleon controls. For more information about how to use properties with Chameleon controls, see Chapter 5 or consult the Chameleon Control Documentation.

Content

Property Name	Data Type
Body	string
FormattedBody	string
ID	int
LastModified	DateTime
Name	string
Title	string

CSApplicationData

Property Name	Data Type
AddFavoritePostText	string
AddFavoriteSectionText	string
ApplicationType	ApplicationType (enum)
CategoryName	string
GroupName	string
Home	string
Name	string
PostName	string
RemoveFavoritePostText	string
RemoveFavoriteSectionText	string
SectionName	string

CSLink

Property Name	Data Type
ApplicationType	ApplicationType (enum)
Name	string
NavigateUrl	string
ResourceName	string
Roles	string
Target	string
Text	string

Group

Property Name	Data Type
ApplicationType	ApplicationType (enum)
Description	string
GroupID	int
Name	string
NewsgroupName	string
SortOrder	int

IndexPost

Property Name	Data Type
ApplicationKey	string
ApplicationType	ApplicationType (enum)
ApplicationUrl	string
BestMatch	string
Body	string
FormattedBody	string
GroupID	int
Name	string
PostDate	DateTime
PostID	int
PostType	PostContentType (enum)
SectionID	int
SectionName	string
SettingsID	int
ThreadID	int
Title	string
Url	string
UserName	string

Link

Property Name	Data Type
DateCreated	DateTime
Description	string
LinkCategoryID	int
LinkID	int
LinkSortOrder	SortOrder (enum)
Rel	string
SortBy	LinkSortBy (enum)
SortOrder	int
Title	string
Url	string

LinkCategory

Property Name	Data Type
Description	string
LinkCategoryID	int
Name	string
SectionID	int
SortOrder	int

Message

Property Name	Data Type
Body	string
MessageID	int
Title	string

Post

Property Name	Data Type
ApplicationType	ApplicationType (enum)
AttachmentFilename	string
Body	string
EditNotes	string
EmoticonID	int
Excerpt	string
ExtendedAttributesCount	int
ForceExcerpt	string
FormattedBody	string
IndexInThread	int
InkID	int
Name	string
ParentID	int
Points	int
PollDescription	string
PollExpirationDate	DateTime
PollTitle	string
PostDate	DateTime
PostID	int
PostLevel	int
PostMedia	PostMediaType (enum)
PostStatus	PostStatus (enum)
PostType	PostContentType (enum)

Continued

Post *(continued)*

Property Name	Data Type
RatingAverage	double
RatingSum	int
Replies	int
SectionID	int
SortOrder	int
SpamScore	int
SpamStatus	SpamStatus (enum)
Subject	string
ThreadDate	DateTime
ThreadID	int
ThreadIDNext	int
ThreadIDPrev	int
TotalRatings	int
UserHostAddress	string
UserID	int
Username	string
UserTime	DateTime
VideoContentType	string
VideoDuration	string
VideoFileFormat	string
VideoHeight	int
VideoImageUrl	string
VideoUrl	string

Post (continued)

Property Name	Data Type
VideoWidth	int
Views	int

PostCategory

Property Name	Data Type
CategoryID	int
DateCreated	DateTime
Description	string
FeaturedPostID	int
MostRecentPostDate	DateTime
MostRecentSubPostDate	DateTime
Name	string
ParentID	int
Path	string
SectionID	int
TotalSubThreads	int
TotalThreads	int

Profile

Property Name	Data Type
Age	int
AolIM	string
Bio	string
BirthDate	DateTime
CommonName	string
DateFormat	string
FontSize	int
Gender	Gender (enum)
IcqIM	string
Interests	string
Language	string
Location	string
MsnIM	string
Occupation	string
PublicEmail	string
Signature	string
SignatureFormatted	string
Timezone	double
WebAddress	string
WebGallery	string
WebLog	string
YahooIM	string

Rating

Property Name	Data Type
ItemID	int
OldValue	int
RatingType	RatingType (enum)
Value	int

Section

Property Name	Data Type
ApplicationKey	string
ApplicationType	ApplicationType (enum)
AutoDeleteThreshold	int
CategorySortBy	PostCategorySortBy (enum)
CategorySortOrder	SortOrder (enum)
DateCreated	DateTime
DefaultLanguage	string
DefaultThreadDateFilter	ThreadDateFilterMode (enum)
Description	string
ExtendedAttributesCount	int
ForumType	ForumType (enum)
GroupID	int
GroupName	string
MetaTagDescription	string
MetaTagKeywords	string
MostRecentPostAuthor	string

Continued

Section (continued)

Property Name	Data Type
MostRecentPostAuthorID	int
MostRecentPostDate	DateTime
MostRecentPostID	int
MostRecentPostSubject	string
MostRecentThreadID	int
MostRecentThreadReplies	int
Name	string
NavigateUrl	string
NewsgroupName	string
Owners	string
ParentID	int
PostsToModerate	int
SectionID	int
SettingsID	int
SortOrder	int
SpamAutoDeleteScore	int
SpamAutoModerateScore	int
TotalPosts	int
TotalThreads	int
Url	string

SiteSettings

Property Name	Data Type
AccountActivation	AccountActivation (enum)
AccountsXml	string
AdminEmailAddress	string
AnonymousCookieExpiration	int
AnonymousCookieName	string
AnonymousUserOnlineTimeWindow	int
ApplicationName	string
AuthenticationType	string
AvatarHeight	int
AvatarWidth	int
CompanyAddress	string
CompanyContactUs	string
CompanyFaxNumber	string
CompanyName	string
CookieDomain	string
Copyright	string
DateFormat	string
DefaultTheme	string
DefaultThreadDateFilter	ThreadDateFilterMode (enum)
DomainName	string
EmailEncoding	string
EmailSubjectEncoding	string
EmailThrottle	int

Continued

SiteSettings *(continued)*

Property Name	Data Type
MailGatewayEmailDomain	string
MailGatewaySecurityCode	string
MaxRssFeedsPerUser	int
MaxTopPostersToDisplay	int
MembersPerPage	int
NewUserModerationLevel	ModerationLevel (enum)
NntpServerLocation	string
PasswordRecovery	PasswordRecovery (enum)
PasswordRegex	string
PointsDownloaderFactor	int
PointsDownloadFactor	int
PointsFavoritePostFactor	int
PointsFavoriteUserFactor	int
PointsPostDisplayLevel	DisplayLevel (enum)
PointsPostFactor	int
PointsRaterFactor	int
PointsRatingFactor	int
PointsReplierFactor	int
PointsReplyFactor	int
PointsUserDisplayLevel	DisplayLevel (enum)
PostingActivityDisplay	UserActivityDisplayMode (enum)
PublicSiteKey	Guid
RawAdditionalHeader	string

SiteSettings *(continued)*

Property Name	Data Type
RoleCookieExpiration	int
RoleCookieName	string
RssCacheWindowInSeconds	int
SearchMetaDescription	string
SearchMetaKeywords	string
SearchMode	SearchMode (enum)
SearchPostsPerPage	int
SectionRatingType	SectionRatingType (enum)
SecureKey	Guid
SettingsID	int
SiteDescription	string
SiteDomain	string
SiteDomainHostUrl	string
SiteDomainUrl	string
SiteName	string
SiteSettingsCacheWindowInMinutes	int
SiteUrl	string
SmtpPortNumber	string
SmtpServer	string
SmtpServerPassword	string
SmtpServerUserName	string
TermsOfServiceUrl	string
TimeFormat	string

Continued

SiteSettings *(continued)*

Property Name	Data Type
TimezoneOffset	int
UsernameMaxLength	int
UsernameMinLength	int
UsernameRegex	string
UserOnlineTimeWindow	int
UserSignatureMaxLength	int

SiteStatistics

Property Name	Data Type
AverageModeratedPostsPerModerator	double
CurrentAnonymousUsers	int
MostActivePostID	int
MostActiveSubject	string
MostActiveUser	string
MostActiveUserID	int
MostReadPostID	int
MostReadPostSubject	string
MostViewsPostID	int
MostViewsSubject	string
NewestUser	string
NewestUserID	int
NewPostsInPast24Hours	int
NewThreadsInPast24Hours	int
NewUsersInPast24Hours	int

SiteStatistics *(continued)*

Property Name	Data Type
TotalAnonymousUsers	int
TotalModeratedPosts	int
TotalModerators	int
TotalPosts	int
TotalThreads	int
TotalUsers	int

Tag

Property Name	Data Type
Name	string
TotalCount	int

TemporaryRssFeed

Property Name	Data Type
Title	string
TotalItems	int
Url	string

TemporaryRssFeedItem

Property Name	Data Type
Description	string
Title	string
Url	string

User

Property Name	Data Type
AccountStatus	UserAccountStatus (enum)
AppUserToken	string
AvatarUrl	string
BannedUntil	DateTime
BanReason	UserBanReason (enum)
CommonNameOrUserName	string
ControlPanelManageView	ControlPanelManageView (enum)
DateCreated	DateTime
DisplayName	string
DummyTotalPosts	int
EditorType	string
Email	string
ExtendedAttributesCount	int
FavoritesShared	FavoriteType (enum)
FilterLanguagesCacheKey	string
LastAction	string
LastActivity	DateTime
LastLogin	DateTime
ModerationLevel	ModerationLevel (enum)
Password	string
PasswordAnswer	string
PasswordQuestion	string
Points	int

User *(continued)*

Property Name	Data Type
PostsModerated	int
PostSortOrder	SortOrder (enum)
PostViewType	PostViewType (enum)
PublicToken	Guid
RecentPosts	int
RoleKey	string
SearchPostsUrl	string
SettingsID	int
Theme	string
TotalPosts	int
UserID	int
Username	string
UserRank	string

UserOnline

Property Name	Data Type
AnonymousId	Guid
DisplayName	string
LastActivity	DateTime
Link	string
Location	string
UserID	int
UserName	string

C

Chameleon Controls — Blogs

This appendix includes a list of controls that exist in the `CommunityServer.Blogs` assembly and also lists the properties of the related Community Server API objects.

Blog Controls

The following table lists controls within the `CommunityServer.Blogs` assembly. All of the controls use the "CSBlog" tag prefix. For more information about the specific properties of each control, see Chapter 5 or consult the Chameleon Control Documentation.

Control Name	Control Type
`<CSBlog:ArchiveDataItemData />`	Single Value
`<CSBlog:ArchiveDataItemList />`	List
`<CSBlog:ArchiveDataItemPropertyComparison />`	Condition
`<CSBlog:ArchiveDataItemPropertyValueComparison />`	Condition
`<CSBlog:BlogFileUrlControl />`	Utility
`<CSBlog:ContactForm />`	Form
`<CSBlog:CSBlogThemePage />`	Utility
`<CSBlog:DeleteWeblogPostFeedbackForm />`	Form

Continued

Appendix C: Chameleon Controls — Blogs

Control Name	Control Type
`<CSBlog:EmailSubscriptionsForm />`	Form
`<CSBlog:GroupData />`	Single Value
`<CSBlog:GroupList />`	List
`<CSBlog:GroupPropertyComparison />`	Condition
`<CSBlog:GroupPropertyValueComparison />`	Condition
`<CSBlog:InlineTagEditor />`	Utility
`<CSBlog:PostAttachmentData />`	Single Value
`<CSBlog:PostCategoryData />`	Single Value
`<CSBlog:PostCategoryList />`	List
`<CSBlog:PostCategoryPropertyComparison />`	Condition
`<CSBlog:PostCategoryPropertyValueComparison />`	Condition
`<CSBlog:SearchForm />`	Form
`<CSBlog:TagBreadCrumb />`	List
`<CSBlog:TagCloud />`	Single Value
`<CSBlog:TagRssLink />`	Single Value
`<CSBlog:ThemeImage />`	Utility
`<CSBlog:ThemeScript />`	Utility
`<CSBlog:ThemeStyle />`	Utility
`<CSBlog:WeblogCalendar />`	Utility
`<CSBlog:WeblogData />`	Single Value
`<CSBlog:WeblogFeedbackList />`	List
`<CSBlog:WeblogList />`	List
`<CSBlog:WeblogPermissionCondition />`	Condition

Control Name	Control Type
`<CSBlog:EmailSubscriptionsForm />`	Form
`<CSBlog:GroupData />`	Single Value
`<CSBlog:GroupList />`	List
`<CSBlog:GroupPropertyComparison />`	Condition
`<CSBlog:GroupPropertyValueComparison />`	Condition
`<CSBlog:InlineTagEditor />`	Utility
`<CSBlog:PostAttachmentData />`	Single Value
`<CSBlog:PostCategoryData />`	Single Value
`<CSBlog:PostCategoryList />`	List
`<CSBlog:PostCategoryPropertyComparison />`	Condition
`<CSBlog:PostCategoryPropertyValueComparison />`	Condition
`<CSBlog:SearchForm />`	Form
`<CSBlog:TagBreadCrumb />`	List
`<CSBlog:TagCloud />`	Single Value
`<CSBlog:TagRssLink />`	Single Value
`<CSBlog:ThemeImage />`	Utility
`<CSBlog:ThemeScript />`	Utility
`<CSBlog:ThemeStyle />`	Utility
`<CSBlog:WeblogCalendar />`	Utility
`<CSBlog:WeblogData />`	Single Value
`<CSBlog:WeblogFeedbackList />`	List
`<CSBlog:WeblogList />`	List
`<CSBlog:WeblogPermissionCondition />`	Condition

Continued

Control Name	Control Type
`<CSBlog:WeblogPostCommentForm />`	Form
`<CSBlog:WeblogPostData />`	Single Value
`<CSBlog:WeblogPostFeedbackData />`	Single Value
`<CSBlog:WeblogPostFeedbackPropertyComparison />`	Condition
`<CSBlog:WeblogPostFeedbackPropertyValueComparison />`	Condition
`<CSBlog:WeblogPostList />`	List
`<CSBlog:WeblogPostPropertyComparison />`	Condition
`<CSBlog:WeblogPostPropertyValueComparison />`	Condition
`<CSBlog:WeblogPostRating />`	Single Value
`<CSBlog:WeblogPostSubscriptionToggleButton />`	Single Value
`<CSBlog:WeblogPostTagEditableList />`	Single Value
`<CSBlog:WeblogPropertyComparison />`	Condition
`<CSBlog:WeblogPropertyValueComparison />`	Condition
`<CSBlog:WeblogSubscriptionForm />`	Form

Related API Object Properties

The following tables list the properties of blog-related objects from the Community Server API that are exposed through Chameleon controls. For more information about how to use properties with Chameleon controls, see Chapter 5 or consult the Chameleon Control Documentation.

ArchiveDataItem

Property Name	Data Type
Count	int
Date	DateTime

Weblog

Property Name	Data Type
AboutDescription	string
AboutTitle	string
ApplicationKey	string
ApplicationType	ApplicationType (enum)
ArticleCount	int
AutoDeleteThreshold	int
CategorySortBy	PostCategorySortBy (enum)
CategorySortOrder	SortOrder (enum)
CommentCount	int
CommentExpirationDays	int
CSSOverride	string
DateCreated	DateTime
DefaultLanguage	string
DefaultPostConfig	BlogPostConfig (enum)
DefaultThreadDateFilter	ThreadDateFilterMode (enum)
Description	string
Email	string
ExtendedAttributesCount	int
ExternalFeedUrl	string
FeedbackNotificationType	FeedbackNotificationType (enum)
FeedBurnerUserName	string
ForumType	ForumType (enum)
GroupID	int

Continued

Weblog *(continued)*

Property Name	Data Type
GroupName	string
MetaTagDescription	string
MetaTagKeywords	string
ModeratedFeedbackNotificationThreshold	int
ModerationTypeDefault	CommentModerationType (enum)
ModerationTypeOverride	CommentModerationType (enum)
MostRecentArticleAuthor	string
MostRecentArticleAuthorID	int
MostRecentArticleDate	DateTime
MostRecentArticleID	int
MostRecentArticleName	string
MostRecentArticleSubject	string
MostRecentPostAuthor	string
MostRecentPostAuthorID	int
MostRecentPostDate	DateTime
MostRecentPostID	int
MostRecentPostName	string
MostRecentPostSubject	string
MostRecentThreadID	int
MostRecentThreadReplies	int
Name	string
NavigateUrl	string
News	string

Weblog (continued)

Property Name	Data Type
NewsgroupName	string
Owners	string
ParentID	int
PostCount	int
PostsToModerate	int
RawAdditionalHeader	string
ReferralFilter	string
RssLanguage	string
SecondaryCSS	string
SectionID	int
SettingsID	int
SortOrder	int
SpamAutoDeleteScore	int
SpamAutoModerateScore	int
Theme	string
TotalPosts	int
TotalThreads	int
TrackbackCount	int
Url	string

WeblogConfiguration

Property Name	Data Type
AggregatePostCount	int
AggregatePostSize	int
ApplicationType	ApplicationType (enum)
BaseTheme	string
BlogEmailSubscriptionTimeFrequency	int
BlogFilesMaxSize	int
BlogFileStorageExtensions	string
BlogFileStorageHiddenFiles	string
BlogFileStorageLocation	string
BlogFileStorageReadPath	string
CommentScoreFactor	double
DateScoreFactor	double
DefaultGroupID	int
DefaultTheme	string
DefautApplicationKey	string
IndividualPostCount	int
PostsToScore	int
RatingScoreFactor	double
RssCacheWindowInSeconds	int
ServicePostCountLimit	int
ThemeLocation	string
ViewScoreFactor	double

WeblogPost

Property Name	Data Type
AggViews	int
ApplicationType	ApplicationType (enum)
AttachmentFilename	string
AuthorID	int
AuthorUrl	string
Bio	string
BlogPostType	BlogPostType (enum)
BlogPostTypeName	string
Body	string
CurrentUserTime	DateTime
Custom	string
DisplayName	string
EditNotes	string
EmoticonID	int
Excerpt	string
ExcerptSize	int
ExtendedAttributesCount	int
FeedbackNotificationType	FeedbackNotificationType (enum)
ForceExcerpt	string
FormattedBody	string
IndexInThread	int
InkID	int
ModerationType	CommentModerationType (enum)

Continued

WeblogPost *(continued)*

Property Name	Data Type
Name	string
ParentID	int
Points	int
PollDescription	string
PollExpirationDate	DateTime
PollTitle	string
PostConfig	BlogPostConfig (enum)
PostDate	DateTime
PostID	int
PostLevel	int
PostMedia	PostMediaType (enum)
PostStatus	PostStatus (enum)
PostType	PostContentType (enum)
RatingAverage	double
RatingSum	int
Replies	int
SectionID	int
SortOrder	int
SpamScore	int
SpamStatus	SpamStatus (enum)
Subject	string
SubmittedUserName	string
ThreadDate	DateTime

WeblogPost *(continued)*

Property Name	Data Type
ThreadID	int
ThreadIDNext	int
ThreadIDPrev	int
TitleUrl	string
TotalRatings	int
TrackBackName	string
UserHostAddress	string
UserID	int
Username	string
UserTime	DateTime
VideoContentType	string
VideoDuration	string
VideoFileFormat	string
VideoHeight	int
VideoImageUrl	string
VideoUrl	string
VideoWidth	int
ViewPostURL	string
Views	int

D

Chameleon Controls — Forums

This appendix includes a list of controls that exist in the `CommunityServer.Discussions` assembly and also lists the properties of the related Community Server API objects.

Forum Controls

The following table lists controls within the `CommunityServer.Discussions` assembly. All of the controls use the "CSForum" tag prefix. For more information about the specific properties of each control, see Chapter 5 or consult the Chameleon Control Documentation.

Control Name	Control Type
`<CSForum:AggregateRss />`	Single Value
`<CSForum:BreadCrumb />`	List
`<CSForum:ChangeViewPopupMenu />`	Single Value
`<CSForum:CreateEditForumPostForm />`	Form
`<CSForum:CSForumThemePage />`	Utility
`<CSForum:DeleteForumPostForm />`	Form
`<CSForum:DeletePrivateMessagesForm />`	Form
`<CSForum:ForumConfigurationData />`	Single Value

Continued

Control Name	Control Type
`<CSForum:ForumConfigurationPropertyComparison />`	Condition
`<CSForum:ForumConfigurationPropertyValueComparison />`	Condition
`<CSForum:ForumData />`	Single Value
`<CSForum:ForumEditableData />`	Single Value
`<CSForum:ForumList />`	List
`<CSForum:ForumPermissionCondition />`	Condition
`<CSForum:ForumPostAnswerToggleButton />`	Single Value
`<CSForum:ForumPostData />`	Single Value
`<CSForum:ForumPostList />`	List
`<CSForum:ForumPostListFilterForm />`	Form
`<CSForum:ForumPostModerationPopupMenu />`	Single Value
`<CSForum:ForumPostPropertyComparison />`	Condition
`<CSForum:ForumPostPropertyValueComparison />`	Condition
`<CSForum:ForumPostRating />`	Single Value
`<CSForum:ForumPostTagEditableList />`	Single Value
`<CSForum:ForumPostTreeForm />`	Form
`<CSForum:ForumPropertyComparison />`	Condition
`<CSForum:ForumPropertyValueComparison />`	Condition
`<CSForum:GoToCurrentPostAction />`	Action
`<CSForum:GroupData />`	Single Value
`<CSForum:GroupEditableData />`	Single Value
`<CSForum:GroupList />`	List
`<CSForum:GroupPropertyComparison />`	Condition

Control Name	Control Type
`<CSForum:GroupPropertyValueComparison />`	Condition
`<CSForum:InlineTagEditor />`	Utility
`<CSForum:MarkAllReadForm />`	Form
`<CSForum:MoveThreadsForm />`	Form
`<CSForum:PostAttachmentData />`	Single Value
`<CSForum:PostAttachmentSubForm />`	Subform
`<CSForum:PostInkSubForm />`	Subform
`<CSForum:PostPollSubForm />`	Subform
`<CSForum:PostTagsSubForm />`	Subform
`<CSForum:PostVideoSubForm />`	Subform
`<CSForum:ReportAbuseForm />`	Form
`<CSForum:TagCloud />`	Single Value
`<CSForum:ThreadCheckBox />`	Single Value
`<CSForum:ThreadData />`	Single Value
`<CSForum:ThreadList />`	List
`<CSForum:ThreadListFilterForm />`	Form
`<CSForum:ThreadPostPageLinks />`	Single Value
`<CSForum:ThreadPropertyComparison />`	Condition
`<CSForum:ThreadPropertyValueComparison />`	Condition
`<CSForum:ThreadRating />`	Single Value
`<CSForum:ThreadStatusForm />`	Form
`<CSForum:ThreadSubscriptionToggleButton />`	Single Value
`<CSForum:UploadPostAttachmentForm />`	Form

Related API Object Properties

The following tables list the properties of forum-related objects from the Community Server API that are exposed through Chameleon controls. For more information about how to use properties with Chameleon controls, see Chapter 5 or consult the Chameleon Control Documentation.

Forum

Property Name	Data Type
ApplicationKey	string
ApplicationType	ApplicationType (enum)
AutoDeleteThreshold	int
CategorySortBy	PostCategorySortBy (enum)
CategorySortOrder	SortOrder (enum)
DateCreated	DateTime
DefaultLanguage	string
DefaultThreadDateFilter	ThreadDateFilterMode (enum)
DefaultThreadStatusValue	ThreadStatus (enum)
Description	string
ExtendedAttributesCount	int
ForumType	ForumType (enum)
GroupID	int
GroupName	string
MetaTagDescription	string
MetaTagKeywords	string
MostRecentPostAuthor	string
MostRecentPostAuthorID	int
MostRecentPostDate	DateTime
MostRecentPostID	int

Forum (continued)

Property Name	Data Type
MostRecentPostSubject	string
MostRecentThreadID	int
MostRecentThreadReplies	int
Name	string
NavigateUrl	string
NewsgroupName	string
Owners	string
ParentID	int
PostsToModerate	int
SectionID	int
SettingsID	int
SortOrder	int
SpamAutoDeleteScore	int
SpamAutoModerateScore	int
TotalPosts	int
TotalThreads	int
Url	string

ForumConfiguration

Property Name	Data Type
AllowedAttachmentTypes	string
ApplicationType	ApplicationType (enum)
DaysPostMarkedAsRead	int
DuplicatePostIntervalInMinutes	int
MaxAttachmentSize	int
MinimumTimeBetweenPosts	int
PopularPostLevelDays	int
PopularPostLevelPosts	int
PopularPostLevelViews	int
PostDeleteAgeInMinutes	int
PostEditBodyAgeInMinutes	int
PostEditTitleAgeInMinutes	int
PostInterval	int
PostsPerPage	int
ReportingForum	int
RssCacheWindowInSeconds	int
RssDefaultThreadsPerFeed	int
RssMaxThreadsPerFeed	int
SupportedInlinedImageTypes	string
ThreadsPerPage	int

ForumPost

Property Name	Data Type
ApplicationType	ApplicationType (enum)
AttachmentFilename	string
Body	string
EditNotes	string
EmoticonID	int
Excerpt	string
ExtendedAttributesCount	int
ForceExcerpt	string
FormattedBody	string
ForumPostType	ForumPostType (enum)
IndexInThread	int
InkID	int
Name	string
ParentID	int
Points	int
PollDescription	string
PollExpirationDate	DateTime
PollTitle	string
PostConfiguration	PostConfiguration (enum)
PostDate	DateTime
PostID	int
PostLevel	int
PostMedia	PostMediaType (enum)

Continued

ForumPost *(continued)*

Property Name	Data Type
PostStatus	PostStatus (enum)
PostType	PostContentType (enum)
RatingAverage	double
RatingSum	int
Replies	int
SectionID	int
SortOrder	int
SpamScore	int
SpamStatus	SpamStatus (enum)
Subject	string
ThreadDate	DateTime
ThreadID	int
ThreadIDNext	int
ThreadIDPrev	int
ThreadStartDate	DateTime
ThreadStarterUsername	string
TotalRatings	int
UserHostAddress	string
UserID	int
Username	string
UserTime	DateTime
VideoContentType	string
VideoDuration	string

ForumPost *(continued)*

Property Name	Data Type
VideoFileFormat	string
VideoHeight	int
VideoImageUrl	string
VideoUrl	string
VideoWidth	int
Views	int

Thread

Property Name	Data Type
ApplicationType	ApplicationType (enum)
AttachmentFilename	string
AuthorID	int
Body	string
EditNotes	string
EmoticonID	int
Excerpt	string
ExtendedAttributesCount	int
ForceExcerpt	string
FormattedBody	string
ForumPostType	ForumPostType (enum)
IndexInThread	int
InkID	int
MostRecentPostAuthor	string

Continued

Thread (continued)

Property Name	Data Type
MostRecentPostAuthorID	int
MostRecentPostID	int
Name	string
ParentID	int
Points	int
PollDescription	string
PollExpirationDate	DateTime
PollTitle	string
PostConfiguration	PostConfiguration (enum)
PostDate	DateTime
PostID	int
PostLevel	int
PostMedia	PostMediaType (enum)
PostStatus	PostStatus (enum)
PostType	PostContentType (enum)
PreviewBody	string
RatingAverage	double
RatingSum	int
Replies	int
SectionID	int
SortOrder	int
SpamScore	int
SpamStatus	SpamStatus (enum)

Thread (continued)

Property Name	Data Type
Status	ThreadStatus (enum)
StickyDate	DateTime
Subject	string
ThreadDate	DateTime
ThreadID	int
ThreadIDNext	int
ThreadIDPrev	int
ThreadStartDate	DateTime
ThreadStarterUsername	string
TotalRatings	int
UserHostAddress	string
UserID	int
Username	string
UserTime	DateTime
VideoContentType	string
VideoDuration	string
VideoFileFormat	string
VideoHeight	int
VideoImageUrl	string
VideoUrl	string
VideoWidth	int
Views	int

Chameleon Controls — File Galleries

This appendix includes a list of controls that exist in the `CommunityServer.Files` assembly and also lists the properties of the related Community Server API objects.

File Gallery Controls

The following table lists controls within the `CommunityServer.Files` assembly. All of the controls use the "CSFile" tag prefix. For more information about the specific properties of each control, see Chapter 5 or consult the Chameleon Control Documentation.

Control Name	Control Type
`<CSFile:CreateEditEntryForm />`	Form
`<CSFile:CreateEntryCommentForm />`	Form
`<CSFile:CSFileThemePage />`	Utility
`<CSFile:DeleteEntryCommentForm />`	Form
`<CSFile:DeleteEntryForm />`	Form
`<CSFile:DownloadEntryForm />`	Form
`<CSFile:EntryCommentData />`	Single Value
`<CSFile:EntryCommentList />`	List

Control Name	Control Type
`<CSFile:EntryCommentPropertyComparison />`	Condition
`<CSFile:EntryCommentPropertyValueComparison />`	Condition
`<CSFile:EntryData />`	Single Value
`<CSFile:EntryList />`	List
`<CSFile:EntryPropertyComparison />`	Condition
`<CSFile:EntryPropertyValueComparison />`	Condition
`<CSFile:EntryRating />`	Single Value
`<CSFile:EntrySubscriptionToggleButton />`	Single Value
`<CSFile:EntryTagEditableList />`	Single Value
`<CSFile:EntryTagsSubForm />`	Subform
`<CSFile:EntryThumbnail />`	Single Value
`<CSFile:FolderData />`	Single Value
`<CSFile:FolderList />`	List
`<CSFile:FolderPermissionCondition />`	Condition
`<CSFile:FolderPropertyComparison />`	Condition
`<CSFile:FolderPropertyValueComparison />`	Condition
`<CSFile:FolderTreeForm />`	Form
`<CSFile:GroupData />`	Single Value
`<CSFile:GroupList />`	List
`<CSFile:GroupPropertyComparison />`	Condition
`<CSFile:GroupPropertyValueComparison />`	Condition
`<CSFile:InlineTagEditor />`	Utility
`<CSFile:PostCategoryData />`	Single Value

Control Name	Control Type
`<CSFile:PostCategoryList />`	List
`<CSFile:PostCategoryPropertyComparison />`	Condition
`<CSFile:PostCategoryPropertyValueComparison />`	Condition
`<CSFile:TagBreadCrumb />`	List
`<CSFile:TagCloud />`	Single Value
`<CSFile:TagRssLink />`	Single Value
`<CSFile:UploadPostAttachmentForm />`	Form

Related API Object Properties

The following tables list the properties of file-gallery-related objects from the Community Server API that are exposed through Chameleon controls. For more information about how to use properties with Chameleon controls, see Chapter 5 or consult the Chameleon Control Documentation.

Entry

Property Name	Data Type
ApplicationType	ApplicationType (enum)
AttachmentFilename	string
AuthorID	int
AuthorURL	string
Body	string
ContentType	string
DisplayName	string
Downloads	int
EditNotes	string
EmoticonID	int

Continued

Entry (continued)

Property Name	Data Type
Excerpt	string
ExtendedAttributesCount	int
FileGalleryPostType	FileGalleryPostType (enum)
FileSize	int
ForceExcerpt	string
FormattedBody	string
IndexInThread	int
InkID	int
MostRecentPostAuthor	string
MostRecentPostAuthorID	int
MostRecentPostID	int
Name	string
ParentID	int
Points	int
PollDescription	string
PollExpirationDate	DateTime
PollTitle	string
PostDate	DateTime
PostID	int
PostLevel	int
PostMedia	PostMediaType (enum)
PostStatus	PostStatus (enum)
PostType	PostContentType (enum)

Entry *(continued)*

Property Name	Data Type
PreviewBody	string
RatingAverage	double
RatingSum	int
Replies	int
SectionID	int
SettingsID	int
SortOrder	int
SpamScore	int
SpamStatus	SpamStatus (enum)
Status	ThreadStatus (enum)
StickyDate	DateTime
Subject	string
ThreadDate	DateTime
ThreadID	int
ThreadIDNext	int
ThreadIDPrev	int
TotalRatings	int
UserHostAddress	string
UserID	int
Username	string
UserTime	DateTime
VideoContentType	string
VideoDuration	string

Continued

Entry *(continued)*

Property Name	Data Type
VideoFileFormat	string
VideoHeight	int
VideoImageUrl	string
VideoUrl	string
VideoWidth	int
ViewPostURL	string
Views	int

EntryComment

Property Name	Data Type
ApplicationType	ApplicationType (enum)
AttachmentFilename	string
Body	string
DisplayName	string
EditNotes	string
EmoticonID	int
Excerpt	string
ExtendedAttributesCount	int
FileGalleryPostType	FileGalleryPostType (enum)
ForceExcerpt	string
FormattedBody	string
IndexInThread	int
InkID	int

EntryComment *(continued)*

Property Name	Data Type
Name	string
ParentID	int
Points	int
PollDescription	string
PollExpirationDate	DateTime
PollTitle	string
PostDate	DateTime
PostID	int
PostLevel	int
PostMedia	PostMediaType (enum)
PostStatus	PostStatus (enum)
PostType	PostContentType (enum)
RatingAverage	double
RatingSum	int
Replies	int
SectionID	int
SortOrder	int
SpamScore	int
SpamStatus	SpamStatus (enum)
Subject	string
SubmittedUserName	string
ThreadDate	DateTime
ThreadID	int

Continued

EntryComment *(continued)*

Property Name	Data Type
ThreadIDNext	int
ThreadIDPrev	int
TitleUrl	string
TotalRatings	int
UserHostAddress	string
UserID	int
Username	string
UserTime	DateTime
VideoContentType	string
VideoDuration	string
VideoFileFormat	string
VideoHeight	int
VideoImageUrl	string
VideoUrl	string
VideoWidth	int
ViewAuthorURL	string
ViewPostURL	string
Views	int

Folder

Property Name	Data Type
AllowedFileExtensions	string
ApplicationKey	string
ApplicationType	ApplicationType (enum)

Folder *(continued)*

Property Name	Data Type
AutoDeleteThreshold	int
CategorySortBy	PostCategorySortBy (enum)
CategorySortOrder	SortOrder (enum)
DateCreated	DateTime
DefaultLanguage	string
DefaultThreadDateFilter	ThreadDateFilterMode (enum)
Description	string
ExtendedAttributesCount	int
ForumType	ForumType (enum)
GroupID	int
GroupName	string
MetaTagDescription	string
MetaTagKeywords	string
MostRecentPostAuthor	string
MostRecentPostAuthorID	int
MostRecentPostDate	DateTime
MostRecentPostID	int
MostRecentPostSubject	string
MostRecentThreadID	int
MostRecentThreadReplies	int
Name	string
NavigateUrl	string
NewsgroupName	string

Continued

Folder *(continued)*

Property Name	Data Type
Owners	string
ParentID	int
PostsToModerate	int
RestrictedFileExtensions	string
SectionID	int
SettingsID	int
SortOrder	int
SpamAutoDeleteScore	int
SpamAutoModerateScore	int
TotalPosts	int
TotalThreads	int
Url	string

Chameleon Controls — Photo Galleries

This appendix includes a list of controls that exist in the CommunityServer.Galleries assembly and also lists the properties of the related Community Server API objects.

Photo Gallery Controls

The following table lists controls within the CommunityServer.Galleries assembly. All of the controls use the "CSGallery" tag prefix. For more information about the specific properties of each control, see Chapter 5 or consult the Chameleon Control Documentation.

Control Name	Control Type
<CSGallery:BreadCrumb />	List
<CSGallery:CSGalleryThemePage />	Utility
<CSGallery:DeleteGalleryPostFeedbackForm />	Form
<CSGallery:EmailSubscriptionsForm />	Form
<CSGallery:GalleryData />	Single Value
<CSGallery:GalleryList />	List
<CSGallery:GalleryPermissionCondition />	Condition
<CSGallery:GalleryPostCommentForm />	Form

Continued

Control Name	Control Type
`<CSGallery:GalleryPostData />`	Single Value
`<CSGallery:GalleryPostExifData />`	Single Value
`<CSGallery:GalleryPostExifList />`	List
`<CSGallery:GalleryPostFeedbackData />`	Single Value
`<CSGallery:GalleryPostFeedbackList />`	List
`<CSGallery:GalleryPostFeedbackPropertyComparison />`	Condition
`<CSGallery:GalleryPostFeedbackPropertyValueComparison />`	Condition
`<CSGallery:GalleryPostImage />`	Single Value
`<CSGallery:GalleryPostList />`	List
`<CSGallery:GalleryPostOrderPrintsRedirect />`	Single Value
`<CSGallery:GalleryPostPager />`	Pager
`<CSGallery:GalleryPostPropertyComparison />`	Condition
`<CSGallery:GalleryPostPropertyValueComparison />`	Condition
`<CSGallery:GalleryPostRating />`	Single Value
`<CSGallery:GalleryPostSlideShowPro />`	Single Value
`<CSGallery:GalleryPostSubscriptionToggleButton />`	Single Value
`<CSGallery:GalleryPostTagEditableList />`	Single Value
`<CSGallery:GalleryPropertyComparison />`	Condition
`<CSGallery:GalleryPropertyValueComparison />`	Condition
`<CSGallery:GroupData />`	Single Value
`<CSGallery:GroupList />`	List
`<CSGallery:GroupPropertyComparison />`	Condition
`<CSGallery:GroupPropertyValueComparison />`	Condition

Control Name	Control Type
`<CSGallery:InlineTagEditor />`	Utility
`<CSGallery:PostCategoryData />`	Single Value
`<CSGallery:PostCategoryList />`	List
`<CSGallery:PostCategoryPropertyComparison />`	Condition
`<CSGallery:PostCategoryPropertyValueComparison />`	Condition
`<CSGallery:TagBreadCrumb />`	List
`<CSGallery:TagCloud />`	Single Value
`<CSGallery:TagRssLink />`	Single Value

Related API Object Properties

The following tables list the properties of photo-gallery-related objects from the Community Server API that are exposed through Chameleon controls. For more information about how to use properties with Chameleon controls, see Chapter 5 or consult the Chameleon Control Documentation.

Gallery

Property Name	Data Type
AboutDescription	string
AboutTitle	string
ApplicationKey	string
ApplicationType	ApplicationType (enum)
AutoDeleteThreshold	int
CategorizationType	CategorizationType (enum)
CategoryListingColumns	int
CategoryListingRows	int

Continued

Gallery *(continued)*

Property Name	Data Type
CategorySortBy	PostCategorySortBy (enum)
CategorySortOrder	SortOrder (enum)
CommentCount	int
CommentExpirationDays	int
CSSOverride	string
DateCreated	DateTime
DefaultLanguage	string
DefaultPostConfig	GalleryPostConfig (enum)
DefaultThreadDateFilter	ThreadDateFilterMode (enum)
Description	string
DiskQuota	int
ExtendedAttributesCount	int
FeedbackNotificationType	FeedbackNotificationType (enum)
ForumType	ForumType (enum)
GroupID	int
GroupName	string
ImageQuota	int
MaxX	int
MaxY	int
MetaTagDescription	string
MetaTagKeywords	string
ModerationTypeDefault	CommentModerationType (enum)
ModerationTypeOverride	CommentModerationType (enum)

Gallery *(continued)*

Property Name	Data Type
MostRecentPostAuthor	string
MostRecentPostAuthorID	int
MostRecentPostDate	DateTime
MostRecentPostID	int
MostRecentPostSubject	string
MostRecentThreadID	int
MostRecentThreadReplies	int
Name	string
NavigateUrl	string
NewsgroupName	string
Owners	string
ParentID	int
PictureDetailsQuality	int
PictureDetailsX	int
PictureDetailsY	int
PictureListingColumns	int
PictureListingRows	int
PostCount	int
PostsToModerate	int
Quality	int
ReferralFilter	string
SecondaryCSS	string
SecondaryThumbnailQuality	int

Continued

Gallery *(continued)*

Property Name	Data Type
SecondaryThumbnailX	int
SecondaryThumbnailY	int
SectionID	int
SettingsID	int
SlideshowDelay	int
SlideshowQuality	int
SlideshowX	int
SlideshowY	int
SortOrder	int
SpamAutoDeleteScore	int
SpamAutoModerateScore	int
Theme	string
ThreadSortBy	GalleryThreadSortBy (enum)
ThreadSortOrder	SortOrder (enum)
ThumbnailBrightness	int
ThumbnailQuality	int
ThumbnailX	int
ThumbnailY	int
TotalPosts	int
TotalThreads	int
TrackbackCount	int
Url	string
WatermarkMinHeight	int

Gallery *(continued)*

Property Name	Data Type
WatermarkMinWidth	int
WatermarkPosition	WatermarkPosition (enum)
WatermarkText	string
WatermarkType	WatermarkType (enum)

GalleryPost

Property Name	Data Type
ApplicationType	ApplicationType (enum)
AttachmentFilename	string
AuthorID	int
AuthorUrl	string
Body	string
ContentType	string
DetailsHeight	int
DetailsWidth	int
DisplayName	string
EditNotes	string
EmoticonID	int
Excerpt	string
ExtendedAttributesCount	int
FeedbackNotificationType	FeedbackNotificationType (enum)
ForceExcerpt	string
FormattedBody	string

Continued

GalleryPost *(continued)*

Property Name	Data Type
FormattedPostDate	string
GalleryPostType	GalleryPostType (enum)
GalleryPostTypeName	string
Height	int
ImageSize	int
IndexInThread	int
InkID	int
MicroHeight	int
MicroURL	string
MicroWidth	int
ModerationType	CommentModerationType (enum)
MostRecentPostAuthor	string
MostRecentPostAuthorID	int
MostRecentPostID	int
Name	string
OriginalHeight	int
OriginalWidth	int
ParentID	int
Points	int
PollDescription	string
PollExpirationDate	DateTime
PollTitle	string
PostConfig	GalleryPostConfig (enum)

GalleryPost *(continued)*

Property Name	Data Type
PostDate	DateTime
PostID	int
PostLevel	int
PostMedia	PostMediaType (enum)
PostStatus	PostStatus (enum)
PostType	PostContentType (enum)
PreviewBody	string
RatingAverage	double
RatingSum	int
Replies	int
SecondaryThumbnailHeight	int
SecondaryThumbnailWidth	int
SectionID	int
SettingsID	int
SlideshowHeight	int
SlideshowWidth	int
SortOrder	int
SpamScore	int
SpamStatus	SpamStatus (enum)
Status	ThreadStatus (enum)
StickyDate	DateTime
Subject	string
SubmittedUserName	string

Continued

GalleryPost (continued)

Property Name	Data Type
ThreadDate	DateTime
ThreadID	int
ThreadIDNext	int
ThreadIDPrev	int
ThumbnailHeight	int
ThumbnailURL	string
ThumbnailWidth	int
TitleUrl	string
TotalRatings	int
TrackBackName	string
UserHostAddress	string
UserID	int
Username	string
UserTime	DateTime
VideoContentType	string
VideoDuration	string
VideoFileFormat	string
VideoHeight	int
VideoImageUrl	string
VideoUrl	string
VideoWidth	int
ViewPictureURL	string
Views	int
Width	int

Theme.config Reference

Node Structure

- **Theme** — Parent node that contains the `DynamicConfiguration`
- **DynamicConfiguration** — Child of Theme node
- **propertyGroup** — Child of `DynamicConfiguration`, can contain `propertySubGroup` and property nodes
- **propertySubGroup** — Child of a `propertyGroup`, can contain property nodes
- **property** — Represents a theme option in the control panel, such as background color
- **propertyRule** — An `IPropertyRule` that exists as a child to a property and defines an action to take when a property changes
- **propertyValue** — A child of property, multiple `propertyValue` nodes can exist at the same level. Used to represent a group of selectable values for a property, such as a font selector

Possible Node Attributes

The Theme node can contain the following attributes:

- `title`
- `previewImageUrl`
- `previewText`

The `propertyGroup` node can contain the following attributes:

- ❏ id
- ❏ text
- ❏ resourceName
- ❏ resourceFile
- ❏ descriptionResourceName
- ❏ descriptionResourceFile
- ❏ descriptionText
- ❏ orderNumber
- ❏ visible

The `propertySubGroup` node can contain the following attributes:

- ❏ id
- ❏ text
- ❏ resourceName
- ❏ resourceFile
- ❏ descriptionResourceName
- ❏ descriptionResourceFile
- ❏ descriptionText
- ❏ orderNumber
- ❏ visible

The property node can contain the following attributes:

- ❏ id
- ❏ resourceName
- ❏ resourceFile
- ❏ text
- ❏ descriptionResourceName
- ❏ descriptionResourceFile
- ❏ descriptionText
- ❏ orderNumber
- ❏ dataType
- ❏ defaultValue

- ❏ editable
- ❏ visible
- ❏ controlType

The propertyValue node can contain the following attributes:

- ❏ value
- ❏ resourceName
- ❏ resourceFile
- ❏ text
- ❏ orderNumber

The propertyRule node can contain the following attributes:

- ❏ type
- ❏ processImmediately

Default theme.config Example

```xml
<?xml version="1.0" encoding="utf-8" ?>
<Theme title="Default" previewImageUrl="~/themes/default/preview.png"
       previewText="This is the default site theme.">
  <DynamicConfiguration>
    <propertyGroup id="layout" text="Layout / General">
      <propertySubGroup text="Layout">
        <property id="columns" text="Columns" dataType="int"
            descriptionText="Select the column layout for this theme."
            defaultValue="2" controlType="
            Telligent.DynamicConfiguration.Controls.ImageSelectionControl,
            Telligent.DynamicConfiguration" selectListWidth="440"
            selectListHeight="400" showImageWhenSelected="false">
          <propertyValue value="-1" text="Two Columns (sidebar on left)"
              imageUrl="~/themes/default/images/preview-2columns-left.png"
              imageWidth="200px" imageHeight="150px" />
          <propertyValue value="1" text="Two Columns (sidebar on right)"
              imageUrl="~/themes/default/images/preview-2columns-right.png"
              imageWidth="200px" imageHeight="150px" />
        </property>
        <property id="width" text="Width" dataType="unit"
            descriptionText="Select the width of the content."
            defaultValue="960px" />
      </propertySubGroup>
    </propertyGroup>
  </DynamicConfiguration>
<Theme>
```

Index

C

F

G

H

I

Themes folder, 3
ThemesBlogs directory, 81
TotalPages property, 51
TotalRecords property, 51
TotalSummaryTemplate property, 53
TrailerTemplate property, 47
transformers, 21–22
TruncateAt property, 41
TruncateEllipsisResourceFile property, 41–42
TruncateEllipsisResourceName property, 41–42
TruncateEllipsisText property, 41–42

U

UrlRewriteProvider class, 15
URLs
    adding, query strings and, 31
    rewriting, 4–5, 15–16
        links, 22–24
        location node, 18–21
        navigation, 22–24
        SiteURLs.config and, 3
        transformers, 21–22
utility controls
    ConditionalAction, 75–76
    ConditionalContent, 76
    ModifiedUrl, 77
    PlaceHolder, 77
    SiteUrl, 78
    ThemeImage, 77
    ThemeScript, 78
    ThemeStyle, 78

V

ValueAutomationRule, 143–144
ValueChanged property, 223
Visual Studio, 8

W

Weblog files, 238
WrappedContentBase class
    AddContentControls method, 176
    AddLeaderControls method, 176
    AddPropertyControls method, 175–176
    AddTrailerControls method, 176
    AutomatedVisible property, 174
    BindDefaultContent method, 173
    CreateDefaultContentControls property, 174
    DataSource property, 174
    DefaultLeaderTemplate property, 174
    DefaultTrailerTemplate property, 174
    EnsureDataBound method, 175
    GetContentTemplate method, 173
    GetContentTemplateWrapper method, 176
    RecreateChildControlsOnDataBind property, 175
    RenderControl method, 175
WrappedFormBase
    AddFormControls method, 194
    AddLeaderControls method, 194
    AddPropertyControls method, 193–194
    AddTrailerControls method, 194
    AttachChildControls method, 192
    AutomatedVisible property, 192
    DataBind method, 193
    DefaultLeaderTemplate property, 192
    DefaultTrailerTemplate property, 192
    GetFormTemplate method, 194
    GetFormTemplateWrapper method, 194
    IsValid method, 193
    RenderControl method, 193
WrappedSubFormBase
    ApplyChangesAfterCommit method, 203
    ApplyChangesBeforeCommit method, 203
    GetPropertyFromHostForm method, 203
    IsEnabled method, 202
    IsValid method, 203
WrappedSubFormBase class, HostForm property, 202